Madonna Magdalene & Beyond

Feminine power Hidden in Empire Culture: How? Why? What's Next?

Madonna Magdalene & Beyond

Feminine power Hidden in Empire Culture: How? Why? What's Next?

Ruth L. Miller, Ph.D.

Madonna, Magdalene, & Beyond: Feminine Power hidden in empire culture: How? Why? What's Next?
Second Edition of *Mary's Power: Embracing the Divine Feminine as the age of invasion & empire ends*
(originally published as *Notre Dame: Mary Magdalene & the Divine Feminine* by WiseWoman Press, Portland, Oregon).
© 2007, 2011, 2021 Ruth L. Miller

Portal Center Press
www.portalcenterpress.com

Cover photo: "The Virgin" in the foyer at the Musée National du Moyen Äge, also known as the Cluny Museum, in Paris, France, from the museum brochure.

Back cover: The window of Marie la Madeleine on the south wall nearest the West Portal of the Notre Dame cathedral in Chartres, France.

ISBN: 978-1-936902-44-6
 Ebook: 978-1-936902-45-3

Appreciation

Special thanks to Martha for making the trip to Chartres and the Ste Baume site possible, for asking all the right questions, and for her commitment to deep comprehension of the important ideas and potentials of life, which is an inspiration.

PREFACE

We live in a culture that tells us, as all cultures do, that how we live now is how humanity is designed to live. We've been told that we're "civilized" and that others who've gone before us or live according to the ancient ways are "barbarians" or "aboriginal" or "primitive." In schools, churches, and the media, we've been led to believe that war is normal, light-skinned men are always in charge, and the only power that achieves anything is physical or financial. Today, this culture, once limited to Europe and North America, is global, and it's destroying the resource base on which it depends.

Over the past few decades there've been many wonderful discoveries concerning the religious and spiritual lives of the ancient peoples who formed the foundation for the culture of Europe and the U.S. A few of those discoveries have seriously undermined the "official story" of our past as it was taught in public schools and many churches through the nineteenth and twentieth centuries. Some of these discoveries, particularly the texts describing the role of Mary Magdalene in the life of Jesus the Nazarene, have captured the imagination of the general public and led to a whole "industry," comprising thousands of books, tapes, and other media exploring the possibilities these texts suggest.

As a woman who was raised on the University of Chicago campus by art historians, who has studied and taught anthropology, ecology, and systems theories at various universities, and is now an ordained minister, I've followed these discoveries with interest. From the Dead Sea Scrolls through the *Gospel of Judas*, from the "chariots of the gods" to the chariot accident that was probably what killed Tutankhamen, I have read and watched and listened to every study, interpretation, and speculation I could get my hands on.

In the process, I came to realize that huge pieces of the puzzle are being totally ignored. Especially as I listened to arguments about *The DaVinci Code*, I've felt as if everyone has blinders on. They aren't seeing all the issues, much less the possibilities!

This book, then, takes an alternative perspective on our culture's development, one that takes into account the fact that only a small percentage of the people living at any given time were men making big decisions in big buildings in cities—even though our histories focus almost entirely on that relatively small group. In general terms, by pointing out often-overlooked patterns, I've attempted to describe how that way of thinking emerged and what was going on around it—and still is, in many places, today.

The world doesn't look or operate the way we were taught in school, and a significant key to understanding it rests with the much-misunderstood Marie la Madeleine—also known as Mary Magdalene.

A powerful woman who affected the lives of thousands, she was, from all accounts and images, a teacher, healer, and mystic who taught many to do and be the same. She embodied an ancient power and principle passed on through the generations, and she had the skill and understanding to help her people move through "the end times" of their world.

Our world, today, is in very much the same situation as her world was, then. So, to the extent that we wish to move through our own "end times" gracefully, and get out of the global mess we're in, we must understand how and why the power that she and her predecessors used were lost to us… and begin to reclaim that power for ourselves and our posterity.

Contents

PREFACE	**I**
INTRODUCTION	**VI**
THE MYSTERY	**1**
Finding Feminine Spirituality in Our Masculine Religious Traditions	2
Discovering a Hymn to the Divine Feminine called *Notre Dame de Chartres*	14
THE OTHER HALF OF PRE-HISTORY: THE AGE OF BALANCE	**33**
Life before Empire	33
UPSETTING THE BALANCE: THE AGE OF INVASION & EMPIRE	**63**
Continued Expansion	76
Rural Conservatives: holding the balance	82
HEBREW CULTURE IN THE AGE OF INVASION & EMPIRE	**89**
Abraham and Sarah: A Patriarch and his Princess Sister-wife	92
The Hebrews Control Egypt	96
Egyptian Rule is Restored	98
Moses, prophet-king	100
"The Law" is Given	102
Miriam's Role	104
David, Solomon, an Ark and a Temple filled with Women	108
THE LIFE AND TIMES OF JESUS THE NAZARENE	**115**

OVERLAPPING CULTURES	115
HEROD'S TEMPLE	117
QUMRAN AND THE ESSENES	120
THE MARYS: STRONG, INDEPENDENT WOMEN OF POWER	122
THE NAZARENES	128
JESUS' TEACHINGS REGARDING WOMEN	132
JESUS' ROLE IN HIS CULTURE	134

CHURCH AS ROMAN/ARYAN EMPIRE — 150

THE CANON—FOUNDATION FOR AN EMPIRE	151
THE CRUSADES—SEEKING CONTROL OF THE HOLY LAND, TOO	156
REDEFINING RELIGIOUS EXPERIENCE	161

WOMEN: A CONUNDRUM IN THE CHRISTIAN CHURCH — 169

OUTSIDE THE CHURCH: POWERFUL TEACHINGS — 177

JERUSALEM CHRISTIANS: JEWS FOR JESUS	178
COPTIC CHRISTIANS IN EGYPT: SEEKERS OF DIVINE UNION	179
THE EGYPTIAN GNOSTICS: UNITING *ANIMUS* AND *ANIMA*	181
THE JOHANNITE MOVEMENT: MAGIC & MYSTERY	186
THE TEMPLARS—OPENING THE DOOR TO NEW UNDERSTANDINGS	197
A GOLDEN THREAD?	202

THE CULT OF THE MAGDALENE — 211

A HOLY COM-UNION — 253

A NEW COVENANT	258

OUR LADY ARISES ANEW — 262

A "New Style" Emerges in France	262
The Mother Mary's Role in Christian Life	271
The Dark/Black Madonna	279
Visions & Apparitions	283
Neo-pagans: Seeking to Restore the Balance	285
Women in Ministry—Embodying the Christ	288
The Feminine Aspect of Modern Science	290

FOR THE FUTURE: FINDING A NEW BALANCE
293

Toward a Balanced, Sustainable Culture	297

APPENDIX A: THE HISTORICAL RECORD 307

From Paleolithic Hunters to Neolithic Villages	307
Urban Empires	313
Anatolia/Asia Minor, Base of operations for the Hittites	327
The Etruscans, founders of Italy	331

APPENDIX B: CHURCH COMMENTARIES ON MARY MAGDALENE 337

APPENDIX C: THE *VEDAS* - EARLIEST HISTORY OF THE ARYANS 342

REFERENCES AND RESOURCES 346

INDEX 350

About the Author	356

INTRODUCTION

The original edition of this book was the result of years of exploration topped off by a few days of profound inspiration. I grew up in a household of art historians, with Gardner's *Art Through the Ages* being the first adult book I tried to read, and I spent long hours studying the artifacts and models in the Oriental Institute in Chicago (in addition to the marvelous science and engineering on display at the Museum of Science and Industry a few blocks away!). I studied anthropology in college and was active in several varieties of Protestant churches as well as the Catholic church growing up and during a career as a mother and futurist, prior to training and ordination as a New Thought minister. One could say that this book is the result of a lifetime of study and exploration, coming to an epiphany over a few days in the dormitory next to the cathedral at Chartres, France.

Some may call these ideas "feminist." My guess is that historians looking back at this and other works like it will call it "Personalist," following the philosophical tradition made popular by Rev. Dr. Martin Luther King, Jr. in the 1960s. Developed by King's academic mentor, Dr. Benjamin Mays, Personalism is a philosophy based on the idea that the divine is available to, and expressed through, each and every individual, regardless of training, gender, or ethnicity, and that not only may each of us experience the divine, but our uniqueness as an individual leads to a unique experience and expression of the divine in our lives. This makes it incumbent on each of us to truly experience and express our unique contribution to the whole.

Another philosophical tradition that informs this work is that of Carl Jung, whose years of analyzing the thought processes and dreams of clients and patients led him to believe that each of us has both a masculine essence, or *animus*, and a feminine essence, or *anima*, and that to deny either one is to live, at least, an unbalanced life, and at worst, a life of mental and emotional instability and illness. Jung saw that western industrial culture is one in which the *anima* is sorely ignored, left out of social, economic, and religious life. Western culture has fallen heir, unfortunately, to the ancient Greek belief that was expressed by Plato as "woman being the failure of blind nature."

Finally, for most of my academic life, I was trained and fully prepared for a career in the "hard" sciences, in which observation leading to inquiry leading to testing of a hypothesis and analysis of the results is the accepted method. All of my work—in metaphysics, in future studies and community development, and in culture studies—is informed and guided by this methodology.

So this is a journey of exploration—through time and across cultures—seeking to answer a few seemingly unimportant, but ultimately earth-shaking questions:

- Who is Our Lady?
- Who is Mary Magdalene?
- Where did they come from?
- What do they have to teach us?
- Why was the Magdalene so maligned in western religions?
- Is she related to the current Age of Invasion & Empire?
- Does she have a lesson for our modern empire culture?
- Can understanding her role affect our lives and world?

The 2011 Edition

The first edition of the book, published as *Notre Dame: Mary Magdalene & the divine feminine in western culture* by Wise-

Woman Press in 2007, was simply an exploration of these questions. The 2011 edition, called *Mary's Power*, goes a little further. First, it emphasizes the kind of power that the Magdalene and women like her had and taught, and is re-emerging in our culture today. Second, it places her in a parallel time in history—the transition between Eons (the age of Aries to the age of Pisces)—as a model and a pointer to the transition we're going through now, from the age of Pisces to the age of Aquarius, and the much longer Age of Invasion and Empire into a new Age of Inclusion and Regeneration.

The 2011 edition was designed to lay the foundation of understanding needed to build the new culture that is emerging while what I've called "the Age of Empire" or "Culture of Control" comes to an end. It reframes the pre-historic data, along with historical and biblical accounts, to a new perspective – one in which the actual role of the feminine can be seen. The role of the Magdalene is pivotal, in that her life and work were a large, though often hidden, part of the transition from the Age of Aries into the Age of Pisces. In spite of all attempts by leaders of the Empire culture to make her disappear, she remains a tantalizing possibility on the edge of our awareness. And in these last years of this culture, she has re-emerged: in novels and histories, legends and channeled guidance; she speaks to women everywhere. And sometimes she reaches men, as well – those who, as has always been the case, "have the ears to listen" and the personal awareness to put aside cultural norms in favor of a higher reality.

The Magdalene can be best understood as the pivot for the previous "dawning of an age," and even in 1200CE, the guild of water-bearers knew her story would be important in the dawning of the next age (Aquarius meaning "water bearer") as they sponsored her window in Chartres cathedral. And now it's clear that her role today is as a model of what is possible for all humanity.

Introduction

This 2021 edition

This new edition is being published while the world is experiencing the trauma of waking up to the reality of the transition we are moving through. And, although dozens of books have been written about the Magdalene since my version first came out—all of which provide insight, often from very different perspectives—none of them place her role and power in the context of who and what we, humanity as a whole, are becoming.

This latest edition, therefore, has been expanded to make that point clear, and to provide guidance for those who are willing to learn from the past a pattern that can help us build a thriving future for all beings.

About the Format...

So many interwoven ideas are braided together in this work that I've taken some liberty with the standard format. My side-comments and notes are in boxes alongside the text, so as not to be confused with formal references, which are in the footnotes. For ease, I've

> These boxes are usually an explanation of something in the text —or a related idea that isn't really part of the text, but may be of interest to the reader.

written all the numbers as digits, rather than spelling them out, as in "50" vs. "fifty." Also,

> quotations from other sources are in this format, indented and in this type font.

And

> My "alternative versions of the story" are written in this format, centered, with a box around it.

There's a long journey ahead, with lots of opportunities to explore. I hope you'll find it useful and inspiring.

~ *Ruth L. Miller, on the Oregon coast of North America*

This is the astrological symbol for *Virgo*, a word that means "the Virgin" and refers to the month immediately preceding the autumnal equinox—the beginning of the ancient Mesopotamian year. Interesting that it's also an "M:" "Mary, Magdalene, Mother, Mater, Matter, Matrix, Material." It ends each chapter.

Ancient Mother, I hear you calling,
Ancient Mother, I hear your song...[1]

THE MYSTERY

OBSERVATION: We live in a culture in which men and women are, ostensibly, equal. We supposedly have the same opportunities for education, employment, and all the other means for the "pursuit of happiness." Yet many a man feels that his life is limited by the women who have taken the places that should have been his, and most women are sure that the men around them are limiting them. Women are, for the most part, only CEOs of businesses they have created or inherited, and men are rarely the ones to clean up after children or the elderly. "Women's work,"—teaching, nursing, librarian, social work—are typically paid about half of what is paid for equivalent years in school for "men's work"—engineering, medicine, consulting, business management. For the past 50 years children in Europe and North America have spent almost all of their waking hours in the presence of women, because the men are somewhere else working. These are not indicators of equality. They are signs of a difficult tension between the ideal of equality and the reality of an imbalance that is deeply embedded in the thought processes of everyone who has grown up in western culture. How can intelligent people accept this as "normal?"

OBSERVATION: Western culture has no clear definition of gender roles and so each new interaction is a struggle to define appropriate boundaries, behaviors, and balances. Our moral and ethical fabric is torn by the discrepancy between what is stated and what is experienced. Our stress lev-

---

[1] Title tune to the album "Ancient Mother," by Robert Gass and On wings of Song, Spring Hill, 1994.

els—and the diseases and addictions that go with them—are off the scale because we're constantly having to negotiate what, in virtually every other culture, is set and understood by all concerned. What happened?

OBSERVATION: Today, western women are alternately repulsed by and envious of the Arab woman's *burkha*, which protects her from prying eyes and, because it makes gender roles clear, gives her a kind of freedom while preventing her from expressing her individuality openly. We wonder: why would anyone accept such an imposition? Some western women journalists have documented that women in the Arab states have a virtually separate culture from the men: separate songs, stories, understandings of how the world works, even some separate vocabulary and an underground economy of their own. How did this occur?

OBSERVATION: The women described in the Hebrew and Christian Bibles are strong, independent, and wise. Yet women in western culture are taught that women "in those days" had no place in the culture. What happened?

OBSERVATION: The religious life of most of the world is centered on a very masculine godhead, teaching that women are secondary at best, but if we look at the daily spiritual practices of these religions, we find very strong feminine presences. Why?

Finding Feminine Spirituality in Our Masculine Religious Traditions

Most students of world religious history have learned that the Roman church adopted and adapted many local customs into the official practice of Christianity. The Christmas tree, with holly and mistletoe, or eggs and bunnies at Easter are typical examples. Such adaptation is even more evident when one considers that the word Easter is a translation of the Greek word *Oestre*—the name of a Macedonian Goddess of Spring whose symbols were eggs and rabbits, and is the root word for estrogen and related female terms. It also appears in the Germanic name for the same goddess, Östera, and as the name of the country of *Österreich*, which English-speakers know as Austria, whose national flower is the edelweiss, a five-petaled symbol of purity and beauty that bears the Latin name, *floarea reginei* (Queen's flower). More, this celebration of Jesus' resurrection is a movable holy day, without a set date, for it occurs on the first Sun-day after the first full moon after the spring equinox—the date used for millennia before Jesus to celebrate the resurrection of life.

Throughout Christendom, we see Christians honoring the Virgin Mary, Mother of God, who holds her infant Son at Christmas as the *Madonna* (from the Latin, meaning "Great Mother"), then on Good Friday holds her dying Son in the statues called *pieta* (in English, "piety, faithfulness"). Protestant Christian scholars have expressed their fear that the Catholic "Cult of the Virgin" or "Marianism" may be a relic of Goddess worship and could be eclipsing the worship of the masculine Godhead. The official Roman Catholic position is that only God, through Christ and the Holy Spirit, is worthy of adoration and worship, while Mary, as Mother of God (in the form of Jesus Christ), is worthy of great veneration and praise. They refer to the angel saying "Hail Mary, full of grace" at the Annunciation of her pregnancy and the not-yet-born John the Baptist, who leapt in Elizabeth's womb upon Mary's arrival in what's called the Visitation, as indications of this worthiness and models of this veneration.

The tendency to incorporate the feminine, often "pagan," traditions into otherwise masculine orthodox religions isn't limited to Roman Christianity. Muslims honor Fatima, the Blessed Prophet Mohammed's youngest daughter, whose name means "Mother of the abstainer" and is the name of the historical Creatrix and Moon-Goddess in the region around Medina. The Islamic fast of *Ramadan,* described as honoring the month in which Mohammed received the *Koran*, continues the ancient Sumerian tradition of fasting while the Goddess weeps for her dead lover/son in winter, and the Jewish *Rosh Hashanah* (meaning "head of the year"), followed by *Yom Kippur* (meaning "day or season of fasting") corresponds to the ages-old autumnal fast of atonement, during which the people made it possible for the risen Son of the Goddess to return, bringing the autumn rains and the new year. Even the Hebrew spirit of God, *Shekinah* ("the Presence," literally, "to dwell, abide"), is described in Goddess terms: "waxing and waning moon...well waters...lily of the valley, Mother Wisdom...gateway and door... mother eagle, serpent...the Sabbath Queen and Bride, the Tree of Life, the menorah, and the earth itself."[2]

Buddhists, followers of a path that is essentially a psychological system for the elimination of suffering, also venerate the divine feminine. The mother of the man who became the Buddha and set the Noble Path is said to have had a miraculous life, ending shortly after the birth of her son. Tibetans, including the Dalai Lama, venerate a female *bodhisattva* named Tara, in Red, Green, or White form, seeking to embody her particular attributes by envisioning her presence and merging with that vision. In Chinese culture, Kwan Yen is also revered as either a goddess in her own right—the source of all life, according to earliest Chinese writings—or as a *bodhisattva* who eternally embodies the qualities of the Buddha and works to eliminate suffering.

> A *bodhisattva* is one who has embodied the Buddha-nature and, though eligible to move on to other realms, has committed to helping others on Earth achieve the same state.

In the Judaic tradition, and maintained in Eastern Christianity, God has a feminine aspect whose Greek name is *Sophia*

> Sophia ... strengthened Abraham, rescued Lot, gave victory to Jacob, stayed in solidarity with Joseph when he

---

[2] Lynn Gottlieb, *She Who Dwells Within*, New York: HarperCollins, 1995. pp.20-22.

went into the dungeon until she brought him to triumph and authority. Most dramatically, she worked through Moses to free the people from bondage ...
The Book of Baruch adds one more element ... She appears upon earth and lives among human beings (3:37)... The wise person is encouraged to walk toward the shining of her light. ... Community of life with her enables individuals to arrive at their destiny, and in the end enables the whole world and its history to be rightly ordered in justice and peace.
Sophia ... mediates between the world and the utterly transcendent God of Jewish monotheism.
...She fashions all that exists and pervades it with her pure and people-loving spirit. She is all-knowing, all-powerful, and present everywhere, renewing all things.
... Her powerful words have the mark of divine address, making the huge claim that listening to them will bring salvation while disobedience will bring destruction. ...
Rabbinic specialists themselves argue that neither wisdom nor word, neither God's name nor Spirit, nor *shekinah* were introduced into Judaism as secondary hypostases to offset the utter transcendence of the divine. Rather, these are ways of asserting the one, transcendent God's nearness to the world in such a way that divine transcendence is not compromised. ... Sophia's activity is none other than the activity of God.[3]

She is also the mother of 3 other "saints," called Faith, Hope, and Love. So the "saint" Sophia, honored in the famous Byzantine church (now mosque), known as the "Hajj Sophia" in Istanbul, is not a woman at all, but the very essence of the lovingly present, or immanent, divine.

Then there are all the other female saints, including the elusive but very present Mary Magdalene.

For those of us brought up in the decidedly masculine tradition of Protestant Christianity, taught that femininity is equated with sexuality and so should be limited to the bedroom—and by no means associated with church and the worship of the Father God—all these practices make little or

---

[3] Johnson, Elizabeth A., *She Who Is: the mystery of God in feminist theological discourse*, Crossroad, NY, 1999. p. 90-91

no sense. They raise a conflict in our understanding of our beliefs and our selves. The more we study, the more confusing it gets. Great men, powerful religious and social leaders, have practiced these traditions—and many still do. *How can we respect someone who so fervently believes something we've been so carefully taught is wrong?*

Approaching Understanding

Generally, American and other Calvinistic Protestant traditions have responded in one of two ways to this conundrum. Some reinforce their childhood lessons and set out to prove how awfully wrong such traditions are. They scour the Old Testament and the letters attributed to the Apostle Paul for language and rulings stating that women have no place in Christianity beyond bearing children and making a home in which those children can grow up good Christians. In the process, they prove to their own satisfaction that what they have always believed is the only true way. Others, in the spirit of Jesus' willingness to relate to women, Samaritans, lepers, a Roman centurion, and other outcasts from his Jewish culture, seek to understand and make allowances for other peoples' ways of doing things, honoring them for "their fruits," and holding the way open for them to find their own path, as did Jesus with the rich man's son.

My own story—and this book—reflects the latter approach. My mother was born in India of Methodist missionary parents and her sister converted to Judaism, while my father's father's parents were Jewish immigrants and his mother's parents were Baptist missionaries in South America. So my own journey of reconciliation of religious beliefs began when I was quite young. I didn't know my father, but I did know both of my grandmothers, and spent long hours with them exploring the magical worlds of other lands and belief systems. While both of them remained active in and occasionally took me to their churches (Methodist and Presbyterian, respectively), they retained a deep appreciation for the appropriateness of other beliefs in other settings. My mother was of a generation that abhorred "organized religion" in all its forms. Her compromise was to send me to Unitarian Sunday school—which I left at age seven because it taught me about the natural world and didn't teach me what the magic of Christmas and Easter were about. My next seven summers were spent on a farm, attending Lutheran Sunday school. That experience was supplemented by participation in a Northern Baptist church choir and youth group during middle school years. Active membership in the choir and youth group of a Presbyterian church during high school rounded out a rather eclectic Protestant upbringing.

College, as it always does, added a new dimension. I was sixteen when I graduated from high school, having been told by the school counselor that if I were a boy I'd make a good minister and having delivered my first sermon, "On Giving," at my Presbyterian church's Senior Sunday the week before.

My mother decided that I would go to a large university in another state, where her sister lived. My aunt was an anthropologist who had converted to Judaism upon her marriage. This was, she told me, partially in response to what she perceived as hypocrisy in the Christian church, and largely because her new husband had grown up in the tradition and it was a psychological system that made sense to her. I spent many weekends in her home, helping with the kids and learning Jewish household practices. I was seventeen, in a strange town in the desert, on a huge campus that was not my preferred school, struggling with the pain of adolescence and feeling very much alone in the universe. The teachings of Christianity seemed less and less relevant as I struggled with my feelings of isolation and low self esteem. If God was love, I was feeling very little of it. My mother had never been good at letter-writing and her hastily scribbled notes were infrequent and disturbingly critical. My older, wealthier, roommate despised me and convinced our neighbors in the dorm to do the same. Fortunately, she married at the end of the first term and I was assigned a new roommate who was far more congenial. She was a Catholic, and, as she was new to town, I escorted her to the local Newman Center—one of many associated with campuses all over the country that provide counseling, classes, and youth activities, as well as Sunday services for college students and faculty. The folk-style service was uplifting and the social-gospel sermons by the scholarly Jesuit priest intrigued me, even though I had begun to doubt the tenets of Christianity.

A class in Comparative Religions during that sane term changed my life. I took the class as an elective, but was very quickly hooked. Week after week we would read of and hear about people around the world who had found reason to believe in a power greater than they, and a way to connect with that power. It happened even if they had no contact with any other groups of people (beyond the anthropologist who was observing them and trying very hard not to influence them in the process). People everywhere found an underlying pattern in their world and an underlying intelligence expressing as various forms of power. Some traditions focused on working with the power in its different forms. Some focused on connecting with the underlying intelligence. Some did both. All the systems they developed were integrally interwoven with the culture as a whole, helping individuals to understand themselves and their relationships with others and the world around them. The more I studied, the more this kind of religion made sense, and as I saw how fundamental it was to all human life, I began to once again consider developing a spiritual life of my own. I was eighteen.

As life unfolded, I completed college, married a Navy officer, moved from town to town, had children, went back to graduate school, and developed a profession as a futurist. I also continued to collect information about religion and spirituality. My husband was Catholic and I attended mass with him and learned the teachings that supported it.

When our marriage was dissolved (in part because he stopped attending church and I needed a spiritual life), I decided that, since we live in a predominantly Christian culture, I would raise my children within that tradition. So we went to a Methodist church, where the service was very similar to the mass they were familiar with, and where the leadership included strong, loving women I was happy to see as role models for my girls. During those same years, as a community-development measure in our small conservative town, I helped to found a Unitarian-Universalist congregation that would provide a place for environmentally and socially conscious folks to gather and support each other.

All the while, the eastern traditions that I had learned about from my grandmother and in college were becoming better known across Europe and America. Many of the sacred texts and practices of Hinduism, with its emphasis on going within to discover the infinite, and developing the individual *Atman* to merge with the infinite *Brahman*, were becoming widely available. So, too, were the interpretive works by master teachers such as Alan Watts, Ram Dass, and Thich Nhat Hanh. Even Tibetan lamas, exiled from their own land, were beginning to teach in other countries the practices and theories that had long been hidden from western cultures outside their mountain sanctuaries.

American mystics like Joel Goldsmith were also becoming known. And a new set of "channeled" works, including the Seth material, *A Course in Miracles,* and *Emanuel's Book,* were underground best sellers.

Always eager to learn, I read everything I could get my hands on, learned to use meditation as a way to take my sense of connection with the divine to a deeper level, and learned a hands-on healing method called *Reiki,* hoping to learn to heal as Jesus did. I studied the various sacred scriptures from around the world, observed and participated in many rituals from many traditions, and, most of all, listened to the people around me as they shared their own spiritual journeys and ideas. Finally, when the children were grown, I trained and was ordained as a minister in the New Thought tradition.

New Thought is a uniquely American form of spirituality that emerged at the end of the 19th century. It combines the philosophy of Ralph Waldo Emerson with the practices of a mental healer named Phineas Pakhurst Quimby through the teachings of a Christian metaphysician, Emma Curtis Hopkins. She drew on a long line of eastern and western philosophical writings to explain the Oneness of all beingness and to demonstrate the presence, within each of us and throughout everything else, of the creative source and power of all that is. At last I had a framework that both mind and spirit could be comfortable in; I had found a spiritual home.

A New Hunger Expressed

Through the 1990s, I taught and spoke and led ceremonies as a "circuit riding preacher" for New Thought churches (including Unity, Divine Science, and Centers for Spiritual Living) across the Pacific Northwest—and for the Unitarian-Universalist congregation that I had helped to found. As I traveled from town to town, church to church, and classroom to classroom, a new theme began to emerge in the questions I was asked and the literature I was encountering. It had to do with what was called, variously, the divine feminine, the Goddess, the Mother, or the Womb-source of all life.

Mostly women, these scholars, ministers, and lay leaders were finding a new, deep satisfaction in recognizing the divine, not as a vengeful, judging Father, but as a nurturing, supportive feminine being, recognizing the phases of the moon as a reflection of their own life cycles, and honoring the earth as the source of our nurturance and supply. They were choosing to live lightly on the planet, using fewer resources, eating fresh foods, and expressing gratitude to each other and to the soil, water, and light on which their livelihoods depended. Some were gathering each month at the full moon to pray and sing and learn from each other. While most often found in the rural areas, more and more women in the cities were doing and saying similar things. These were intelligent, educated people, many of whom were active leaders in their communities, doing things that, 300 years ago, would have led to their being burned at the stake!

I could feel their hunger. I, too, had felt something missing, and my study of both psychology and spiritual traditions helped me understand the logic of their choices. Having studied the work of Carl Jung, I was aware of the need to develop both the *animus* (masculine soul/mind/spirit) and the *anima* (feminine soul/ mind/spirit), with the goal of ultimately merging the two into one whole Self. I had, almost subconsciously over the years, simply adopted Jesus' Comforter, the Holy Spirit or *Shekinah*, as the feminine divine, and taken the biblical stories of mother Mary and Ruth as my role models. But the women around me were asking for a more tangible acknowledgement that the power that creates and controls the universe is not entirely masculine in nature.

We had grown up in spiritual traditions that denied the existence of the feminine spirit. I had lived the problem a woman faces trying to be whole in a world dominated by a Father and Son, with only a formless Spirit to balance them. For others it was dominated by a demanding Lord Jehovah, who sometimes acted as a nurturing parent and sometimes as angry judge. For still others it was dominated by the one *Allah* (blessed be the Name) and his one very masculine prophet.

Indicators of the shift were evident outside of my limited circles, as well. Visions of Mary the Mother were being documented around the world. Catholic scholar Matthew Fox (author of, among others, *Original Blessing* and *The Coming of the Cosmic Christ*) was working with the self-proclaimed "witch" Starhawk, at their Institute for Creation Spirituality in a decidedly integrative approach to spirituality that went far beyond traditional doctrine in the Catholic church by identifying not only a need, but a clear role for the sacred feminine in spiritual life. Riane Eisler, an attorney inspired by the work of anthropologist Marija Gumbutas, wrote the best-selling *The Chalice and the Blade*, explaining how it came to be that women were so disempowered in our culture. As the decade progressed and the new millennium began, more and more books were published by women about women's spiritual history—and the need to recognize the feminine aspect of divinity as well as the masculine.

Somewhere along the way, I discovered *The Feminine Face of God*, by Sherry Ruth Anderson and Patricia Hopkins, which is not, in spite of the title, a description of God as feminine, but a set of stories describing the journeys women were taking through the 1980s and early 1990s to discover their spiritual identities and the practices to support them. The authors found a wide range of thought processes and experiences, with one consistent factor. They found that religion without the feminine qualities of nurturance, kindness, unconditional love and acceptance, along with the possibility of growth and development, was not sufficient to heal the heart and nurture the soul of women in the late 20th century. More, they said, these women were going to great lengths to find and define those qualities.

Joan Borysenko perhaps most accurately identifies the issues—and the process—in her lovely book, *A Woman's Journey to God*. A self-described "medical scientist and psychologist," Borysenko was director of Harvard's clinic and research program exploring the use of various meditation practices in medicine. She has since published a number of books that help to explain the integrated nature of mind and body—and the processes through which the total system develops. She says, "Spiritual growth is inextricable from psychological growth. And psychological growth is, in part, a gender issue. Men and women are different, our bodies as well as our brains." [4]

> Women are intrinsically mystical, that is, we tend to experience direct connection with the Divine. ... For women there really is no journey. Life and spirituality are one and the same. ... going through menarche, infertility, stillbirth, cesarean sections, normal births, the decision not to bear children, the loss of a child, menopause—these are women's mysteries and passages that are intimately related to our spiritual lives, and for which we seek meaningful ritual to celebrate, to find strength, and to mourn.[5]

Borysenko goes on to assert that

> "Almost all spiritual exercises and systems were developed by men, for men.... Step by step, according to psychological theorists as diverse as Jean Piaget, Erik Erikson, and Daniel Levinson, men ascend the ladder of psychological development. ... Several male Jungians, among them James Hillman and Thomas Moore, likewise conceive of spirituality as an autonomous journey traveled in a vertical dimension."[6]

This distinction between the feminine journey of deepening relationship and the masculine journey of ascending a ladder is fundamental to understanding Western spiritual culture. As Borysenko points out, for those of us in the Judeo-Christian tradition, the Bible is a road-map for the masculine spiritual journey: "... biblical Scripture, written by men for men... is concerned largely with public life rather than the details of private life, so little is known about the role of women."[7]

Starhawk put it this way in her book, *The Spiral Dance*:

> Since the decline of the Goddess religion, women have lacked religious models and spiritual systems that speak to female needs and experience. Male images of deity characterize both western and eastern religions ... Women are not encouraged to explore their own strengths

---

[4] Borysenko, Joan, *A Woman's Journey to God* 1999. p.69.
[5] ibid. pp. 5-7.
[6] ibid. p.70-72.
[7] Borysenko, Joan, *A Woman's Journey to God* 1999. 1999. p.7.

and realizations; they are taught to submit to male authority, to identify masculine perceptions as their spiritual ideals, to deny their bodies and sexuality, to fit their insights into a male mold." [8]

Biblical scriptures have guided western culture for over 1500 years. Directly and indirectly, they've led millions of individuals to a God-centered life of love and provided the basis for much of the material progress we have experienced in Europe and America over the same centuries. That's not all bad!

Today, however, too much conflicting evidence exists for the thoughtful person to simply accept the Bible *verbatim* as history, or even as the final word in spiritual life. More and more, thoughtful people seek a deeper understanding than most of us have found in the Bible, *Torah,* or *Koran.* We have come to a turning point in western culture in which, after over two millennia of denying the validity of the feminine experience, we are being called—required, even—to restore balance. In the process, something long buried is re-emerging; some long-ignored, inner hunger is being acknowledged and fed; some ancient understanding is being rediscovered. And many of us are discovering that this understanding is not new, just hidden in the best possible place: full view.

Discovering a Hymn to the Divine Feminine called *Notre Dame de Chartres*

My first memory of seeing the cathedral in Chartres, France, is a slide that was shown at a gathering of faculty and students at Rockford College following a "summer abroad" that my grandmother had helped chaperone. Frankly, it's the only slide I remember from that warm, sleepy evening. There, silhouetted against the blue sky, was the most compli-

---

[8] Starhawk, (Miriam Simos), *The Spiral Dance.* Harper San Francisco, 1979. p.8

catedly beautiful structure I had ever seen (and living on the University of Chicago campus meant that I had seen plenty of interesting buildings!). I was fascinated, and the presenter's voice was full of wonder, tinged with regret that the group couldn't spend more time examining this marvel.

Decades later, a guided meditation that was called a "past life regression" ended with a vivid image of me sitting within the partially-constructed walls of that same structure, teaching workers during its construction. A brief run from Paris on a stopover several years later gave me the opportunity to validate the experience. On that trip, walking up from the train station, I came around the corner and found myself right at the spot where I had been sitting in the "vision." It was an eerie feeling, not unlike *déjà vu*. I knew I would come back another day.

An Ancient New Kind of School

During the year I began writing this book, 2006, a celebration was underway in the city of Chartres, France. It was the thousand-year anniversary of the founding of a school there by a man named Fulbert (*Fulbertu*s in the Latin texts of his time).[9] His school was associated with the Roman Church, as were all schools at that point in European history, but it went so far beyond the normal teachings of church schools that Chartres became the intellectual center of Europe for the next 200 years. It was so beloved that parts of the cathedral that Fulbert built still stand today, as the foundation of this great mother of all gothic cathedrals, on the promontory above the town. Fortune and a good friend made it possible for me to spend almost two weeks there for

---

[9] 2006 was also the first year of a new series of classes being offered by a new university, Wisdom University, of San Francisco (formerly the Institute of Creation Spirituality), in which the school's president, Jim Garrison, was leading a modern "Mystery School" each year at Chartres. Participation in the 2006 session is part of what inspired this book.

this once-in-a-lifetime event and to experience the cathedral and its founder in much greater detail.

Fulbert was a remarkable man. He was comfortable speaking at least 5 languages and had read not only the Bible (which was unusual at the time), but many of the ancient Greek philosophers and early church theologians in the original Greek, as well as Latin and Arabic histories and philosophical texts. He had traveled extensively, serving multiple bishops and a pope in his journeys. Along the way, he discovered a great hunger in the hearts of his fellow clerics: a deep desire to experience the kind of connection with God the Father that Jesus had. He also found that there was a dismal lack of understanding of how to fill that hunger.

In his readings Fulbert had learned that the ancient Greeks had developed a spiritual ladder. It was a process by which, through study and experience, a man could begin to feel the Spirit's love move in his heart and the power of God move in his soul. In his travels Fulbert had observed that two groups of mystical scholars, Jewish (students of the Kabbalah) and Arabic (the Sufis), seemed to have mastered this process. Under the guidance of his mentor, Gerbert of Aurillac, who went on to be crowned Pope Sylvester II, Fulbert proceeded to learn this process and apply it in his own life—which led, inevitably, to people wanting to know what the secret of his joyful, loving, powerful presence was, and, of course, the demand that he teach it.

So, with the blessings of his bishop and pope, Fulbert founded a school—a mystery school in the ancient Greek tradition—through which his students might transcend the limitations of their limiting belief systems and begin to experience the mystical Oneness that they longed for. It was a place where Jesus' "two-law" ("Love God with all your heart … and your neighbor as your Self") was paramount, where mental discipline was the primary skill to be developed, and where the intellect was constantly challenged with new ideas and opportunities for synthesis. It was a cauldron (*grail*, in the Celtic language that many of them spoke*)* in which hearts and minds were opened and Wisdom was honored for her own sake.

Second sons of noble families and wealthy tradesmen flocked to be tutored by this wise and famous man. Designated by tradition for the priesthood, many of these young men had traveled and learned other languages, but had not found, in the monastery schools of their childhood, explanations for their experiences.

Fulbert offered them the skills and opportunity to find their own explanations, while giving them a new career path, that of scholar, and they loved him dearly for it. A letter (translated from the Latin it was written in) from one former student to another helps us see this:

> Beloved in Christ, fellow-pupil and foster-brother, a greeting in the Lord, from Adelman.
>
> I have called thee foster-brother because of the fair time we have spent together, I by a few years the elder and thou as a young man, in the Academy of Chartres under our beloved and venerable Socrates. We indeed have an even greater right to glory in our life together with him than had Plato when he gloried and gave thanks to nature that she had created him in the time of Socrates not as an animal, but as a man.
>
> It was ours to know the still more blessed teaching of this catholic and most Christian man, and we must now hope that in the presence of God he helps us though his prayers, for we ought not to believe that the loving thoughts with which in his goodness he enfolded us as in the womb of the mother have had an end, or that the Christ-like love with which he received us as his sons is now extinguished in him. Without doubt he is much more mindful of us, has a much more all-embracing love for us than when he made his pilgrimage here in this mortal body.
>
> And through his wishes and silent entreaties he turns our minds to him, adjuring us by those secret evening talks in the little garden by the chapel, when he spoke to us so often of that kingdom, in which if God so wills, he now sojourns as a senator.

And most earnestly he implores us by those tears which many, many a time broke forth from him in the middle of his discourse, flowing over from the surging of his holy passion, that we should zealously struggle thither in that we walk straightly in the kingly path ...[10]

Fulbert was clearly a tremendous influence in the lives of these young men! Many of them took these teachings home to share with other family-members. Some became the heads of families and communities; others stayed in the monasteries to become significant scholars in their own right.

An Ancient Curriculum

Fulbert introduced and explained to his students the thought process, symbols, and metaphors of the Greek tradition, and the mystery schools associated with it. The Liberal Arts, as defined by the ancient Greeks, were the ladder by which the students would climb to the ultimate mystical union:

1. *Grammatica,* learning to receive the word by learning the letters, basic reading, syntax, and grammar;
2. *Dialectica,* learning to describe one's experience through speaking and writing one's own word and by analyzing the written word;
3. *Rhetorica,* learning to speak clearly, articulate well, and compose thoughts into beautiful sentences and verses;
4. *Arithmetica,* learning to understand numbers and numeric values, to count and account, and to see the mystical nature of numbers through numerology;
5. *Musica,* learning to relate number and time, perceive rhythm, analyze and compose melodies and harmonies;
6. *Geometrica,* learning to perceive numerical values and relationships in space, to perceive and analyze the basic shapes in two- and three-dimensional space, to com-

---

[10] reprinted from *The Golden Age of Chartres: The Teachings of a Mystery School and the Eternal Feminine* by René M. Querido, Rudolf Steiner College Press, 1987.

pose harmonious spaces and structures based on them, and to experience the mystical value of different shapes;

7. *Astronomica*, learning to see numerical relationships in space-time, to understand the rhythms and cycles of the stars, the sun, and the moon, and to see how they affect life while learning to use observation of the stars as a means to deepen one's mystical sense of oneness with the universe.

It was a carefully designed curriculum, developed in ancient Athens around the time of Plato and much evolved over 1,300 years of implementation, with each step preparing one for the next.

These "Liberal Arts" were taught through the written works of their foremost Greek expositors. Plato and Socrates opened the door to the world of language. Pythagoras explained the nature of number and music, as well as geometry (remember the Pythagorean theorem? It's just one of the many contributions he made to our current world!). And all of them were taught as the seven aspects of the soul, whose mastery was a path of purification: part of the process of encouraging "that mind which was in Christ Jesus" to come alive in the student.

> Although most of the great works of the ancient Greeks had been lost to Europe during the fall of Rome, the Muslim Arabs, through their conquest of Alexandria and other Hellenistic cities, had preserved and studied both the documents and the methods. Fulbert, having spent time in the Arab-influenced Mediterranean region, had learned them well enough to restore their teachings at his school in Chartres.

On completion of the 'undergraduate" curriculum, the young men who attended this cathedral school were welcome to go home, but rarely did. Here at the school they were free as they could never be at home. They were challenged by ideas, not weapons, and they were not required to pay taxes nor marry as long as they could find a way to support themselves here.

As a result, many students went on to "graduate work." Having mastered the Arts, they began what would be for most a lifelong study of the two sacred Sciences (*scientia* being a Latin word meaning "way or form of knowledge"):

- *Astrologica*, (astrology) the science of relationships between the macrocosm and the microcosm, the stars and humanity, the within and without, was studied through observation of the essential characteristics of each of the constellations and the planets and how they affect each other, as illustrated in human life and history—and the application of that understanding to decision-making and design;
- *Alchemica*, (alchemy) the science of the interactions of things, exploring the role of consciousness and catalysts in transformation—in matter, in spirit, and in human lives—which set the foundation for the modern sciences of chemistry and psychology.

These are, perhaps, the most ancient of sciences. Astrology was practiced in ancient Chaldea, the region of Abraham's birth, as well as Egypt, as far back as the earliest written records. Students would spend the night charting the paths of the heavenly bodies and then compare them to observed events and identify patterns. Alchemy appears to be more recent, usually credited to an Egyptian mage under the Ptolemys whose name is reported as Hermes Trismegistus (meaning "thrice-great"). The word alchemy, however, is Arabic in origin, and the method has often been confused with sorcery (remember cartoon images of old men in long robes chanting in laboratories high in the tower or deep in the castle keep?). Nonetheless thousands of scholars and seekers have practiced it over the centuries, including Isaac Newton, who was among the last Europeans to practice the discipline, and all indications are that he accomplished his goal—

becoming head of the British mint soon after shutting down his laboratory.

Building as a Teaching

That these Arts and Sciences were held sacred is demonstrated in the many reminders of their importance in and around the cathedral and its associated structures. Over the 200 years that the Chartres school was operating, the original church burnt down and was rebuilt several times—each time more lavishly. The underground "crypt" of today's cathedral is, in fact, Fulbert's last basillica.

The great Western porch, called the Royal Portal, with its three entrances, was begun by Fulbert in 1020 and completed by Thierry of Chartres over the next 20 years. It remains standing today, recently cleaned and polished so the hundreds of sculptures that adorn it are easily seen and their remarkable personalities shine through. A series of seven sculptures arch over the right door, called "the Wisdom door" of this portal. In these sculptures, each of the liberal arts is embodied, in the ancient Greek tradition, by a female figure holding the tools of her craft.

The following are the pagan scholars whose work formed the curriculum of the greatest Christian school in the world for over two centuries:

- Priscian for Grammar
- Aristotle for Dialectic
- Cicero for Rhetoric
- Boethius for Arithmetic
- Euclid for Geometry
- Ptolemy for Astronomy
- Pythagoras for Music
  (because *Musica* holds the instruments that he used to develop his theory of intervals)

Musica and *Grammaria*, on the shoulders of the philosophers who defined the fields, on the Western Portal at Notre Dame de Chartres.

Adjacent each of the Liberal Arts is the symbol for a day of the week: the Moon for Monday, Mars/Thor for Tuesday, etc. Then at the center of the pointed arch, on the tympan, is carved a lovely Madonna with Man-child on her lap (a version of the ancient statue located in the crypt, the remains of the original sacred site on which the cathedral was built), and an angel on each side. With this image the pattern of the "undergraduate" studies of the school is clearly presented, even for those who cannot yet read: the infant soul/spirit is embraced by Mother Wisdom (in Greek, "Sophia" who "was with God even before the Creation") and nurtured through the seven levels of understanding, or arts.

The left-hand, north, doorway of this remarkable entrance illustrates the first area of "post-graduate" study: astrology. The bay over the door is lined with the symbols for the signs of the zodiac next to carvings of workers performing the tasks associated with the month in which each sign emerges.

The Mystery

Signs of the Zodiac (Virgo at the top) and associated labor, in the arch over the Left (north) door of Western Portal at Notre Dame de Chartres.

At the center of the arch on this doorway is the Christ ascending, with an angel on either side. Again the message is clear, having completed the cycle of the zodiac, man is no longer mortal, tied to the chains of matter (*mater* meaning "mother" in Latin, and is the root for "material" and "matter,"); completion of this study is to ascend with the Christ. The tympan of the great central portal, with its double doors lined up directly with the labyrinth and altar within the cathedral, represents the pinnacle of achievement: Christ in glory, framed by the *vesica piscis* or *mandorla* (the pointed-oval sign of the sacred feminine), supported on the lintel by the 12 apostles and 2 additional figures.

> The *vesica piscis*, or *mandorla*, is the space in the overlap of two circles: the product of the two coming together. It sometimes represents the vagina, the entrance to the womb. Turned on its side, it's also the "fish" sign associated with early Christians.

He's surrounded by the 4 animals that, since at least 400CE, have symbolized the authors of the four gospels.

They're also the 4 "living creatures" in Ezekiel's vision and surrounding God's throne in John's *Revelation*.

Lion = Mark
Ox = Luke
Eagle = John
Angel/human = Matthew

Christ in the *Vesica Piscis*, over the central door of the Western, Royal Portal of Notre Dame de Chartres.

This set of connections is from St. Jerome. Others have linked them in different orders. St. Augustine, for example, said,

> ...those who have taken the lion to point to Matthew, the man to Mark, the calf to Luke and the eagle to John, have made a more reasonable application of the figures than those who have assigned the man to Matthew, the eagle to Mark, and the lion to John.

With this central door, we see that the alchemical transformation is complete. The seeker is no longer animal in nature but is now one with the Christ, who is enthroned and blessing all who enter this sacred space.

An Ongoing Lineage

Fulbert died around 1029 and was followed by a succession of scholar-priests whose works have been woven into the fabric of the Roman Church, as well as the nations of Europe, over the centuries. By and large, these were men who had studied at Chartres, gone out into the world, and were later called back to lead further generations. Among them:

- William of Conches, who attempted to reconcile the atomic theory of Democrites and the Epicureans with the physical theories of Plato's *Timaeus*, and who defended the use of reason against the opponents of natural science. For example: "We do not place a limit upon divine power, but we do say that of existing things none can [reconcile earth and fire], nor in the nature of things can there be anything that would suffice..."

- Peter Abelard, who at one point in his life was the most renowned logician and dialectician in Europe, summarizing the essence of the school's teachings with, "The man of understanding is he who has the ability to grope and ponder the hidden causes of things ... those from which things originate, and these are to be investigated more by reason than by any sensory experience"

- Thierry of Chartres, Fulbert's immediate successor (d. 1155), who took on the first attempt to explain the universe in terms of natural causes, declaring that it was impossible to understand the story of Genesis without the intellectual training provided by the *quad-*

rivium, "for on mathematics all rational explanation of the universe depended."

- John of Salisbury, one of William of Conches' pupils, who in 1170 was elected Bishop of Chartres, was a close friend of Thomas à Becket (Henry II's chancellor and later Archbishop of Canterbury) and considered the leading statesman of his time.
- Bernard of Chartres, who expressed both in words and the windows of the cathedral, "We are dwarfs on the shoulders of giants ... so ... we perceive more than they do." (This was centuries before Isaac Newton, who may have used the quote as a code reference.)

Building As a Spiritual Experience

Several of these chancellors had the task of rebuilding the cathedral after a great fire. The final rebuilding occurred, remarkably, in the 26-year period between 1194 and 1220. The entire building, except for the great Western Royal Portal, with its huge rose window and imposing towers, was demolished by fire in the fall of 1194. But, under the rubble, hidden in its reliquary, the precious fabric known as *La Chemise*, the cloth donated to the cathedral by Charles the Bald, grandson of Charlemagne, in 876, and believed to have been worn by the Virgin Mary when she bore Jesus, was found unscathed.

It was a great miracle that called for great and pious action on the part of the people whose lives were touched by this building and the school it housed. One of the pamphlets available at the cathedral shop says that during the next few years:

> Every person there set to work, then people came from the neighboring provinces, neighboring kingdoms, even from England, then at war with the king of France, Philip Augustus. Those who could not come sent offerings. This was communal effort as redeeming as a crusade, uniting serf and artisan, lord and lady, under the same yoke in

order to heave, like beasts, the stones and timbers, sand and lime.[11]

Historian of religion Karen Armstrong describes the process as an alternative to the military crusades—one that focused on peace and healing, rather than war:

> A building association was formed that organized lay men and women, rich and poor, to quarry stones themselves and convey them to the site. An awed monk wrote to a monastery in England of the extraordinary scenes he witnessed. Men and women yoked themselves to the huge wagons "like beasts of burden." Nobody could join the building association unless he had reconciled himself with all his enemies, and even though a thousand or more lay people were working together at a time, there was absolute silence, save for the prayers of the priests who accompanied them, "exhorting their hearts to peace." ... All night long there was singing of hymns and canticles.[12]

René Querido, of the Rudolf Steiner College located in Sacramento, California, has written a detailed history of the cathedral and its school. He says,

> Laborers, apprentices, journeymen, and masters of architecture, stained glass and sculpture were assigned tasks commensurate with their inner development as well as skill in the craft. In architecture, for example, those in the first degree might be allowed to hew stone used outside the building. Second degree workers would graduate to the task of cutting stone to be used for the pillars within. Third degree workers would be permitted to sculpt the architraves and capitals...while fourth degree were instructed on the relationship between the inner and outer forms, and so on. A mason would not be allowed to work inside the building unless he had a certain attitude of soul, otherwise, it was felt, he might interfere with the spirit of the building by bringing to it the wrong forces.[13]

---

[11] *Chartres Cathedral*, Editions Valoire, 4th page.
[12] Armstrong, Karen, *Holy War: the Crusiades and Their Impacct on Today's World.* pp. 222-223
[13] Querido, René, *The Golden Age of Chartres*. Rudolf Steiner College Press, 1987. pp 49-50.

It also happens that the Grand Master of the Knights Templar during this time was one William of Chartres, and many indications of Templar involvement in the cathedral's construction are evident in the artwork that adorns this remarkable building.

Building on a Sacred Site

The cathedral is known to have been built on an ancient Celtic sacred site, to which pilgrims have traveled since long before the Roman Empire. Histories of the Druids suggest that they had major gatherings there. The promontory of limestone, or "chalk," and granite on which it rests, is the classic formation for ancient sacred monuments throughout Britain and Europe. Adjacent the site is a set of *dolmens*, or "cairns," standing stones that may be the basis for the name of the people who lived there during the Roman Empire: Carnutes. The cairn is so fundamental to the city's identity that it's in the city's seal today, and also in the medal given to pilgrims visiting the cathedral since at least the 1200s (though it's upside down on the medal) shown below the sacred relic, La *Chemise*, being carried by two monks or priests in its reliquary.

The Seal of the City and the medieval pilgrim's medal for Chartres with a dolmen in the circle between the 2 monks carrying *La Chemise* in its case.

Beneath the cathedral is the "sacred well," tapping into a spring (in French called *source*) that was part of what made this place, like hundreds of other across Europe, sacred to the divine feminine, or "Mother Earth" by the ancient—and many modern—Celtic people. An ancient image (which many believe was originally carved into the stone, a Neolithic petroglyph, and is now replicated as a statue carved in pear-wood) called *Notre Dame de Sous-terre* ("Our Lady of Under-Earth") confirms the dedication. Many believe that it was because of the presence of this image that the early Christians claimed the site as the oldest Christian church in Europe, saying that the locals had been honoring Mary, the Virgin Mother of God, even before the Christians arrived!

**Madonna of the Crypt: "Our Lady of Under-earth,"
Notre Dame de Chartres**

Homage to the Divine Feminine

From the beginning, then, the sacred site of Chartres has been associated with the divine Mother, so it's not too surprising that the Madonna (meaning "Great Mother") is the dominant image in this great structure. Unlike most modern Christian structures, which focus on the death of Jesus; this one is filled with images and reminders of birth. In all, over 150 images of the Madonna and child may be seen in this amazing structure—ranging from the famous "black Madonna" sculptures in the crypt below the altar and on the pillar just inside the North porch, to the glowing *belle-Verriere* (meaning "beautiful window") over the South Porch.

The great rose windows are, in themselves, homage to the divine "Rose of Sharon," one of the names for the feminine found in the Song of Solomon. Below them, in the lancets, we find on the North side an image of "Sancta Anna" holding "her daughter, the Virgin Mary" (see photo on p. 233). Across from her, over the South Porch, is *Notre Dame de belle-Verriere,* "Our Lady of the Beautiful Window", crowned and holding the Child on her left arm, much as she is represented in the far more ancient image, in the crypt, below.

This very visible adoration of the Virgin-Mother, however, was more than acceptance of church doctrine. Each of these images was a reminder to the student that, when the study was complete and the soul had been purified, it would become virgin-like, ready to give birth to a new level of knowledge, a new way of being—the spiritual seeker would be "re-born," a new Son of Man, nurtured in the arms of Mother–Wisdom.

This realization is reinforced when one sees that, alongside all of these images of mother-and-child are many images of women with books.

***La Vie Contemplative*, Notre Dame Cathedral at Chartres.**

Now this building was built between 1190 and 1230 CE. There was no printing press; books were hand-copied or hand printed with wood blocks. There were no public grammar schools, and only men were allowed to go to the schools run by the Church. There were, in those days, only three acceptable careers for women: wife, housemaid, or nun. The only other way to survive was as a courtesan or prostitute—who might learn to read if they chose. (The video *Dangerous Beauty* illustrates that very issue quite accurately). Wives were mothers and housekeepers, kept "barefoot, pregnant, and ignorant." Housemaids were even less well educated. Nuns might learn to read a few prayers in a breviary, though there were a few shining examples, such as Hildegarde of Bingen, who not only read books, but wrote poetry and music and administered large landholdings for their convents. What then could all these images possibly refer to?

One lovely sculpture provides a clue. It's called, *La Vie Contemplative,* "The Contemplative Life." It's located by an arch near the heart of the building and tells us that these images are, as is almost everything in this amazing "encyclopedia in glass and stone," a metaphor for the attainment of Wisdom—they are the feminine aspect of the divine, as She is absorbing and integrating ideas within each of us.

Once we peel back the many assumptions that we bring from the Judeo-Christian perspective, the cathedral at Chartres is clearly the perfect starting point for developing a deeper understanding of the role and history of the divine feminine in our empire culture.

*In the cool of the evening, the people gathered
in a circle in the meadow, beneath the old oak tree.
In the center stood a woman,
A healer and a teacher of the wisdom of the earth...*[14]

THE OTHER HALF OF PRE-HISTORY: THE AGE OF BALANCE

In order to understand the true message in the cathedral at Chartres and comprehend the role that Mary and the divine feminine have played in the traditions of Mediterranean peoples and our own culture, we need to step back and re-examine the history and pre-history of Europe and the Middle East.

Life before Empire

It's hard to believe when we look at the history of Asia and Europe, but humanity as a whole has not always lived in fear of being raided by marauders or overrun by neighboring peoples. For most of the people of the world, over most of human occupation of this planet, each cul-

> The "war parties" and "sorties" of cultures like the Plains Indians of North America were never intended to take land or do real harm, but were a sort of competition, designed to provide a relatively safe outlet for the excess testosterone of adolescent males.

---

[14] Title tune from the record album, "Burning Times," by Charlie Murphy.

tural group has lived on land that has been theirs for as long as they can remember. Their language, their social structure, and the land that they live on are one. They could no more "pick up and move" than fly to the moon: they would have no way to communicate, no way to relate, and so no way to identify themselves, or possibly even survive, if they did. They would no more try to take their neighbors' land than they would try to steal the ocean; it would be an impossibility. They were born in one place, they lived their lives in that place, and they looked forward to a good death and burial in the earth that sustained them.

We can observe this way of thinking today among the few remaining remnants of the once vast array of human cultures: tribal aborigines in Australia, "Bushmen" and forest "pygmies" in Africa, "Indians" in the Amazon, "Eskimos" in the Arctic Circle. And, based on the documents of invaders over the millennia, it seems to have been the case for most of the (currently accepted time-span of) 200,000 years of human culture. The experience is beautifully illustrated in David Abram's *The Spell of the Sensuous*, particularly where he describes how certain songs must be sung by aboriginal Australians as they move through certain lands—even when they do so in cars, when the song must be sung very fast, to keep up with the landscape going past![15]

Building for A Long-Sustained Way of Life

For many thousands of years, virtually all peoples on this planet were brown-skinned gardeners and gatherers, living in a way that had evolved over millennia to maintain a harmonious balance with nature, within the community, and in each person's body-mind. Evidence for this way of life abounds in archeological sites and in the ethnology of Neolithic cultures documented over the past hundred years, from

---

[15] David Abram, *The Spell of the Sensuous; perception and language in a more-than-human world.* New York: Vintage, 1996.

Hopi-land to Tibet, from the Andes to the Kalahari, and from Lapland to Alaska.

One of the oldest towns to be excavated so far is called Catal-Huyuk, in southern Asia Minor, an area once known as Anatolia. It's so old that some have called it the missing link between the "Paleolithic" (old stone) age of wandering hunting/gathering tribes (200,000-10,000BCE and in hidden tribes around the world today), and the "Neolithic" (new stone) age, that started about 11,000BCE and may be seen around the world through the early Industrial era, and now in the village farming cultures of Central Asia."[16] Because of its age and the extent of excavation that has been completed there, Catal-Huyuk serves well as a model of life before the current age, which has been defined by Invasion and Empire.[17]

With an average population of about 1,000 people, the town-site known as Catal-Huyuk was occupied for over 5,000 years, evolving from a village of scattered huts with shared gardens (about 9000BCE) to a well-planned town with covered sewers, plastered-brick houses with doors and courtyards, and open plazas, by 6000BCE. Buried in layers of brick walls, dirt, burials, and trash are remains of furniture, tools, musical instruments, pottery, and many kinds of foods, with the walls of shared food-storage facilities.

The town is open and orderly, looking very much like Taos Pueblo in New Mexico, today. Plazas are surrounded by single-story houses or apartments, set stepwise, one on top of another. Each house has a courtyard, a kitchen area, sleeping alcoves, and a sacred altar-space. The kitchen areas have storage facilities and access to outdoor clay ovens. Covered latrines drain into covered sewers along the streets. The

---

[16] James Mellart of the British Institute of Archaeology at Ankara, *the Neolithic of the Near East* (1975), quoted in Riane Eisler's *The Chalice and the Blade*, pp 7-10.

[17] The most detailed description of this site is to be found in Marija Gimbutas' *The Civilization of the Goddess*. A remarkable re-creation of the town may be found in Forte and Siliotti's *Virtual Archaeology*.

baked-brick walls are plastered and painted, often with multi-colored murals. Trees and fountains are found in some courtyards.

A Model of Catal-Huyuk.

In the later periods, there are lovely copper implements and jewelry, alongside beautifully worked stone and pottery. Some of the pottery and stonework have a form of "sacred script" on them, dating from 5500-5000BCE. Most strikingly, according to an analysis of burial remains of one period of over 800 years, no one died a violent death.

The Neolithic Pattern

Comparing the town-pattern, art forms, and tools of Catal-Huyuk with other sites in Europe and the Middle East, it looks as if the Anatolian-style culture emerged over several thousand years across Macedonia and northward into Europe, southward along the Mediterranean coast, onto the islands of Crete and Cyprus, and eastward through Mesopotamia and into India. Jericho and other ancient Palestinian sites repeat this pattern. Early Egyptian villages repeat this pattern Sites along the Danube River do, as well.

Between about 8000BCE and 4000BCE, throughout Asia and Europe, wherever a river created a fertile flood plain, the Anatolian pattern can be found. And with this pattern we see artifacts of the triune Goddess religion evident in every home and public area.[18]

One of the interesting things about these towns is that there doesn't seem to be a hierarchy; there's no great difference in wealth among the residents. All households appear to be essentially self-sufficient. While some homes have priestly objects and others have artisan's tools, for thousands of years, houses, jewelry, and other art forms, food storage and preparation areas are all similar in size, number, and capacity. The Anatolian pattern of community appears to have been very egalitarian.

It was also very inventive. Not only were baked bricks, plastered walls, covered sewers, chimneys, tiles, and ceramics well advanced by the 8th millennium BCE, metallurgy began in these communities, as well. As a result, by the time Crete was settled, around 4500BCE, bronze and copper implements were common. And, as mentioned earlier, a form of "sacred script" associated with sanctuary spaces was developed, along with the other art forms. These were used first as individual symbols on objects, and then evolved into story-scripts associated with the use of the objects.

Clothing ranged from leather outerwear to finely spun, intricately woven cotton and linen gowns and curtains. Woolen rugs and wall hangings had complex designs. Jars of ointments were carved from stone or made of pottery. Musical instruments were also present in many homes.

Residences were well insulated, built of local materials, usually rock and clay with wooden support beams with win-

---

[18] This understanding of such findings was pioneered by University of California archeologist Marija Gimbutas and is documented in *The Goddesses and Gods of Old Europe*. Riane Eisler, Monica Sjoo, and other feminist writers have drawn extensively on her work, and Merlin Stone's *When God Was a Woman* takes it several steps further.

dows for ventilation. Community centers such as the stone circle and temple-mound, however, would be built using materials hauled from several miles, and sometimes hundreds of miles, away.

A stone circle, oriented to the sun, moon, and evening star, would usually be built near the town on a limestone or basalt hill under which a "blind spring" (underground water source, feeding other springs in the area) was located. The stones making up these circles vary in size, from mere boulders to the huge stones we find in places like the 8000-year-old Stonehenge outside of Salisbury, England. Similar megalithic stone circles can be found throughout Europe and Western Asia and have been dated in Brittany (northwestern France) from 4000BCE.

Sacred mound at Sillbury, Britain; one of many from about 4000BCE.

The other common structure in or near these village sites is the temple mound. Typically, this structure would have three rings of courtyards around an inner chamber with one small door and no windows, the interior walls of which were usually painted with red ochre or ox-blood. These, too, are found from Egypt and Mesopotamia to Italy, Yorkshire, and Ireland (often built into the shelter of hills), dating from about 5000BCE.

Honoring the Feminine

In most sites from that era, many artifacts and wall-paintings focus on feminine figures. Wall paintings, pottery, and jewelry show various interactions of these icons: the Virgin-Maiden alone or with a serpent, bull, or moon, the Mother bearing all life, Maiden and lover, Mother with infant Son, the consort/lover as hunter, the Son injured and dying, the Crone alone or with the waning (crescent-shaped) moon or a bull (with crescent-shaped horns) or in the process of restoring her Son's life, and many more.

Some figurines from various sites in the Fertile Crescent are shown below. Note that the ancient feminine ideal was not the slender, athletic figure of today, but far more like what comfortably fed and housed middle-aged women's bodies actually look like!

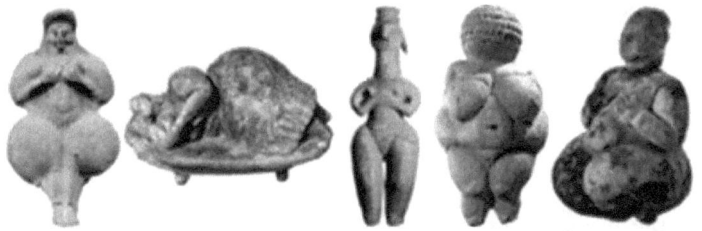

Grand-Mothers, sometimes called "Venus figures," from various Neolithic sites.

Looking at these icons, one can almost imagine a young girl or young wife missing her mother picking up a bit of clay or rock or wood and crafting a figure that is reminiscent of the absent one. Or a barren woman, wishing to become pregnant, creating an image of herself with child. One can see how later generations might venerate the beautiful carving—and the person it represented. The Mother, the beloved Maiden, and the Grand Mother were at the core of life in these times and places.

Daily Life in River Garden Villages

The pattern of life that we see in these ancient sites remains fairly consistent in Neolithic cultures around the world—through the ages and across the continents. As in early Anatolia, the cycle of one life-form giving up its own life to another, as well as the cycle of the year, are celebrated in annual rituals, ceremonial art, and oft-repeated stories. From Hopi-land in southwestern North America to rural Tibet in the mountains of central Asia, and from Finland south to Botswana, similar stories are told and similar rituals are celebrated among indigenous peoples. Some of these refer to events dated as early as 20,000BCE that have been substantiated by archaeologists.

So, if we use descriptions of life on Crete (Minos, the heart of the great Minoan culture) and the other Goddess-oriented cultures that were described in ancient literature, and combine them with modern ethnographies, we can imagine what it must have been like to live in these towns tens of thousands of years ago.

Daily life would have revolved around the cycles found in household and field, punctuated by seasonal activities. People would have known who they were in the community and the larger world, and what was needed from them each day, and, while this knowledge was comforting, it was also a little confining, so they would look forward to regular seasonal festivals as opportunities to break out of those molds for a while.

Activities would have been based on the circle, or spiral, of life. The circle of the sun, the moon, and the seasons would set the tone. When the rains came, how long the dry season lasted, and the first and last frosts would have determined what most people were doing at any given time. Virtually everybody in town would participate in planting, and again at the harvest. There would be seasonal hunts to provide variety in the diet and limit the animals and birds that threatened the crops. Then there would be feasts of thanksgiving and fasts of purification to help keep the earth, sky, and people in balance. Special events and "impossible" tasks and projects would be set up to stretch the wits and bodies of young people, and those who completed these tasks would be honored for their courage, talent, and skill.

And through it all, the trained teachers and healers at the temple and stone circle would guide and counsel, mediate and arbitrate, and, when necessary, prophesy and heal, to help the people find a balanced, healthy way through the spiral of the years.

In western Asia, as in most parts of the world, specific stories and rituals are defined by the natural cycles of the place. For Turkey, once called Anatolia, the land and seasonal changes defined a very specific set of stories, art, and ritual, much of which is still in place, even in today's "godless" society.

There were two seasons in the region: dry (summer) and wet (winter). The year would begin at the height of summer, the midpoint between the summer solstice and the autumnal equinox (our July 31/August 1—called *Lughnasa* by the Celts, and Whitsunday in old England), which would typically also be the beginning of the harvest. Winter would begin at the fall equinox (around our September 21), when the rains came and the harvest was in, then would end at the spring equinox (around our March 21), when summer would begin. The summer solstice (around June 21), the shortest night of the year, would mark the halfway point through the season, or "midsummer's night," just as the winter solstice (around December 21), the longest night of the year, marked the halfway point of the wet season.

During the dry season, while the crops ripened in fields and gardens, many outdoor activities would go on. Athletic events would be held. Homes and common spaces would be built or repaired. Travelers would wander through. There would be trading among the towns, and occasionally great fairs, where traders from all over Asia and Europe set up camp in the plaza or a dormant pasture to exhibit delightful objects and raw materials from other places. People would sleep in their courtyards or on their roofs, out under the stars. Great processionals through the town and services at the temple and stone circle would honor the turning of the year.

Then, with the shortening days, the rains would come, and the colder weather. Activity would move indoors. Crops would be prepared for storage. Tools, furnishings, and fabrics would be made or repaired. The interiors of homes and public buildings would be decorated. Children would be taught the skills necessary for a good life, and all would listen to and learn the stories and songs of praise to the great Mother that was the source and sustainer of all, who, out of her own being bore all that is, including her own divine Son who, born in the dark of winter, would grow up to become her companion and lover—beginning the cycle again.

Sun Cycles

Each winter, as the sun reached its nadir (low point) on the horizon, the people would gather at the stone circle and call it back. At the solstice (which means "standing still," usually between our December 21 and 24), they would light bonfires and lamps, wear gold and copper jewelry that they had made for the season, and sing songs of praise for the sun's warmth and light. They would feast and share gifts, and dance the great circle dances, knowing that what is praised and appreciated grow,

> Anthropologists call this practice of attempting to create something in the world by doing what it does, "imitative magic;" In the New Thought tradition, it's called "living the Law of Attraction."

and then, when they could see the sun begin its journey once more on the horizon, they would carry new fire to the temple-mound, to remain lit for the next year, as a reminder of

The Other Half of Pre-History

the presence and importance of the light. In later years, under Roman rule, it would be the job of the Vestal Virgins to maintain this fire.

The next few months, dark and gray, with long nights and occasional snow falls, would be spent quietly, eating little, sleeping a lot, telling stories of the past and dreaming about the year to come: what might be planted and hunted and built and created in the next turn of the year. Teachers and elders would go from home to home and stay a few days, sharing songs and stories, teaching the young ones, and offering healing services.

When the first lambs were born and sun rose at the midpoint between the solstice and equinox on the stone circle (our February 1 or 2, "groundhog day" "St. Bridgit's day" or "Candlemas"), the temple leaders would call the people together to start a new cycle. As a group, with the guidance of the highly intuitive and wise teachers

> The term "marriage" is used loosely here. The evidence suggests that marriage as we know it didn't exist, but couples would come together with the intention of having children, who would then be raised by the whole extended family, while the couple typically broke up and each went their own way—lifelong partnership was rare.

and healers of the community, the people would decide who would do what work, manage which fields, and contribute in what way to the whole. It was a time to make vows: of marriage, of ministry, of stewardship, and to the wellbeing of the community. Everyone would wear white and drink the fresh lambs' milk as they sang and danced and began a new year, and new life, together. One young woman would be dressed in white and covered in a veil to represent the goodness of the Goddess, present in her Maiden form, and would be honored by everyone as such for the coming year. (In northern Europe and the US, brides—from the Irish name for the Goddess, "Bridgid" or "Bridget"—wear white, with a veil, as an indication of their maidenhood.)

As the sun's cycle continued, food stored from the last harvest would be running low. A few greens from carefully tended south-facing gardens, along with mushrooms from nearby forests and fish from the river, would be supplemented by milk, cheese and yogurt from cattle, sheep or goats who were nursing their newborns. As the river rose with snowmelt from the mountains, even fish might be hard to find. In hard years, the adults would do without, or fast, letting the youngsters and sick folk eat what remained of the food. (We call this period "Lent," from an old Saxon word that means "lengthen.")

> One of the rules for "keeping Kosher," following the ancient Jewish law, is not to "eat the meat of the calf in its mother's milk." Given the nature of the Hebrew language, this may originally have been a rule against eating the young during the season Christians call Lent.

But when the sun reached the spring equinox, and the day was finally as long as the night (equinox meaning "equal night"), it was time to decide which of the young males from the herds would live to serve at stud, and which would be set apart, or "made sacred" (which is the root meaning of the word "sacrifice") to be ritually slaughtered with great thanksgiving, and prepared as the first meat of the year. The people would gather at the stone circle, where the judging and butchering would take place. One man would be given the honor of cutting the young rams' or bullocks' throats and letting their blood flow into a bowl (to be saved for a variety of uses) and, always, a portion returned to the soil. In later years, Sumerian and Babylonian texts tell us, the calf's head would be cut off and floated down the river, as a gift to the power that controlled the flow.

Afterward, the remaining young ram or bullock would be decorated and praised as worthy of siring healthy offspring, as would all the newly adolescent men. And the people would process back into the town, leading the young men and the bullock to the temple-mound to be blessed by the woman representing the Goddess. Then each family would carry their share of the precious meat home.

The spring equinox festival would also signal the time for planting, and over the following weeks all would go to their agreed-upon fields, singing songs of praise for easy growth and good harvest. They would till the fields and plant the seeds that had been carefully saved from the previous year in communal storehouses—often located in or near the temple-mound. The procession from storehouse to field would be gay and happy, as the whole town came out for the first planting of the new year, honoring the great Mother-source which would sustain the plants and the Father-sun whose light and heat would ripen the crops.

At the midpoint between equinox and solstice (which we call May Day), the town's mothers would be honored, and the girls who had entered womanhood would be blessed. The new mothers in the herds would be led through the town, in procession with the young women and the woman chosen to represent the Goddess in her Mother form, arriving at the temple to be blessed, along with the early harvests of young greens and vegetables.

By the summer solstice, the crops would be well established and a few fruits would be ripe. Again, the people would gather at the stone circle and the sun would be honored as it reached its apex (high point). Games of athletic skill would follow, and dancing and picnics, with songs and stories, would be enjoyed around campfires through the short night—honoring the heights of human capacity and divine potential. The champions among the men would be recognized for their prowess, and lead another procession to the temple-mound for blessing—and, for the greatest athlete, a mystical union with the Goddess.

Over the next several weeks, life was easy. It was time for the men to watch for predators, to hunt birds, and to trap fish and small game. It was time for the children, women, and elders to gather at the temple to learn answers to the questions they had pondered over the winter months. It was time to develop new skills—to ride the sacred bull or handle a boat or to shoot an arrow or throw a spear without losing it, for the men, and to discover the healing plants and minerals for the women.

By the mid-point between the summer solstice and fall equinox, the young animals born last spring would be mature and the harvest would have begun. It was time for all the people to gather in the fields, again, and at the threshing floors. To feed the people while they worked, the oldest bulls from previous years would be slaughtered, butchered, and smoked over great pits in the stone circle. People would snack on this barbecued jerky during the next several weeks of work in the fields.

Then, when the crops were harvested, and the threshing done, the seed-grain would be carried in great processions into the storehouses, which would be sealed by the temple leaders for use next year. A great harvest festival would be held, with new games and dancing and songs of thanks and praise for the wise and nurturing Goddess who supplied the people with all that is good.

Moon Cycles

Within this larger cycle, another set of cycles was recognized. The phases of the moon, and its location in the sky, were every bit as important as the location of the sun. And in some places, especially near the equator (where there's little seasonal variation in the location of the sun), it's even more important. These 13 moon-cycles "plus a day" remained the measure of a year for villagers throughout Europe, Asia, and Africa well into the 18th century.

Many researchers believe that the first calendars were made by women tracking their bodies' cycles by the moon. The phases of the moon not only correspond with tides in lakes and oceans, they also map the 29-day menstrual cycle of most women. So the moon, in most cultures, is associated with the life-giving, creative power of women and the earth, which power is represented in virtually all cultures, as the Goddess. Like the moon, the Goddess has phases:

- Growing, she is the Maiden or Virgin.
- At her fullness she is the pregnant or nursing Mother, then the administering Matron.
- Waning, she is the wise woman, the Grandmother, the Crone, who has the experiences of a lifetime to draw on as she observes and assists her family and community.

And each phase of the moon, like the positions of the sun, was honored with appropriate rituals.

The moon was not worshipped, but its presence was used as a reminder of the presence and characteristics of the Goddess. Through the first quarter, the young women would be honored, and any girl who came into her periodic cycle would be welcomed into the circle of women. As the moon reached its full phase, the mothers would be honored, and any pregnant women would be comforted, massaged with oils, and otherwise cared for. As the waning crescent moon hung low in the sky, the older women would be given their due.

The Women's House

In most cultures around the world, menstruating women have a special place to go while they let the "blood of life" flow from their body into the earth. In these places, they take care of each other, massaging aching backs, tired feet, and swollen ankles, and they learn from each other: about sex, about love, about becoming mothers, about all the things that women experience, everywhere. They also get a break from the routines of homemaking. While nursing babies are allowed in the space, no one else may intrude on the women, there—it's a sacred (meaning "set apart") space. For hard-working mothers, the 3 or 4 days spent in "the women's hut" each month are blessed days, indeed.[19]

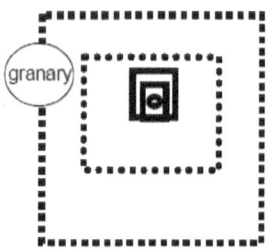

"Women's House" plan.

A special fence would often be built around the dooryard of this house, to let the little ones play safely while their mothers rested inside. Boys and men, older women, and pregnant or pre-menstrual sisters and daughters would leave food and drink for the women while they were there—outside the fence so the little ones wouldn't get into it

Sometimes the women's space would be a cave rather than a hut; the women would gather inside Mother Earth to return their life-blood to the soil. Still, there would be a safe place established around the opening and an area beyond where people could come by and leave their gifts.

In the early stages, each village of Anatolia would have had such a women's house. This sacred space would have been honored as the place where women came into their power as life-givers. Over time, the little houses in the villages along the rivers evolved into house-sized buildings, with plaster-covered brick walls. This women's house, with its interior and exterior courtyards, was still set apart from regular houses, though, with special decorations—mostly in the color red.

---

[19] Anita Diamant's book, *The Red Tent,* is a marvelous description of the experience of such a place.

As the population grew, and more women used the space, it would grow to accommodate them. Since it was the one place that all the women visited, it would be logical to store the annual supply of seed-grain in or near it. Since it was where women went to learn from each other, the courtyards became places where people went to find answers to questions about life and death and relationships—with men allowed only in the outer spaces—beyond the inner fence.

Widowed older women whose children were grown or gone might choose to stay permanently in the women's house, caring for the younger women, healing any injuries, and sharing their wisdom with those who asked. Small sleeping-spaces would be built within the safe, inner courtyard for these older caretakers, and they would be offered a share of the food left for the women.

> The idea of a man choosing to live a woman's way of life is strange to most Europeans and Americans, but is considered an acceptable option in many cultures. From the Plains tribes of America to the steppes of Asia (and, dare we say, within the Christian church?), to have the capacity to think like both a man and a woman and put on a woman's long robe has often been considered a path to true power—and worth the price.

Sometimes older, widowed or injured men, or the occasional young boy would choose to live in the courtyards. To maintain the spirit of the law, they would be required to wear the robes of women to do so—in later years, they were often castrated, as well, becoming eunuchs in the service of the Lady.

So now we have a sacred building surrounded by walls and courtyards, where men and children may not go, where the cycles of the moon are monitored and recognized, where blood flows and is offered to the Earth, and where women come into their power and understanding as givers and nurturers of life—buildings which archeologists, much later, called Moon temples.

The Stone Circle

Typically, the stone circle was out in the open, usually on a hill outside of the town, where the night sky could be seen and the rising and setting sun would be observed at the moment it touched the horizon. One pair of stones would mark where the sun rose and set at the summer solstice, another at each of the equinoxes, and another pair at the winter solstice.

Eight more stones might be used for the midpoints between those dates, which correspond roughly to our Groundhog Day or Candlemas (also known as St. Brigit's Day, or *Imbolc*—which means "in milk" in Celtic), May Eve and Day (*Beltane* to the Celts), High Summer (July 31-August 1, *Lughnasa* in the Celtic and "Lammas" in Christian tradition), and All Souls & All Saint's Days (Samhain in the Celtic calendar, with Halloween—All Hallows ("All Souls") Eve— the night before).

One of many stone circles across Europe, dating from about 8000BCE.

This meant that there would be at least 8, and sometimes 12 or 16, stones in any circle, their size and type depending on what was available in the region. In or adjacent to the circle would be at least one more stone—usually a different color, and often smaller than the others. This would serve a number of functions, from altar to viewing point, or "eye" stone.

Aligning these stones precisely to the appropriate position of the sun would have been an important task for the men of the village, and would have required some engineering and agility. The tasks of finding, cutting, and moving the stones, then setting them in their proper positions would be shared by younger men—might even serve as rites of passage, as well as tempering testosterone flows. As the moon was the women's guide, the sun, with its influence on the plants and animals of forest and field would be the men's guide—and this circle would be a site for masculine rites of passage, with the trainings and exhibitions that go along with them.

Once the stones were in place, the circle would also provide a place for the whole community to celebrate the turning of the year, coming every few weeks in great processions from the town. Individuals may have used it as a place to study the sky and the stars and to learn about the planets (a Greek term that means "wandering ones") and their relationships with community life. Young men and women might practice their dances among the stones. Older folk might use the stones as an aid to meditation and prayer—as later cultures use labyrinths and "stations of the cross." The community would share the first meat of the year as the young males were culled from the herds in the spring and butchered here. The winter solstice and spring "cleansing" bonfires would burn here. And, sometimes, the death of a leading member of the community would be commemorated with a great funeral pyre on the altar stone.

Though the stone circle was considered the men's responsibility, there would be, now and then, a woman who was uncomfortable with women's roles in the community and preferred the activities and company of men. Like her male counterpart at the women's house or temple, she would "cross-dress"—and sometimes would have one or both breasts removed. Her men's clothes would allow her to engage in the sports and hunt along with the men in the community, so she would help maintain the circles, and learn about the stars and planets and other men's "secrets" with her co-workers. These "amazons" would often have reduced or nonexistent periodic cycles and would be excluded from the women's "moon house," having identified themselves with the men. Sometimes, however, the balance of life might be restored by honoring these women as another aspect of the Goddess—a form that, in later years, was called Diana, Athena, and Minerva, the divine feminine as huntress and warrior, an athlete with a mind like a man's.

Maintaining the Balance

Harmonious balance is the fundamental necessity in all sustainable cultures. All of the above-described rituals around the sun and moon and the seasons, the honoring of women's cycles and men's prowess, and the structure of the houses and towns, are part of the process for maintaining balance in these long-lived cultures.

We can observe in the ancient icons and murals that both men and women maintained local sacred spaces, or sanctuaries, where grain was returned with thanks to the Earth mother in burning-bowl ceremonies, drums and flutes were played, pottery was made, and sacred stories were retold. Women's gatherings would have included stories and songs and activities that strengthened women's bodies and spirit and skills for bearing and raising families and fostering healthy relationships in the community. Men's gatherings would have included opportunities to challenge the body and intellect, to develop new skills in hunting and fishing, and to protect themselves and the community from predators.

All forms and activities of human life were recognized as part of the whole and kept in balance through right action and prayer-full rituals. As the women worked within the village and gardens, the men worked in the fields and forests and on the rivers. As the women chose when and how to marry and bear children, the men chose when and how to propagate the herds and limit the predators. As young adults explored life around and in other villages, older people kept the home.

We could know more, if we could translate the sacred writings on the clay jars that line the walls of these ancient communities. However, although we have no real way to translate the language of ancient Anatolia, much research has been done on the Egyptian language—where a very similar, and possibly related, culture was in place by about 5000BCE. There, the word for "right action" with implications of truth and justice, was the same as the name of the earliest form of the Great Mother: *Ma'at,* a word that may well be the root of the much-later Hittite/Syrian word, *mat,* and the even later Greco-Roman word, *mater,* both meaning "mother."

Illustrations in tombs and temples in Egypt show Ma'at as the weigher of souls: if one's word was good, she would permit eternal life; if not, then the soul was condemned to destruction. A funerary inscription of the famous "Negative Confession" to be recited by an Egyptian man's soul on facing Ma'at after death tells us about "right action" from this period:

> I have not been a man of anger. I have done no evil to mankind. I have not inflicted pain. I have made none to weep. I have done violence to no man. I have not done harm unto animals. I have not robbed the poor. I have not fouled water. I have not trampled fields. I have not behaved with insolence. I have not judged hastily. I have not stirred up strife. I have not made any man to commit murder for me. I have not insisted that excessive work be done for me daily. I have not borne false witness. I have not stolen land. I have not cheated in measuring the bushel. I have allowed no man to suffer hunger. I have not increased my wealth except with such things as are my own possessions. I have not seized wrongfully

the properties of others. I have not taken milk from the mouths of babes.[20]

Egyptian drawing of weighing the soul, with Anubis and "the monster" at the scale, and with many people praying, above.

Through such choices, such right action, all human activity could be kept in the balance that Ma'at, as the source and nurturer of life, required.

Although everyone maintained essentially the same standard of living in Anatolian-style cultures, different levels of skill and learning, with appropriate initiations and inductions, were recognized. Someone who had mastered the healing arts, or who understood the ebb and flow of the river and the ways to direct it into the fields, might be at a higher level of respect than the less-experienced homemaker or farm worker. Higher still, in the sense of knowing more and being able to do more, would be those who understood the basic principles of all such activities. These people would be honored at seasonal celebrations and when significant events occurred in the life of the community. One woman and one man, in particular, would typically become the "mother and father," elders, for the community.

---

[20] From Sir E. A. Budge, *Dwellers of the Nile,* p. 254. Very likely women had a similar, but role-appropriate, version.

As the community grew, the gifted women—those with a marked ability to take in information and also develop their intuitive skills—would spend more of their time as healers and teachers in and around the women's house, which, over time, became the Moon temple. There, they would spend time alone, connecting with the earth in the safe, dark central building, and learn from each other through observation and dialogue. As new generations experienced change and insecurity, one of these women would emerge as the mother-teacher for all. Like the mother-superior of a modern convent, she would guide others in their own learning process and administer the operations of the temple community. To the uninitiated, looking in from the outside, it would appear that she was second only to the Goddess: Her representative on earth.

Similarly in the men's circle. Boys would learn to run and leap and hunt and fish and build and lead. In the evenings and in poor weather, boys would be instructed in the wisdom of the world, beyond what was taught in the home. Holidays and feast days would provide opportunities for them to demonstrate their prowess. Strenuous rites of passage would help to channel testosterone. Through their own training process, focusing on skills and ideas very different from the women's, the men developed their own hierarchy of knowledge and their own measure of the ideal.

After a time, one man would emerge as the One who Knows, taking on the role of the knowledgeable, intuitive, and powerful son of (meaning "right hand" of), the Sun, around whom the men's rituals centered.

Sacred Marriage

Over the years the positions of Mother of All and Son of the Sun became ritualized, and the concept of "holy marriage" (called, years later, in Greek: *heiros gamos*) emerged in the various river valleys. Each year, these two were publicly united. As long as the community flourished, their union continued. If any problems emerged in the community during their time together, or if the man showed signs of infirmity, then the man, as the Mother's consort, was let go at the spring equinox (with "the passing" or "Passover") and a strong new Son of the Sun was installed at the height of each summer (August 1, now known as *Lughnasa* or *Lammas*), to restore harmony and bring the life-giving harvest and autumn rains.

This ritual became the manifest fulfillment of the nearly universal explanatory story for the seasons: the Goddess losing her lover/son, weeping for her loss, going into the underworld to find him and negotiate with her sister goddess for his life, then bringing him back to life as her son/lover—restoring harmony and well-being to all creation.

Each village or tribe would have their own names for the characters involved in this story, just as individual tribes and nations do today. Many of the Anatolian tribes had a name for the Mother/ Source/All with the syllables "An-a." In later years, these would be written as Inanna (in Sumer, the oldest written name), Diana (around Ephesus, in today's Turkey), Anat (in Canaan), Anna, Athena, and many others.

The consort of the Goddess had two names: one for the youthful son and another for the mature lover. Often the name of the son would have the syllable "us" or "uz" at the end. In Egypt the son was Horus and the lover, Osiris. In Sumer the son/lover was Marduk, in Chaldea/Babylon he was Dimuzi or Tammuz , in Greece, Bacchus, and in Rome, he was Dionysius.

> It's possibly because of these special male role models that the masculine form of most Greek and Roman nouns and names ends in "-us."

After the ceremony, the men and women involved in the rituals would return to normal life, until the next occasion for ritual came around on the cycle. Like a prom king and queen who must return to class and take exams with everyone else, "the Mother" and "the Son (or Consort)" were understood as temporary titles and states, taken on as part of the annual cycles of the community. In this way equality of responsibility and opportunity were maintained in the harmonious balance of the whole.

Emergence of the Temple as Institution

Prayer-full ritual and right action provided not only a way for balanced life, but also a means to influence the various powers of nature—all of which were recognized as aspects of the one power from which everything flowed. Throughout Neolithic cultures, everyone bears responsibility for such ritual and action.

To honor the individual powers was a relatively easy way to honor the overarching one—the forces of nature and the powers of animals were visible and tangible to those who had not yet been initiated, and images and icons, which the Egyptians later called *neters*, were kept visible as one way to remind them. Sanctuary houses and household prayer spaces had many images of full-bodied, sometimes-pregnant women. In later years, these homes also were replete with bulls' horns, whose crescent shape is reminiscent of the crescent moon, which is always associated with the feminine aspect of the divine, while the bulls, themselves, are clearly masculine in nature. The massive horns decorated sanctuary walls and served as an elevated seat near a fire pit—again harmonizing the masculine and feminine aspects of life. Other images, of bird-women and snake-women, as well as hunters and fishers, abound, as well.

To honor the source of power that these images represented required abstracting from direct experience to principle and developing the ability to do so required, for many people, long years of training in the Sun circle or Moon house. As a result, the leaders in these centers were highly respected as people of wisdom, and were also relied on as healers and teachers, counselors and mediators—skills that take time to learn. We know that music and dancing was an important part of the balancing act, and many people were musicians—which also takes training.

So the Moon house and Sun circle became both temple and university. Women would spend their "blood time" every month that they weren't pregnant or in the first months of nursing a child, (whenever their menstrual flow would stop) to learn, as well as to relax and be cared for. Young women would spend time with them prior to marriage. Older women would return when their children were grown. Men would follow a similar pattern, setting up their own, parallel, learning institution at the stone circle.

The future leaders of these institutions would go through training and initiations that taught them to become the "right hand of the divine," which, in the ancient languages, means, "manages the work of." [21] The work to be managed varied from community to community, depending on the number of people, the amount of land needed to sustain them, and the storage requirements for food. In smaller communities, of a few hundred or less, the man and woman selected to represent the Goddess and her Consort would act as mediators and arbitrators for whatever conflicts or misunderstandings might arise, as well as guides for life decisions and chief healer—bringing the wisdom and power of the Goddess and her Consort for everyone. In larger communities (sometimes as many as several thousand, living in self-sufficient households), these roles were distributed among many well-trained people, working under the direction of the selected pair.

The merging of the educational function and the religious function of the temple continued for thousands of years. Well into the 19th century, even in Europe and in the US. Local churches were the sites and organizers of local colleges all over the Eastern and Midwestern states of the

---

[21] Aramaic scholar George Lamsa has provided more accurate definitions of a number of biblical phrases according to ancient usage in his *Idioms in the Bible Explained* and *A Key to the Original Gospels*.

U.S.—many of which were seminaries, built to train ministers, more than for any other purpose. It's not until the concept of federally funded "land grant" colleges was introduced at the end of that century and socialist countries built public schools that education was seen as separate from religious development in western culture.

An Evolving Structure

As we go northward from Anatolia into England, we find sacred spaces built, not above ground and open to the weather, but inside great mounds—some of which have been called tombs because they were also used to honor the bones of those who had made a profound contribution to the community.

Moving southward into Egypt, we find the same. At first, sacred spaces were covered over with dirt, then they were built into terraced mounds, then evolved into the great pyramids, some of which also became tombs. Eastward into Mesopotamia, the temples were built according to the same design as we've seen so far, but aboveground, and the inner *sanctum* was typically elevated above the courtyards, sometimes as much as 70 feet.

How this might have come about makes for interesting speculation. It's possible that the height was needed for astronomical observations: as the number of people increased, the smoke and light pollution would make it difficult to track the moon and stars from "street level." It's also possible that the ancillary use of the space (or an adjacent building) as storage for shared supplies of grain and other foods required extra protection from pests and predators. But another possibility comes to mind. Consider the situation: women come together every month to let their life-blood flow into the earth. After a time, as anyone who has used ox-blood to harden a dirt floor knows, the earth in their space would become hardened and unable to absorb more blood. At first, more soil or sand would be brought in, to absorb the flow.

In time, though, the floor would be so close to the ceiling that no one could use the space.

So a new space would be created—often simply on top of the old one. The new space would therefore be elevated. It would have a higher ceiling. And it would have plenty of good, fresh soil or sand to absorb the flow of blood from the women who gathered there.

After a time or two of rebuilding the sacred space, someone would have figured out that the precious blood could be drained from the room into a receptacle—or even down into the earth below the courtyard—by the same means as wastes were drained from the latrines. So a grooved drain would be built into the floor and the women's blood would be allowed to flow into the earth, below, where it belonged.

As the population grew, of course, there's no way all the women could come to one room at one time, and other Moon Houses, sacred houses, temples, and retreats were developed. But the main town temple, with its roots in the original "women's house," remained a place where blood was restored to the land, and where women—and the men who dressed and acted like women—could learn and heal and be healed. And so it continued, well into the Roman Empire, and in some places, even today.

Based on written descriptions, illustrations, and more recent structures of the same style, we have pretty clear ideas about the way these temples were used. It was very like the original women's houses. The outer, largest courtyard was a place where anyone might gather, at any time, to bring gifts, hear the stories, dance the dances, and enjoy divine blessings. During festivals and good weather, this area would have been filled with people. Arguments would be settled, promises would be made and broken, and visitors from other places would have been met here.

The second, slightly smaller courtyard was only for those who had been initiated (literally meaning "begun, introduced") into the community, and teachers and healers would meet with students, disciples, and aspirants there, providing esoteric (meaning "inner circle") knowledge.

The smallest, interior courtyard, originally for women, babies, and older widows, now became a place for secret teachings. It was restricted to those who had made a commitment and demonstrated a willingness and ability to learn and serve: priestesses, priests (who, in most places, had become eunuchs and wore the robes of priestesses), and their novice-assistants. Here rituals were prepared and occult (meaning "hidden") teachings were shared.

Within this courtyard, the inner sanctum, the "Holy of Holies," was kept sacred, which would be in keeping with the sacred nature of the "women's house" on which it was based. Originally it was a place for the women to gather and be re-empowered, but as wisdom evolved, it became a place where those who understood the deeper meanings of things and had developed their spiritual and mental capacities would experience unity with the power of the All and channel that power for the well-being of the community. This space was reserved for certain people on certain days. Artifacts sacred to the local representation of the Nurturer/Provider/Protector were placed therein, to be seen or used only by the highest initiates.

The sacred days, according to stories and illustrations that we can see today, were—as they had been for thousands of years—determined by the position of the sun, moon and Daystar/Evening Star, as seen by their alignment in the stone circle. If those who tracked the night skies saw that it was time to give thanks for harvest, or to cause the rains to start, then it would be necessary for the priest/priestess to commune with the divine powers in the inner sanctum. On rare occasions, it might be necessary to enter the sacred space to find guidance for the community—as did the priestess at Delphi. The space was also used as part of the initiation process of the priests/priestesses. According to

Egyptian records, to be sealed into this "inner sanctum" for three days and nights and to rise again as a new being, part human and part divine, enabled them to "sit at the right hand" of, or "manage the work" of, the divinity.

These temples emerged throughout the "Goddess" cultures, and especially clearly in the Minoan culture of Crete, which was destroyed by a volcanic eruption about 1500BCE, before being overrun by invading horsemen. There, the temple at Knossos, once assumed by archeologists to be a palace, is now understood to have been a store-house and educational facility, as well as temple. At the center of its maze-like corridors is the "holy of holies," a place of danger for the uninitiated, where the divine and animal aspects of a human being were united through a series of trainings and initiations into a powerful form that, in later years, the Greeks feared and called "the Minotaur." Not far away is an arena, once a stone circle, where young men and women demonstrated their lack of fear and athletic prowess by dancing with bulls—which seems to have been a common accolade to the divine feminine among Anatolian-style communities that continues still, after a fashion, in bullfights and the "running of the bulls" in Spain.

Upsetting the Balance: The Age of Invasion & Empire

Traditional scholarship has assumed a gradual developmental shift from the horticultural river-town pattern of life to the "classical" urban design associated with empires, but there's increasing evidence that such was not the case. Instead, the shift was punctuated and erratic, and it seems that regular waves of cattle-herding, armed invaders riding their horses out of the Caucasus and Taurus Mountains into the river valleys below were a prime causal factor. [22]

It looks, from the archaeological records, as if taking over someone else's land was not a possibility in human experience until about 6,000 years ago. That was when the first herder-warriors came out of the Caucasus and Taurus mountains and drove their herds into the river valleys of the Middle East.

The original Caucasians, they called themselves "Aryans," "golden ones," and "sons of the light." And, starting about 4000BCE, these invaders rode down out of the mountains every few generations, to claim new lands for their herds and new women for themselves.

> BCE replaces the old dating system of B.C. (meaning "before Christ"); it's read as "before the common era" with "A.D." (*anno domini,* or "the year of our lord") now CE, to be read as "common era." The numbers of the years remain

---

[22] Again, Gimbutas provides the seminal work in this area, but her ideas are supported by the historically documented "waves of invaders" across Europe and Asia, as well.

The first two waves of these migrations had little effect on the peoples of the valleys, as the men tended to look for high-meadow pasturelands for their cattle. However, the third wave of these "Indo-Europeans" (called such because their language became woven into every language from England to India) emerged out of their mountainous homelands about 3,300BCE. Using historical and archeological timelines, it's possible to trace a pattern of invasions of light-skinned people nearly every 200 years since then. (Appendix A details this cycle.)

These large, light-skinned, blond and redheaded men were descendents of the ancient ice-age hunters of the woolly mammoth. Their forefathers had followed the snows to higher elevations as the glaciers had retreated 5,000 years before. There they had evolved their way of life from following herds of game for hunting to managing herds of sheep, goats, horses, and cattle. They lived lives and told stories of heroic proportion. (See Appendix C for their own descriptions of themselves, from the ancient text: *Rig Veda*.)

These men and their herds are the leading edge of a shift from the Age of Balance to the Age of Invasion and Empire—an age that we still live in, today. They spread in all directions: southwestward into Asia Minor, the original "Anatolia," down the Tigris and Euphrates into Mesopotamia, along the Mediterranean into Egypt, westward into the valleys of the Danube and the Ural, northward toward the North Sea, southeastward into the Indus valley, and eastward across the high plains to the Yellow River.

The various descriptions we have from those days make it clear that these men were the first emperors—in Sumer, Egypt, China, and India—and that their descendents remained the nobles, priests, and warriors of the countries they controlled. They were the ones "favored of the gods" and were the heroes and heroines of every recorded story. Even today we can see the remnants of this pattern: in almost every country, from Scandinavia to Java, the lightest-skinned,

Upsetting the Balance: Invasion & Empire

lightest-haired people are usually the highest class, the heroes of the traditional stories, and the most popular celebrities and leaders. And many studies have demonstrated that, in a wide range of cultures and across generations, well-muscled blond, blue-eyed men and women are considered "more attractive" than their darker, less athletic-looking counterparts.

Traditional scholarship has long recognized that emigrants from the Caucasus called themselves Aryans and are associated with the origins of the Indo-European language group. The branch who went to India under the name Aryans, which means "noble ones," is usually called the Indo-Iranian group. In fact, the word "Iran" is derived from the Persian word for Aryan.

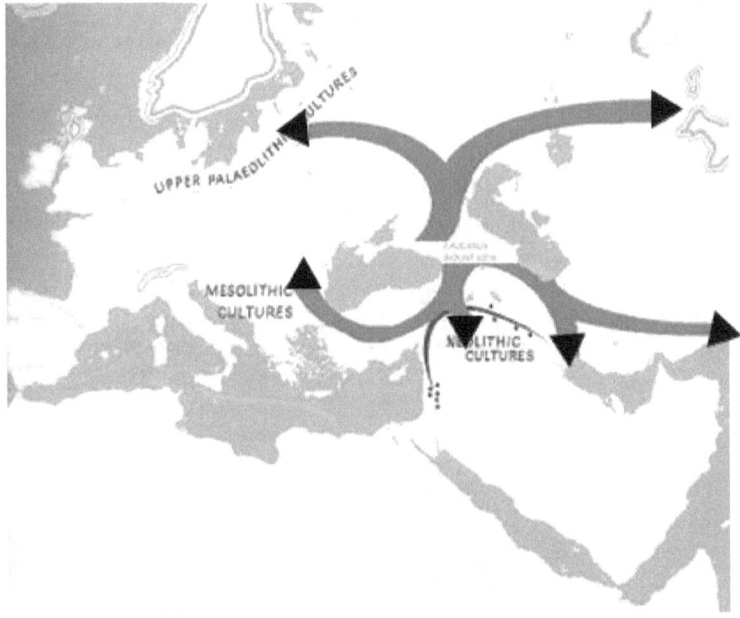

Migration pattern, 4000BCE and ongoing.

Other branches spread into Greece and western Asia, where they were known as Hittites, Kassites, Hurrians, and Mitanni. A rock inscription found at Boghaz Koi dated about 1400BCE and commemorating a treaty between the

Mitanni and Hittites, invokes the Aryan gods Indra, Varuna, Mitra, and the twins Nasatya (Asvins).

They were big, loud, boastful men, the original cowboys. Their tales of heroism, evolved from the ancient practice of hunters reenacting the hunt in evening stories, became the basis for the most ancient Sanskrit texts known as the *Vedas* and contributed to the Sumerian mythos—which in turn became the basis for the Babylonian and Chaldean tales woven into the Old Testament. Their names, in time, became the names of gods and kings, and were frequently the titles taken on by later generations of empire-builders seeking to emulate them. Their physical prowess and total lack of regard for the gentle, non-confrontational standards of behavior that had evolved among the smaller, dark-skinned men in the balance-oriented Anatolian-type communities made it easy for them to overpower whatever minimal defenses such communities may have had to protect themselves from predatory animals.

One illustration of this behavior pattern in one of the oldest Sumerian texts, called today "The Epic of Gilgamesh."

> Gilgamesh is making everybody crazy: he's going into the markets and taking whatever he wants, he's bedding whatever woman catches his eye, he's fighting with any man who catches him the wrong way; he's just being barbaric in a civilized community. He's bigger and bolder and louder and brasher than anyone else in town, but he's the rightful king and the people simply don't know what to do with him. So a council of elders meets and decides he needs a friend and a quest. They know of a "wild man" who lives not far outside of town with the herds and they decide to tame him and bring him to Gilgamesh.
>
> Unfortunately, however, nothing works—until they send a "temple harlot" out to him. She uses her "womanly wiles" to persuade him to clean up and come into the city, where the council names him Enkidu and introduces him to Gilgamesh. Immediately the two men get into a brawling fight that does much damage to their surroundings, but after Gilgamesh has pinned Enkidu, the two become

fast friends. As they get to know each other, it turns out that Gilgamesh has behaved this way because he fears death and wants to be immortal. The council sends them off on a quest to find out how to be immortal and the two friends have all kinds of adventures, while the town is left in peace.

These brash "cowboys," warrior-herders, lived by a set of rules based on "more is better." More land, more cattle, more horses, more women, more children, more jewels—and ultimately, more power over the lives of others—these were the goals they set for themselves, and taught their sons to set for themselves and their families. Recognizing that the women they were capturing to bear those sons were from a different culture that had different values, these men implemented a standard practice of removing male children from their mothers at age six or seven, to ensure that the boys would adopt their fathers' traditions, rather than the women's (not unlike the tradition among British of the upper classes well into the 20th century).

How could this happen? What factors could lead to this particular set of behaviors and assumptions? Consider the possibility:

> The rugged, stormy, volcanic mountains of the Caucasus were one of the last remaining sites of glaciers following the retreat of the great ice sheets. Herds of horses, deer, and cattle from the Ice Ages were isolated in these mountains and at least one tribe of hunters followed them there.
>
> In these hunting tribes, as ethnographic records document today, groups of men typically would spend three to five days following game animals, then another day or two bringing the kill home. They would frequently endure miserable weather and push their bodies to the limit. On their return, the rigors of the hunt would be offset, not only by the food and other products that came home with them, but also by the enthusiastic response of those who stayed home to the entertaining reenactments of the hunt that followed the feast, and to the retelling of favorite heroic exploits. These hunters were encouraged to show off their skills; they depended on each others' strengths in the hunt and they competed with each other

for attention and access to good things at home. In their world, a man's life revolved around the hunt; women existed to make and maintain home, to prepare food, to nurture babies, and to provide sex. Starting about age six or seven, boys would have spent most of their time away from the women to be prepared for the hunt with the men. By ten, they would be working with the older men to prepare for initiation experiences that would set the pattern of their adulthood as strong, skillful hunters and entertaining storytellers.

Over the generations, as the herds dwindled, the men shifted their focus from killing prey to keeping the sole source of food—herds of sheep, goats, horses, and cattle—strong, and many of these same traditions were maintained. Men who had spent days out protecting the herds would share their adventures around the evening fire "in the field" and at home, recalling the heroic exploits of previous generations as part of the entertainment. Very young boys would listen to these stories and take them as models for their own future activities, and, as soon as they were old enough be trusted, they would be taken out of the home and assigned a time and place to watch the herds of smaller animals. As a result, boys' lives would be centered on men from a very early age.

Then, because the only model for female that most of the boys-turned men would have was a vague memory of mother (tinged with sub-conscious anger at her "disappearance") and their own observations of females in the herds they cared for, there would be no tradition of respect for women. And, since having lots of babies was good for the herd, it must be good for the tribe, as well, so keeping women "barefoot, pregnant and in the tent" would be the norm. Then, too, because women were a scarce commodity and easily stolen while a man was out with his herds, no man would want other men to see his woman, so he would insist that she stay home as much as possible and cover herself completely when outside of the tent.

Inside the men's tent, a woman would be a sexual object, expected to simultaneously atone for the sins of and fulfill the maternal role the boy had been deprived of when taken from his home. She would be expected to behave according to the rules that the boys had been

Upsetting the Balance: Invasion & Empire

> taught by the men, or, just as the boys had been, she'd be beaten for her infractions.
>
> However, since her man's wants were few, what she did with her time when he was gone was her own. So the women got together. They talked about their old lives, before being taken away from their homes. They reminded each other about the Goddess and the rituals and the dances. Sometimes they would dance for each other as they had in the villages before the invasions. And, on those few occasions that they menstruated (when they were not pregnant or nursing), they would set up a special tent to be alone or with the other menstruating women and allow the blood to flow into the earth, as they had been taught it should, for the good of all. The women would live their lives and love their children and do what was expected by their men—as much to avoid a beating as out of respect or affection. And so a separate women's culture emerged, complementing, but almost completely separate from, the men's ideas and activities.

Sound familiar? This is precisely the pattern of the culture that emerged out of the Caucasus Mountains 6000 years ago and has dominated the Asian steppes and the region from the Mediterranean to India, ever since. Regardless of religion or emperor or the Internet, it remains. Wives are "stolen" from neighbors' families and kept hidden from other men. Young boys are removed from their mother's care about the age of 7 and raised as their

> Removing boys from their mothers' home is also the practice in British middle- and upper-class homes. Boys are sent off to boys' schools at age 7—and have been since at least the 1500s. Prior to that they were sent off to work as pages at that age, following the culture's traditional pattern of arranging for young boys to grow up among men. Another form was to apprentice boys to a trade, a practice that continued, even in North America, into the late 1800s. Is it possible that the propensity for building empires is sustained by that practice?

fathers and uncles were. Strangers are always both suspect and a potential source of riches. And the strongest man is in charge.

Behind and beneath this "man's world" are the fears of a young boy taken away from the comforts of mother and a nurturing community and made to rely on his wits and puny strength in a dangerous world. And, since they weren't able to move through the ages and stages of normal development, these men now have to deal with those stages as adults. So, throughout the regions dominated by Aryan culture, we see the pattern of invasion and control, as the preadolescent boy strikes out in his man's body and declares, "Look at me! Look how strong and wonderful I am!"— the very words that records show were spoken by new kings and emperors in Mesopotamia for millennia.

The conflict raised by this process was reflected in fragments of one of the earliest Sumerian texts, in which the Goddess, Inanna, is choosing a consort. Dated about 2700BCE, it's called "Inanna Prefers the Farmer."

> Inanna says: The much-possessing shepherd I shall not marry;
> In his new [...] I shall not walk,

| Similar stories may be seen in the biblical tales in Genesis. First, we have the reversal: the sacrifice of Cain, the farmer, is not accepted by God, but the first-born lamb offered by his brother, Abel, is, according to Muslim commentaries, spectacularly accepted with a bolt of light and fire. Later, we have the story of Jacob, the shepherd, who steals his father's blessing from his brother, the farmer-hunter. |

> I, the maid, the farmer I will marry;
> The farmer who makes plants grow abundantly ...
>
> *The shepherd says:* The farmer more than I? The farmer more than I?
>
> The farmer what has he more than I? ... [*then he goes on to list the things he has, comparing them to what the farmer has*]

The farmer replies: Thou, o shepherd, why dost thou start a quarrel?
Me with thee, O shepherd, why dost thou compare? ...23

The farmer, representing the original, earth-centered culture, is preferred by the Goddess, but the shepherd, representing the new culture and whose self-worth is based on the size of his flock, was raised to compare and compete, so can't see why. He can't see what the farmer has to offer that he doesn't have, so he goes into the competitive mode that is familiar to him and starts listing all that he has—which the farmer can't understand at all. Having things is not what the farmer's life is about—he only wants to live in balance with the beauty and power of nature, which is, of course, pleasing the Goddess.

Holy Marriage & Divine Rights

The Inanna story is a ritual text referring to the ancient river-town tradition of "holy marriage," (described in detail above, and called later by the Greeks: *heiros gamos*) in which the most able man in the community would publicly wed the woman who was recognized as representative of the Goddess. The ceremony is one of the oldest in human culture.[24]

> The assumption is usually made that Egypt's Pharaoh was a man, when in fact, Pharaoh was always a pair: man and woman, husband and wife, usually children of the same father. The only known exception to this pattern prior to Greek occupation was the widow Hatsepshut, who sat on the throne alone until her son matured and even had statues made of herself with a beard, rather than join with a new man and thus potentially lose the throne for her son.

---

[23] In *Sumerian Mythology: A Study of Spiritual and Literary Achievement in the Third Millennium B.C.* by Samuel Noah Kramer, New York: Harper, 1961, p. 101.

[24] Merlin Stone has developed this idea very effectively in her book, *When God Was A Woman*.

The annual marriage of Inanna to Tammuz (or, in later years, Marduk) in Mesopotamia is the basis for some of that region's oldest writings, and the annual wedding of Isis and Osiris is one of the oldest images in Egypt. It was well-documented even into Roman times, with much of the language of the biblical *Song of Solomon* coming from the same source. It continues today in variations of Celtic tradition and neo-pagan, or *Wiccan*, practices and is referred to in *The DaVinci Code*.. The ceremony was a public recognition of the necessity to honor and utilize both masculine and feminine qualities; it was one of the many ways that balance was maintained in the river communities—and it was a way that excellence and contribution to the community was encouraged.

Ironically, however, the sacred marriage also gave the Aryan invaders a "way in" to the existing hierarchies of the Anatolian-style river towns. If their warrior chieftain could arrange a "marriage" with the representative of the Goddess, he and his people became the accepted leadership of the community they were invading. And, since the herders' diet was high in protein which, as recent history has shown, encourages much larger bodies than a diet based on grains and vegetables, (the norm for Neolithic gardening communities), the Aryans were, typically, larger and stronger and in many ways more athletic than the relatively gentle river people, it wasn't hard for them to establish themselves as "the best man" in the village, the one worthy of the Goddess.

The bridegroom of the woman selected to represent the Goddess, whom we call a "priestess," was revered as consort to the Goddess. The Goddess was the power and the source of all life, *Creatrix* and therefore the only "owner" of the world, and the priestess managed the town's land in Her name. Her consort was given all the honors of a god-king, and their child, or an appointed man, was called the "son of God."

Traditionally, evidence suggests, the consort's role was to help train boys, to mediate disputes and assist in the management of community property, and to coordinate hunting and fishing expeditions. However, as Aryan men, with their "more is better" value system, began to occupy this role, they used it to begin the pattern of "nationalistic" increase that led to the formation of city-states and empires.

Nonetheless, holy marriage as a requirement to sit on the throne continued into Roman times and beyond: Julius could not become Caesar (which means "emperor") without marrying Hera/Demeter's high priestess—as did virtually every other emperor after him. Even in Medieval Europe and later, many kings and emperors were only granted the title by marrying into it.

> Some say that the requirement continues today; that in spite of outward appearances, certain men marry certain women (e.g., Jack Kennedy and Jackie; Charles and Diana) because of this ancient heritage of "divine right."

Part of the marriage ritual involved separation and danger for the divine couple. An epic poem describes Inanna's descent into the underworld in search of her lover, Tammuz. To paraphrase:

> Tammuz has died and Inanna, the queen of heaven, can't go on without him. Afraid of being killed in the underworld by her elder sister Ereshkigal, Inanna instructs her brother Ninshubar to notify the assembly of gods if she is not back in three days. He is to go to Enlil at Nippur for help; that failing, then to Nanna at Ur; if that fails too, Ninshubar is to go to the temple at Eridu, where Enki, knowing the food and water of life, will restore her. Inanna, having fastened the seven divine decrees to her body, is stopped by Neti, the gatekeeper of the underworld. As an excuse to get in, Inanna says that her sister Ereshkigal's husband has been killed. Ereshkigal tells Neti to open the seven gates; but as each gate is opened, one of the divine decrees is stripped off of Inanna's body until finally she is naked. Then the seven judges pronounce judgment and fasten upon her the eyes of death and hang her up. After three days, Ninshubar cries for her in the house of the gods. He enters Ekur, the temple of Enlil, to plead for Inanna, but

Enlil does not stand by himr. So he goes to the temple of Nanna in Ur, but he does not support him either. In Eridu he weeps before their father Enki, and Enki provides the water and food of life to sprinkle on the corpse; Inanna arises and ascends from the underworld...

The end of the Sumerian version is lost, but in a later, Akkadian version of the story, Ereshkigal instructs the gatekeeper to return to Ishtar (which is Akkadian name for Inanna) the clothes she lost at each of the seven gates, beginning with her breechcloth and ending with her crown; then the underworld goddess allows Tammuz to be washed, anointed, clothed, and given a flute as the lovers go forth in freedom—into the lives of millions of people for the next several millennia.

So the downside of this arrangement for the men was that traditionally, at the end of the 7-9 years it takes for the planet we call Venus and the Chaldeans called Tammuz to return to the same spot in the sky at sunset or dawn, an older man would be replaced with a man who was more virile or attractive—in the name of keeping the region healthy, strong, and secure. However, with their commitment to accumulation rather than to balance, the new kingly consorts were disinclined to let go of their power. They were unwilling to step down and definitely not willing to let someone else take over.

> An interesting parallel is in the Hebrew tradition of years of atonement—when all debts and contracts are released—every 7 years.

The result of all this was that, after millennia in which violence among human beings was virtually unheard of, these warriors introduced ritual killing into the cities they were forming—and the ancient stories were rewritten to justify the assassination of the old king/consort to the Goddess to be replaced by a new, younger, god-king in order to return the community to a healthy state. One can imagine the horror felt by the first priestesses, as representatives of the Goddess, when they realized that, for the good of the peo-

Upsetting the Balance: Invasion & Empire

ple, and in order to restore balance, they must abet a murder. In time, though, assassination of the aging or failing king or emperor became part of community life—typically at the time of "Passing," the first full moon after the spring equinox (our mid-March to mid-April), but sometimes at the fall equinox.

The old "god-king" must be replaced by a new one, and the ending of his life was typically the burden of his most trusted lieutenant—whose charge was to do what was good for the people and not let his leader make a fool of himself. This drama was played out for millennia all around the Mediterranean and into Europe. Jeremiah tells us about it when he complains that the "women still weep for Tammuz"

> In the early days of anthropology, this kind of ritual was written off as the rite of a "fertility cult" with the assumption that only ignorant people would believe in such things, lacking the know-how to fertilize, etc. The evidence shows, however, a high level of technical skill and understanding in these cultures, belying a need for "magical" aid.

and still, centuries later, when Julius Caesar's oracle told him to fear the "ides (the 15th) of March," on which date his best friend and protégé participated in his fatal stabbing in front of the Senate. It may also have been the basis for Judas' betrayal of his beloved teacher, Jesus, son of the "Virgin" and called the "Son of God," on the night of the Passover feast.

Sometimes a substitute sacrifice would be arranged for. A man would be given a short tenure as "son of the highest," having all power for whatever he wanted during his reign (which might last for days, weeks, or months), at the end of which he would be killed as the requisite sacrifice. In the meantime, the old monarch (a word meaning "one over all") would go hunting or on retreat or on a military campaign, returning to a hero's welcome. The Roman midwinter festival of Saturnalia may well have been a vestige of this pattern, since "slave became master" and all the usual rules and standards were turned upside down. It's likely that Homer's story of Odysseus has some of this element in it as well, and the return of Richard the Lionheart to dethrone "bad Prince John" in England may be a remnant.

Continued Expansion

Amassing great amounts of wealth requires designing and building systems and structures to maintain it and protect it. At first, when these people were nomadic, like the early Hebrews, armies of men were sufficient, and the herds supported the armies. We see descriptions of this way of life throughout the books of Genesis and Exodus in *Torah* and the Christian Old Testament.

In time, however, the amount of wealth collected required walls, so the walled city became the chosen mode of life. Strategically situated Anatolian-style villages would be taken over and immense building projects begun, turning self-sufficient communities into walled cities. In these cities, residents lived clearly defined social and economic roles, determined in part by birth and in part by skill. After a few generations, to feed and house an increasing population who no longer produced their own basic needs, these walled enclosures expanded into city-states with field-agriculture and large-scale irrigation systems. We can see examples of the process all over the world. Jericho is the first known such city. David and his son Solomon did it in Jerusalem. Several Egyptian pharaohs built them in various places along the Nile. Chinese warlords built them to create bases from which they fought others like them.

As the traditional stories of western history tell us, the value of "more is better" and its obvious corollary, "more control is safer," led to the walled city-states being dominated by one powerful king in kingdoms of several city-states, then forming empires of several kingdoms, each level requiring increased use and power of military force. The first known emperor was Sargon, who dominated the Euphrates region about 2350BCE. He set the pattern that was followed soon after, all across Asia, from the Yellow River (the Sang or Shang empire) to the Nile. From then on, it was a matter of taking over each other's empires—sometimes by simply replacing the emperor. (The details of this process are documented in Appendix A).

2000 years later, when the little city of Rome began to show its muscle, the Greek empire, established when Alexander took over the Persian empire, included the entire Aryan region, from the Greek peninsula and the Nile to the Indus Valley. Rome took over the Greek empire and expanded it into Europe and the rest of Mediterranean Africa. Islamic leaders took over all but the European portion of that empire 500 years after the fall of Rome. What we call Western Culture, then, continues the Culture of Invasion and Empire with only minor modifications to this day.

The Urban Temple and its Priests

Yet even these powerful men recognized the need to maintain a semblance of the age-old patterns of spiritual life. So they usually allowed the local seasonal holy days and customs to be maintained—often even using them as means to expand their own power-base. As a result, over the centuries, in the tradition of "more is better" and "mine is bigger than yours," the new warrior-kings typically enhanced and enlarged the existing temple structures. Each one wanted to create something greater than the last. Sun circles were expanded into theaters, arenas and, ultimately, massive coliseums for the display of men's prowess. Moon houses became veritable palaces for the divine—the great temple of Artemis in Ephesus and the Parthenon of Athena in Athens are but two examples from ancient times.

> The Hebrew word usually translated as "prostitute" or "harlot" is, in the masculine form, translated as "temple devotee."

While the "holy marriage" continued to be an essential way to legitimize the king's rule, it, too, became subject to the new values. Following the value of "the biggest man takes the best," the homes of the high priestess and her assistants were integrated into the king's home as what we call, today, the "harem." The first documented example of this is Solomon's temple in Jerusalem, the first permanent structure for Hebrew religious rites, in which he built a residence for what are called today his thousand "wives," many of whom practiced religious rites to the Goddess in their residences in Solomon's temple.

Over time, following the Aryan value of "if he has it I want it," union with the Goddess was degraded by being made available to whomever could provide an appropriate sacrifice. Men and women of means would go to the temple to experience the sacred mysteries and the priestesses and healers who remained in the temple were relegated to the roles of either "temple prostitutes" or "vestal virgins."

Finally, since the high priestess herself now "belonged" to the god-king and was hidden from public view as a queen in his palace, the representative of the Goddess was replaced by the castrated priests who had once served her. As documented in the book of Exodus, these, in turn, were replaced by a new breed of married priests who spoke to a new, all-powerful, male God. Still wearing the robes of their female predecessors, these new priests began to preside over a new kind of ritual—the slaughter of animals, rather than the sharing of menstrual blood—to provide the blood of life that they knew must be returned to the divine Mother Earth through the soil.

So the innermost chamber of the temple, that safe place surrounded by courtyards, where once women sat and shared and learned from each other as they released into the soil the "blood of life" that regularly flowed from their wombs, now was a place of mystery and terror. By the days of cities with king-priests, only the "high priest," who inherited the position from his father and was trained to be in direct communion with the divine, could enter this blood-colored chamber and expect to come out alive. And only on certain days of the year was it permissible to enter. This basic structure remained the model for all sacred spaces in European-Mediterranean culture, including tombs. In fact, even the Christian church, with its altar rail separating the members' space from the space for the priests and acolytes, and its sacred *Christorum* (container for the sanctified wafers of the communion ritual) within that space, follows the same model.

Transforming Temples into Churches and Mosques

Over the centuries, the temples around Europe and the Mediterranean were either destroyed by the Christian or Muslim priesthood or taken over and dedicated to saints—though often, as prescribed by the great church leader Augustine, the "saint" being honored was merely the local name of god/goddess, given a more acceptable representation—and story—within Christian or Muslim theology.

One example of this progression may be seen at Ephesus, in today's Syria. Archeological records indicate that around 700BCE a group of women from south Russia (near the Caucasus) moved to what had long been a sacred grove outside of Ephesus, a place where a meteorite had landed and created a crater, with its associated magnetic anomalies, in the forest. These women are known now as Amazons, because of ancient stories and the prevalence of images and artifacts of women as warriors throughout the area. The stone circle and sacred house that they built near the site is filled with such images and artifacts—and the inner sanctum honors a deity without a clear form. This grove and surrounding area continued to be a place of women's ceremonies for millennia.

In 556BCE, the Persians conquered the area and built a huge new temple a few miles away, at the port of Ephesus—

the gateway into their empire from the Mediterranean. The temple was covered in gold and was visible for 5 to 6 miles, especially at sunset, when it reflected the last rays of light like a lighthouse. The temple was built to honor the powerful feminine protector of the region; in it stood a huge statue of the goddess, called "Artemis" by the Greeks who wrote about it, dressed in armor with 1000 "breasts" (oval objects all over her chest that archeologists think—and my examination of the statue in the Vatican museum concurs—is more likely armor decorated with figs, eggs or bull testicles).

Then, on the night Alexander the Great was born, in 356BCE, that temple burnt to the ground—an event seen by many historians as an ironic portent, since Alexander was to conquer that same Persian empire within thirty-five years. Over the next 100 years, under its new Greek rulers, the temple was rebuilt to its original specifications, and stood another 600 years, called the temple of Diana, the huntress. Then,, in the mid-200s CE, it was plundered by invaders and torn down—with all its contents disappearing when the ships carrying them were sunk in transit.

A much smaller temple of Diana was built near the site soon after, and was a site of pilgrimage during the Roman empire. Then, along about 370CE, the Christian church "allowed" locals to continue their worship of the divine feminine on this site by converting the Diana temple to a Basilica of Mary. Officially, they were honoring the tradition that Jesus' youngest disciple, John, brought Jesus' mother, Mary, to Ephesus, where they both taught and healed and where, ultimately, her body died and her soul was "assumed" by angels into Heaven—as illustrated in countless paintings and sculptures of "The Assumption of Mary."

Numerous other examples of such takeovers may be traced across Europe and around the Mediterranean, from Bridget's sacred grove in Kildare, Ireland, across the Irish Sea to Bath, across the English channel into Britany and Chartres, in France, up into the Alps, across Greece and Italy, and even in northern Africa. Over and over again, the local representation of the Goddess has been renamed Mary, Mother of God or turned into a Christian saint. In Arab regions, the prime example is the very center of Islam: the great cube, called the *Kaaba* in Mecca, was originally dedicated to the Goddess, whose rituals included the priests walking seven times around the cube.

These urban temples, now called churches, synagogues, and mosques, idealized the masculine as the

> One common element in many of these "takeovers" is that the presence of a dark stone, usually a meteorite, that sometimes bears the name of the Goddess, as in the Cybele, and sometimes is given another role, as in the stone in the *Kaaba*, said to be the foundation stone of Abraham's house.

only form of divinity. For Christians, "The Father" replaced "The Mother." "The Son" became "Lord," and his mother was demoted to a "Holy Virgin" who was to be honored but not worshipped or adored.[25] In traditional Judaism, *Adonai Elohim,* meaning "Lord of hosts" is the term used to refer to the divine, and only mystics seek to learn about *Shekinah* who, the Hebrew scriptures tell us, was present with the Creator from the beginning as the feminine principle of wisdom. In Islam, the blessed *Allah* is the only divinity, and His only prophet is Mohammed (blessed be his name). In all three traditions, until very recently, only men could study the holy scriptures and teach others to interpret them.

---

[25] See Chapter IX for a detailed description of the role of Jesus' mother in the Christian Church.

Rural Conservatives: holding the balance

Looking over the events and personalities of recorded history in the Middle East[26], it's quite clear: wherever the "Indo-European" invaders, first calling themselves Aryans, and later taking on the names of their leaders, took over a region and imposed their Indo-European language, the culture became a patriarchal hierarchy. But if a different language pattern remained in place, a different kind of cultural pattern was the norm, usually egalitarian and agrarian with a great emphasis on the arts and on maintaining "right relationship" with the natural forces. In modern times, we see this by looking at the Basques, the Welsh, and the Fins. None of these languages are Indo-European and all of these culture groups have very different ideas about the nature of the universe and of gender roles.

The word "pagan" is Latin, meaning "of the country." People who live in the country live a different kind of life from folks in urban areas, even today. With activities governed by the natural cycles of light and growth and weather, they tend to maintain values and behaviors that are more closely related to nature than apartment-dwelling urbanites whose lives are often totally unrelated to natural cycles. They also have fewer forms of information, indoctrination, and entertainment: there are few if any theaters, galleries, and places to walk to and "hang out"

> Yes, even in people who lived in the ancient Rome lived in apartments—over their shops, or in crowded tenements. This, in part, is why "bread and circuses" were used to keep the masses satisfied there. When there were economic difficulties, no "honest labor" was possible in such an environment.

---

[26] See Appendix A for a brief overview of the waves of invasion and empire.

with other folks in small towns.

As a result, long after the king-priests had built their elaborate temples and coliseums, and long after they had taken over the rituals and ceremonies of the Goddess' representatives, people in the country tended to keep on doing what they always had. They might change a name or two to keep the current ruler happy. They might even add a few prayers or hymns, using whatever name for the divine that the king wanted them to use, but in the quiet of their own hearts, the old names and old hymns remained alive. And in their homes and in the old sacred places, they would share the stories, often as a nursery rhyme, legend, or myth, which once defined their spiritual lives—and this still happens today.

Such conservatism in rural areas can be seen today in politics around the world. In the U.S., urban areas are typically "liberal" or "progressive" in their politics while rural areas are almost uniformly "conservative" in theirs, and legislatures have historically been very nearly evenly divided along such lines. In other countries, the division may seem to be an ethnic one, as rural populations, living on ancestral lands, object to the rulings of their urban "leaders" who typically come from different ancestry.

So, historically, to be a "pagan" is to be one who has not been acculturated or indoctrinated into urban thought patterns and continues in the age-old nature-centered life and spirituality of the ancestors. To be a pagan is to have nature's rhythms and cycles guide one's actions and to honor the power of nature to bestow or to destroy, just as one would honor a powerful mother who usually provides shelter and nourishment, but if she's upset, can make life miserable. To be a pagan is to do whatever it takes—however insistent the king and his government may be to do otherwise—that will ensure that nature bestows her blessings upon oneself and one's family, rather than to incur her wrath.

As a result, today we find, all over the world, regardless of the "official" religion of the state, vestiges of ancient practices, either woven into the "official" religion, as in Christian Easter and Christmas traditions, or practiced alongside it, as in Haitian "Voodoo" or Mexican "Day of the Dead" festivities. This was equally true in years past. Jeremiah, the Hebrew prophet in the days leading up to the Babylonian exile, wailed that the women still "weep for Tammuz," the ancient "Son of God" and consort to the Goddess, each spring as they had for over two thousand years in that part of the world. Centuries later, Greek and Roman bureaucrats would bewail the "backwardness" of their rural citizenry and their unwillingness to adopt the "civilized" gods, values, and behaviors of their urban rulers.

Throughout history, then, conservative (which comes from root meaning "to save") country-folk, have maintained at least vestiges of their ancient, nature-oriented traditions. The farmers have continued to focus on living in the beauty and balance of nature, while the shepherds and cowboys have continued to build larger flocks and herds. The ancient tales and rituals, from celebrations of the feminine/masculine relationship such as young girls dancing around the May pole to the singing of songs like "Old John Barleycorn," whose growing in the light, being crowned in glory, and being hewn down, is a metaphor for both plant and god-king, live on in the countryside. And, in doing so, they have helped maintain some of the balance necessary for the wellbeing of many people.

> In modern times, the word "conservative" has come to mean something else entirely. In his book, *The Cultural Creatives*, sociologist Paul Ray suggests calling these folks "Traditionals" instead, to more accurately reflect their desires and intentions.

Remnants of Anatolian-style Cultures

For Anatolian-style villagers over-ridden by the Aryan horsemen, the concern was not just the survival of their belief system, but of everything that mattered in their world. While some stayed, many moved as far away from the disruption as possible. First, they moved westward from Asia Minor into Macedonia and what is now called Greece. There, they re-established their way of life. Only a few hundred years later, though, another wave of invaders came in from their old territory, this time bringing some of their own language, family-members, and traditions with them. Again, some stayed and some moved on. Some went north into the Balkans, while others followed the coastline of the Mediterranean. In each place they recreated the ancient pattern, including the Moon house and Sun circle, and we can see evidence of both from Asia Minor across Italy to Ireland and Portugal.

The Celts

Archeological evidence shows variations on Anatolian-style settlements, with wagons and metals used as tools and weapons in ways characteristic of the Aryan invaders, in place across Europe by 4000BCE, when the great stone circle at Stonehenge is believed by many to have been completed. Today we call this integration of Anatolian and Aryan cultures "Celts." Based on archeological and historical evidence it's safe to say that these groups were the remnants of Anatolians who had migrated several times away from the invading Aryans and yet, through repeated invasion and other contacts, had adopted many of the Aryan characteristics. They were a hybrid culture, made up of people from all over the area between the Caucasus and the Atlantic.

By the time of the Roman empire, Anatolian-style river villages populated by small, dark-skinned people were scattered across Europe, with warrior-tribes of large, light-skinned blonds and redheads moving back and forth across the continent in near-constant battles for control of land, women, herds, iron, and silver. Jean Markale, a French scholar who has written dozens of books on the subject, says,

> ... the origin of the Celts is central Europe, in a triangle located between Bohemia, the Alps *autrechiennes* and *le Harz*, it's also known that they ranged, until the 3rd century before Jesus Christ, over a large portion of Europe, even across the Dardanelles and forming, in the heart of Turkey, the kingdom of Galatia. ... More, there never has been a celtic race. The Celts have always been a conglomerate of people of diverse origins who speak the same language, practice the same religion ... They have never formed an empire and among them the concept of centralization has never existed... For the Latins, the abstract notion of *civitas*, which is to say the community of citizens, is intermixed with the concrete experience of the City, which is to say, Rome. For the Celts, this is an aberration: different people have always lived one among the others in an autonomous manner, only relying on great foundational principles, on the same culture. ...As such ...the Celts were the first to model Europe...[27]

Julius, the general who became the first Caesar, called them "Gauls." His famous journal entry, *"Gallia in tres partis divisa est," ("Gaul is divided into 3 parts."),* is the beginning of the definitive description of those peoples at that time, detailing his observations of the 3 warrior tribes he encountered and the territories they occupied.

The Romans were well acquainted with the Celts and considered them great fighters: in fact, most of the footsoldiers of the Roman army were enlisted from Celtic villages in northern Italy, southern France, and Macedonia. So, when Julius Caesar traveled into what is now northern France, about 70BCE, the people he encountered were not entirely strange to him. He already knew them to be proud, independent people with light skin and blond or red hair

---

[27] Markale, Jean, *Sites et Sanctuaires des Celtes,* Paris: Tredaniel. Translated from the French by Ruth Miller.

whose men, and many of whose women, were powerful warriors.

What he had not encountered before, however, was the power of their spiritual leaders. And when he did, at a site that many believe was very close to the modern city of Chartres (an area he called the land of the Carnutes), he described those leaders in great detail in his journal, calling them Druids. Nor had he encountered the power of independent communities and leaders voluntarily coming together to defend themselves and their lands—which lack of understanding almost defeated him before he was able to regroup and, ultimately wipe out most of the warriors of the northern Celtic tribes. It was a later emperor who rounded up the Druids on an island off the coast of Britain and systematically slaughtered them as a means of maintaining control of the region.

As a result of Julius Caesar's exploits, Roman soldiers were stationed all across the European continent and Roman temples were built on many Celtic sacred sites, following the Aryan tradition of transforming local deities into the ruling government's deities.

In the usual way, people further removed from an urban setting were more likely to continue their ancient practices and speak the ancient language. The rest were assimilated into the Hellenistic culture of the Roman empire.

So the Celtic language—and religious practice—was isolated in pockets. Ireland, Wales, Scotland, the Baltic mountains, and parts of the Iberian Peninsula are now the best-known regions of Celtic identity, and while the stories and traditions we hear about Celts today tend to be strongly influenced by the locale from which they've been gleaned, they are the same at the core. The modern Wiccan, Starhawk, gives us a summary of the central story on which Celtic culture is based:

> ... The Sun Child is born at the Winter Solstice, when after the triumph of darkness throughout the year's longest night, the sun rises again. ... the embodiment of innocence

and joy, of a childlike-delight in all things. His is the triumph of the returning light. At Brigid or Candlemas (2/2) his growth is celebrated. At the Spring Equinox, He is the green, flourishing youth who dances with the Goddess in her Maiden aspect. On Beltain (5/1) their marriage is celebrated with maypoles and bonfires and on the summer solstice it is consummated, in a union so complete it becomes a death. He is named Summer-Crowned King... the crown is of roses: the bloom of culmination coupled with... thorns. He is mourned at Lughnasa (8/1) and at the Fall Equinox He sleeps in the womb of the Goddess sailing on the sunless sea... At Samhain (11/1), He arrives at the Shining Land in which the souls of the dead grow young again, as they wait to be reborn. [28]

This Cycle of the Sun dominated religious and secular activities among the Celts, closely followed by Moon cycles and the honoring of the crescent moon.

The heroic tales of the Aryans were woven into the more-ancient tales of the Goddess and her consort, and these, in turn, were directly connected to the season and the sun's position. In later years, these would be woven into the Christian story and become holy days.

---

[28] Starhawk, (Miriam Simos), *The Spiral Dance.* Harper San Francisco, 1979, p.99.

[HE:] A garden locked is my sister, my bride ... a spring sealed up...
[SHE:] My beloved was knocking ... I arose to open to my beloved; and my hands dripped with myrrh...[29]

HEBREW CULTURE IN THE AGE OF INVASION & EMPIRE

Since the Hebrew scriptures were written by men for men, we don't get much of a glimpse into the women's culture during those centuries. We only get small glimpses of the lives of the women whose impact was so great they could not be ignored. Modern archeologists and ethnologists, however, have been able to piece together some of the elements of the dynamics of Hebrew culture not explained by the standard texts.

Many of us studied the Old and New Testament in Sunday school, or *Torah* in *shul* or temple, or in religious studies classes in high school or college. In these classes we learned about the Bible as a story of the Israelites' moving toward and then falling away from Jehovah, their Lord of Hosts (the meaning of the term, *Adonai elohim*), and a description of the hypocritical, male-dominated society in

> *Torah* is the Hebrew name of the first 5 books of what Christians call the Old Testament. These 5 books are called the Pentateuch by Christians. "Jehovah" is the anglicized (thru the German) version of the "tetragrammaton," the 4 consonants (YHWH) that are used to represent the unspeakable name of God

---

[29] *Song (or Canticle) of Solomon,* ch 4 - 5.

which Jesus was living.

Later, we may have learned about the scholarship that verified the biblical stories. We learned how many men had studied and made decisions hundreds of years ago about Jesus and the Hebrew people that affect our way of thinking today. These men were, among many others, Augustine, Thomas Aquinas, and Martin Luther. What they thought we should know and what we're beginning to understand don't always agree.

Most of us grew up with stories about the ancient Hebrews. We heard about Noah and his ark (from comedian Bill Cosby, if nobody else!) surviving the flood. We heard about how little David struck down the invading giant, Goliath. We heard about Jonah being swallowed by a whale and we sang about Joshua bringing down the walls of the city of Jericho with the sound of many trumpets. In the late 1940s, the story in Exodus of Moses' epic journey leading the Israelites out of Egypt became the justification for carving a new country out of Palestine, called Israel, which would be allied with the U.S. and Europe in a region that had historically seen light-skinned people as conquerors. In the 1950s and 1960s the Exodus story became part of the basis for the Civil Rights movement and the ending of legal sanctions against African-American rights in the U. S.

In recent years many wonderful discoveries have verified the historical descriptions in the Old Testament. At the same time, however, a significant amount of historical and archeological evidence is undermining the understandings and assumptions that we've been handed by the great scholars of the past. The translations of the Dead Sea scrolls and the *Nag Hammadi* codices have contributed greatly to a new understanding, as have the explorations and findings of researchers from many disci-

> *Codices* is the plural form of *Codex*, referring to pages of parchment or papyrus stitched into stiff leather covers like modern scrapbooks or photo albums.

New Understandings of the Hebrews 91

plines across Asia Minor, Palestine, Egypt, and the Sinai Peninsula. In addition, there are new understandings of how the cultures of the area evolved, some of which have informed the ideas so far presented in this book.

The first shift in modern thinking has to do with the identity of the Hebrews. Most of us were taught that about 4000 years ago, one small tribe, whose leader was called Abraham, became the whole Hebrew nation. A more accurate historical picture might look something like the following.

> For a thousand years, groups of herders had migrated out of the Caucasus Mountains into the Fertile Crescent and along the Mediterranean, in search of grazing lands and wives. Over generations, they intermarried with people who had migrated there out of Africa thousands of years before, and formed family and economic liaisons that allowed them to control large tracts of land and build huge herds and households. Customs among these Caucasian clans were similar, but their languages differed somewhat, based on the combination of tribes that had been integrated within them. One such group was known by the Egyptians as *Habiru,* or Wanderers. They were Semites, and their leader, Abraham is called in Genesis, "great among the Hittites." They maintained their Caucasian heritage as herders while amassing great wealth. One branch of he Hittites, however, focused on horses and cattle, and learned to build and ride chariots and wield bronze swords as a means to acquire land and wealth, while the *Habiru* focused on sheep and goats, and bargained for their land and material goods. The horseback Hittites (or *Hyksos* as the Egyptians called them) moved faster across the landscape than the *Habiru,* making their holdings much greater in size. Between the two, however, they managed to cover most of the region between Asia Minor, the Euphrates, and the Nile, moving their herds back and forth and increasing their family holdings along the way. At one point, about 1700BCE, a large family group of *Habiru,* who called themselves *Amo Israel* ("people of the rule of God") moved into Egypt, joined with the *Hyksos,* and one of them became a ruler in the land: Joseph son of Jacob.

Abraham and Sarah: A Patriarch and his Princess Sister-wife

The usual telling of the story of this patriarch focuses on his fathering Ishmael and Isaac and, through them, all Arabs and Jews. According to the book of Genesis, a man named *Abram* (which means "high or lofty father" or "patriarch") and his wife *Sarai* (which is usually translated as "princess") were traveling with their father and his herds and hired helpers out of the region around the Chaldean city of Ur when Abram began to enter into silent communion with a presence he called *El*, usually written and read as "the Lord." And the Lord told him that if he would move to Canaan, he would become "the father of nations," even though he and his wife were both well past child-bearing age. So he packed up his many belongings and helpers, wondering how that prophecy could ever come to pass, and moved to what is now Bethel (meaning "place, or source of God"), where he built an altar and, in his silent communion, was told that his descendants would fill the land "from the river of Egypt to the Euphrates."

Some years later, during a famine, he took his people (now several hundred strong) and herds into Egypt. There he was welcomed as an honored guest, described years later, by the Roman-era historian Josephus, as the one who brought Chaldean mathematics and astronomy to Egypt. During this trip, Sarai, who at Abram's request referred to him only as her brother, was taken by Pharaoh as a wife into the royal household—until several plagues came upon Pharoah's family, which his priests told him were because of this almost-adultery. Embarrassed and angry, Pharaoh commanded that Abram and his household "be escorted away" with all their belongings and many gifts of atonement. Years later, Abram did the same thing to another king, Abimelech, calling Sarai his sister and letting her go into the harem in order that, as he later explained to the enraged king while being given many goods in recompense, "they will not kill me because of my wife."

What was it about his wife that he was so afraid? Why would a man who, according to Genesis, has over 300 trained soldiers in his retinue, be afraid that he might be killed? A clue is in her name, which has been translated as "Princess." She is clearly related to royalty, but there's more. The first part of her name, *Sar*, is translated as "captain, governor, lord, ruler." The second part of her name is from a root meaning "how" or "whence," which might also be said as "the means by which." And there we have it. According to the pattern being suggested here, to be married to Sarai was the means by which a man could rule. They were, according to the scripture, the children of the same father; she was Abram's half-sister. This type of marriage was common among the royalty of the time, keeping the power to a limited few. She was also, according to the traditions of the people who still live where she was buried, a priestess in her own right; in the tradition described above, she was the representative of the Goddess whose consort would rule over all. And, since the Hebrew/Hyksos culture was one in which the aged husband/consort would be killed in order for a younger man to wed the "means by which" one ruled, the elderly Abram was rightfully concerned. By presenting her as merely his sister, rather than his sister-wife he would not be hunted down and killed. By putting these other rulers in the place of having wronged him (and thereby incurring their divinity's and his Lord's punishment), he made it so they must be conciliating rather than murderous toward him—and gained many possessions in the process.

In the course of the story, Sarai, who had acquired an Egyptian maid in their travels, was concerned that Abram's prophesy of many progeny could not be fulfilled—and therefore, we can infer, there would be no son to present to her successor "means by which to rule." To move things along, she offered to let her husband take her Egyptian maid as a concubine and beget a son by her. He did so and the child was named Ishmael (meaning "hearing" or "obedient to" "the mighty one" or "God").

With this birth, the Lord changed Abram's name to Abraham, which, with the syllable *ah* meaning "beloved" and nearly always referring to the divine, now means "beloved of the most high Father." Then, when Ishmael achieved the age of manhood, the Lord told Abraham to circumcise himself and all other men in his following, including Ishmael, as a sign of his covenant with the Lord. At the same time, Abraham was instructed to change his wife's name to Sarah, again introducing the *ah* syllable, meaning "love" and referring to the divine, making her name perhaps most accurately defined as "beloved of the ruler," as Genesis says, "for she shall be a mother of nations; kings ... shall come from her." The princess has become Queen Mother.

Time went on and one day, Genesis tells us, while Abraham was communing with the Lord, three men appeared in front of him. Abraham welcomed them (calling them "my Lord") and had Sarah arrange for a feast for them on the spot where they appeared. During the meal, Abraham was told that in a year the Lord would return and Sarah would have born a child. Sarah, well past menopause, laughed at this, but in spite of her age and unbelief she did indeed conceive and bear a son, who was called Isaac, in Hebrew, *Yitshaq*, meaning "laughter," in the sense of mockery.

When the child was weaned, according to Genesis, Sarah caught Ishmael mocking them and so had him and his mother thrown out of Abraham's camp. Fortunately, an angel helped the two outcasts find water in the wilderness, so Ishmael went on to become the father of all the Arab tribes. The promise to Abram that his seed would populate the land from the Nile to the Euphrates was therefore fulfilled in Ishmael's offspring, most of whom today are Muslim, and all of whom honor Abraham as their patriarch.

New Understandings of the Hebrews

The book of Genesis tells us that, some years later, the Lord told Abraham to offer Isaac as a "burnt offering" "in the place I shall show you." Abraham took his son to a rock on a hill and was actually in the act of killing him when the voice of the Lord stopped him, told him he had "passed the test," and showed him a ram to use as an offering, instead. So, in paintings and sculpture, Abraham is usually pictured with a boy and a ram.

> Tradition has it that the rock that Abraham was guided to is the same rock David was told to place the ark on and build Jerusalem around, that Solomon built his Temple on, and from which Mohammed ascended into heaven; it's now covered by the Dome of the Rock on Mount Moriah in Jerusalem.

Looking at this story from the perspective of the pre-existing Goddess culture, this miraculously averted sacrifice might well have been a reference to the already ancient tradition of the death and resurrection of the miraculously born son of the king, the consort of the Goddess' representative on earth. It was a young man, not a boy, who was tied to the rock, and it was a young ram that was substituted, suggesting the paschal season. It's possible that the whole story of Abraham was written, in part, to describe the transition from one set of practices to another.

An important, often overlooked detail in Abraham's story is that when Sarah died, a Hittite named Ephron offered a site for her burial, saying, "You are a mighty prince among us. Bury your dead in the best grave we have." And when Abraham died, he, too, was buried in the Hittite tomb.

As Genesis proceeds, Isaac grew up to father Jacob and Esau, who embodied the split in values of their day: Esau preferring the world of nature and balance; Jacob going for the goods. Jacob, after a number of mishaps and misdeeds, and a night spent wrestling with an angel until he was allowed to see the face of God, took on the name Israel, *Yis'rael,* meaning "he who rules (as) God."

In Jacob's story, we get another glimpse at the world of women in that time. Jacob, sent by his mother to stay with her cousin until Esau "cools off" meets a daughter of the household at the well and immediately wants to marry her. Her father, however, has other ideas. He makes Jacob "buy" her through 7 years of indentured servitude, then substitutes his older daughter for the desired one, on the grounds that the oldest one must be married before the younger one may be (still a practice throughout the Middle East). Then he requires a further 7 years to "purchase" the younger. Jacob does well by his mother's cousin, and they prosper. Then, when it's time for him to leave with his wives, Rachel decides to take the "household gods" with them and hides them under her skirt on the saddle—then insists that no one can search her as she is having her menstrual flow and so is "unclean."

> The "household gods" were important because the carvings themselves, were believed to be the source of protective power for the family. This is in sharp contrast to Abraham's experience as presented in Genesis.

Over the next decades, Jacob built up his own herds and huge household and fathered 12 sons, who in turn fathered the 12 tribes of Israel, becoming known as the Hebrew people.

The Hebrews Control Egypt

As the story in the Hebrew scriptures continues we're told that one son of Jacob/Israel, Joseph of the coat-of-many-colors, through his continuing connection with God and his ability to interpret dreams, overcomes prejudice and a prison sentence to be married to the daughter of the high priest of *On* and become the First Steward of Egypt.. This means that a Hebrew was in charge of all production and distribution of goods, the entire economy, of Egypt. As

New Understandings of the Hebrews

such, he was also responsible for building canals and the redistribution of lands to the farmers after the annual floods erased most boundaries.

But how could this happen? How could the proud Egyptians effectively turn over their country to foreigners?

The answer is, they didn't. Recall that the Hebrews were Semites, of the same language group—and value system—as the chariot-riding Hyksos/Hittites who had plundered Babylon and swept through Syria between 1900 and 1700BCE, and that Abraham, the wandering herdsman from Chaldea, is described as related to them. After some years of trading daughters and other acts of diplomacy and appeasement on the part of the Egyptian throne, the chariot-riding Hyksos rode in and wiped out the chariot-less Egyptian army, taking over the Nile delta, and adopted the role and lifestyle of the Egyptian Pharaohs and ruling class from 1720 – 1567BCE.

Abraham is generally thought to have left Ur, in Chaldea (Sumer), sometime after 1900BCE. His great-grandchildren, sons of Jacob-Israel, apparently arrived in Egypt soon after the Hyksos took over, nearly 200 years later, as illustrated on the wall of a tomb at *Bene Hasan* south of Cairo.

> The first Semitic emperor was the Akkadian *Sargon*, who took over the fertile crescent after the floods and re-established the city of Ur, from which Abram is said to have come.

So Semitic people were, at the time of Joseph, the ruling class of northern Egypt, controlling the rich farmlands of the lower Nile valley. Their leader had, following their usual practice, taken the Egyptian priestesses and royal wives and daughters as his own, and had taken the title of the local king, which we know as Pharaoh. Joseph's role as "seal-bearer" is documented in the archeological finds at Avaris, north of Cairo, where a walled city with palaces is being excavated and where, among other things, a set of royal seals, including a fragment of a finger-ring sized one with the name

Yaakov ("Jacob," probably fully *Yusef ben Yaakov* or "Joseph son of Jacob") has been found.[30] The Wanderers had found a home.

Egyptian Rule is Restored

But the Hyksos never quite persuaded the Egyptian people, nor, more importantly, the Egyptian priesthood, that they belonged on Pharaoh's throne. So it was that, in 1567BCE, the rightful heir to the throne of the double-kingdom, Kamose, rose up out of exile in the southern city of Thebes and, with the help of the priesthood, reclaimed his heritage. He then went about erasing any indication of the occupation and restoring the ancient lands to their original (or his preferred) owners and caretakers. His brother, Amosis, took over in 1532 and, using the Hyksos military technologies of chariot and composite bow, expanded Egyptian control all the way to Asia Minor to protect against future invasion.

The Semitic people were no longer in a position of power in their adopted country. Some high-ranking officials were sent to the turquoise mines (there are written calls to *El* on the walls of those mines in an ancient form of proto-Hebrew to prove it). Others were merely exiled. The rest no longer owned land but had to work for a living. They were no longer the dominant minority, but instead felt like an oppressed minority. And, as the book of Exodus tells us, their numbers were growing so fast that they might even overrun the Egyptians, who, unlike the Semites, followed the precepts of the goddess and tended to control their population.

Initially, according to Exodus, Pharaoh tried to control the Semitic population by controlling the number of children

---

[30] A wonderful summary of current archeological and geological understandings concerning the Hebrew experience in and exodus from Egypt may be found in the History channel's documentary "The Exodus Decoded."

New Understandings of the Hebrews 99

allowed to grow up. But neither Egyptian religion nor law allowed for infanticide or human sacrifice, and tension between the two peoples was merely intensified by the effort.

For the proud Semites, conditions were intolerable. For the Egyptians, the Semites were a burden. Something had to be done.

Most of us were raised with the idea that the Israelites were slaves in Egypt, working and living under great hardship. The historical record—even the biblical text—however, does not support that image. For one thing, Egyptian records suggest that temples and pyramids were built, not by slave-labor, but rather through a form of tithing—each Egyptian adult giving several weeks a year in loving service to their preferred temple. For another, both the book of Exodus and some contemporary murals on ancient Mycenian walls indicate that the Hebrew people left Egypt heavily armed and well-supplied. That the Hebrews, in the last years of their occupation of the Nile valley, were required to work for a living, after years of living in luxury, appears to be a more accurate description of their situation. If we read Exodus carefully, we see that the Hebrews had their own homes, controlled their own family life, and, as they were leaving the country, took all sorts of riches with them, compounded by the gifts they were given by their former employers as they left. This understanding is confirmed by the word used in the book of Exodus, *eved,* which may be translated as "slave," bondsman," or "servant," depending on the context. They were wage-earners, earning enough to get by on the economy, but unable to own their own land, much as most "middle class" Americans and Europeans are today.

What happened to cause these people to leave the land that had become their home? Remember, they had been in northern Egypt as long as the U.S. has occupied North America, so their being required to leave the country would be something like the Native Americans rising up and kicking the European-Americans out. How did these two peoples resolve their dilemma?

The resolution seems to have been in the person of Moses.

Moses, Prophet-King

We don't yet have any Egyptian records of Moses and his life, but that's not too surprising since the restored Pharaoh would have worked diligently to rid his kingdom of all signs of any occupation; besides, the story tells us that Moses was just one of several sons being raised together.

According to biblical accounts, Moses was a son of the Hebrew tribe of Levi who was adopted by one of Pharaoh's daughters, who had found him

> Some researchers believe that Egyptian religion is the basis for *huna* among the Polynesian cultures. Edgar Cayce connects it with Atlantis. Recent studies of the ancient hieroglyphs suggest that the medical, psychological, and paranormal skills and understandings of this great culture far exceed those of most of Western history.

while praying for a child at the river. He was given the Egyptian name Moses, and raised as Pharaoh's son. He went through all the training that would prepare him to administer a vast nation, lead an army, and serve as High Priest in religious ceremonies. He was trained in reading and writing, in the logical, rational, thought processes of mathematics and military strategy, and in mind-body control techniques. He was privy to the secret workings of palace and temple and had, before he went into exile, demonstrated great skill as a warrior.

If we place this prince's life in the time of the restoration of the Egyptian dynasty, Moses' exile into the desert makes sense: as a Hebrew with a prince's training, he would no longer be welcome in the country, but, because of his military training and standing in the priesthood, he could not be easily killed. Recognizing that he was trained as a high priest, privy to all of the powers and processes of the Egyptian religion, helps make sense of his capacity to listen to the divine—and to out-do the Egyptian priests at their own showmanship when he returned to Egypt.

We have another clue in the name: there's very little difference between *Moses,* and the Pharaohs' names *Kamose,* and *Amosis,* especially since neither language had vowels at that time, which could be an indication of their relationship. Some scholars suggest that they actually worked together to resolve the problem: that the Exodus was a planned strategy to remove a troublesome population from the Nile valley while expanding Egyptian cultural (and defensive) presence up along the Mediterranean coast into Canaan. This version of the story would explain why the Israelites so systematically wiped out the residents of the area, rather than following their ancient tradition of assimilation through purchase of land.

This scenario would place the exodus at about 1500BCE, as suggested by Josephus in the first century CE. A contemporary document says that shortly after 1500BCE Idrimi, the son of an Aleppo king, wandered among the *Habiru* in Canaan. It would mean that the Hebrew people were used as an extension of Egyptian culture, providing a buffer against the more militant Hyksos invaders. They would therefore have been closely allied with the Egyptians for the next 200 years, until, under Akhenaten, the monotheist who turned the religious

> Some scholars, using the traditional, later date (c. 1250) for the Exodus, suggest that Moses was supposed to become Amenhotep IV, who disappeared and may have been a follower of the "One-God/Sun-God" teachings of the pharaoh Akhenaten, who was exiled when that pharaoh died and his temples were demolished, and later took the "true-believers" out of the country to practice the new religion.

hierarchy upside down, Egyptian control of the eastern Mediterranean was eroded.

Placing the exodus shortly after the end of Hyksos rule of Egypt, but about 250 years before the pharaoh Ramses II, whose reign has long been accepted as the date, makes even more sense when we consider recent geophysical and climatological research. Several geologists are now suggesting that the plagues described in Exodus as befalling Egypt during the negotiations could well be the result of a volcanic eruption in the Mediterranean that happened about that time. The eruption of Thera, on the island of Santorini, could explain every one of the ten plagues: as the ash covers the sky, day becomes night. As it settles on the soil and in the rivers, gases from the ash pollute rivers and lakes and turn them red, ecosystems are upset, fish die, frogs escape to the land, locusts migrate, and so forth. Heavy carbon dioxide, flowing from the polluted river, would have suffocated the first-born sons who slept in their privileged position in low beds on the ground floor, the coolest spot in the house. A tidal wave would have caused the waters all along the Mediterranean shore to pull back, leaving dry land for a few minutes, only to become an overwhelming wall of water soon after—especially in the marshy lands between Egypt and the Sinai peninsula known as the "Sea of Reeds," which is the most accurate translation of the place named in Exodus: *Yam Cuwph*. All of these events are described in an Egyptian scroll called the *Ipuwar* papyrus.

"The Law" is Given

Regardless of the exact date of the Exodus, Moses is the long-recognized Law-giver to the Hebrews. He was the great prophet who spoke to God, listened to God's word, lived by it, and taught his people to do the same. The resulting set of books were called *Torah*, known by Christians as the Pentateuch, the first five books of the Old Testament, has guided

New Understandings of the Hebrews

the lives of millions of people since. And, while probably not actually written by Moses, as some traditions hold, these five books are clearly derived from his teachings and rulings.

According to these books, it was Moses who re-introduced the idea of the sanctity of human life as well as the importance of focusing on the power and presence of divinity to the formerly herding culture's values. His "Ten Commandments" were, in fact, derived from the Egyptian moral code, called "the 10-words: *Idolize-not, Murder-not, Covet-not, Steal-not,*" etc. He also established the principles of diet and hygiene that evolved into "keeping Kosher" and have defined the Jewish culture for all the centuries since.

> In Moses' day humanity was living through a stage in the zodiac called the "Age of Taurus," during which, for 2000 years, the region's spiritual life was dominated by images and ideas of bulls and calves, such as "the golden calf" created by the Israelites at the foot of the mountain. The age he began was the "Age of Aries," the ram, during which Israelites were called to worship with ram's horns, sacrificed young rams at Passover, and sent a young ram or goat into the wilderness to "take away the sins of the people." That age ended at the time of Jesus, who was the last "Lamb of God," and who dominated the "Age of Pisces," represented by fish. We are now entering the "Age of Aquarius," the water-bearer—been carrying your bottle of water around lately?

Then he transferred the priestly duties and authority exclusively into the hands of one group of men among the Hebrews, declaring that they should receive the first tenth of all that the Hebrew people produced to support them. He laid down the law that the sons of Aaron, of the tribe of Levi, would perform all sacrifices and would be the only ones allowed into the "holy of holies" and commune directly with God, whose Spirit would abide "above the mercy seat" on the Ark of the Covenant. Many of the rulings laid down in these sacred texts were descriptions of how the new priesthood was to interpret symptoms in the body and in the home and to help the people remain healthy. If the number of times the people rebelled against his rulings is any indication, he was completely revamping their spiritual life and traditions—requiring them to integrate their own heritage as warriors with the spiritual and moral code of their Egyptian experience with the norms of the herding peoples they had descended from and he had been exiled into.

Moses did all this, not within the safe framework of an existing temple and its well-disciplined students, but out in the open, with several hundred thousand (some say millions) of urbanized, materialist men, women, and children, most of whom expected to have their own way now that they were no longer under Egyptian control. Life as nomads was not at all what they were used to and they

> "Forty" is a number used throughout the biblical scriptures meaning "many: more than two of us can count on our fingers and toes, together; enough to be complete."

were all-too-ready to tell him about it. So, when they didn't pick up on the gift of a new kind of culture that he was giving them, he did the only thing a far-sighted ruler could do: keep everyone busy till the old "sticks-in-the-mud" either changed or died off and the new generation, growing up in the new way, could take over. Hence the reported "forty years" of wandering around Sinai before entering Canaan.

Miriam's Role

Moses, however, was not alone in his leadership. He had two powerful co-leaders: his brother Aaron, who became the first high priest of the Hebrew people, and his sister Miriam. Interestingly, the name Miriam appears in the Old Testament only once—as part of the Exodus story. There are no other women named Miriam in recorded Jewish history.

New Understandings of the Hebrews

In Exodus, however, there are two main references: she leads the women in singing a song of celebration when they successfully cross the "Sea of Reeds" (often mistranslated as "Red Sea"), and, much later, she and Aaron are called before God in the meeting tent for speaking unkindly of Moses' taking a non-Israelite, a Cushite woman, as his wife. During this divine chastisement for her rebelliousness against Moses' absolute authority, her skin turns leprously white, for which she is banned from the camp and sent to the "outsiders camp" for the lawful seven days necessary to purify anyone who has been declared "unclean"—just like any woman who has "so much as been slapped by her father." Aaron and his sons became God's anointed high priests, responsible for all aspects of the spiritual and physical health of the Hebrews, while Miriam, though clearly a major leader at the start of their journey, is never heard from again (though at her death, a nearby spring is named after her).

Miriam starts a dance of celebration after the crossing in Exodus (from a Coptic scroll).

Taking all this into the context of the long history of separation of male and female activities described in the previous chapter adds another dimension. Though they had grown up in a relatively egalitarian Egypt, they were, in fact, descendants of the Hyksos/Hittites, who lived by the ancient tradition of separation of "subjugated" women from "dominant" men in virtually all aspects of life. This was in stark contrast to the Egyptian tradition of conjoint rulership of brother and sister in a sacred union that represented the union of the masculine and feminine at the heart of all reality. In Egypt, therefore, Moses' sister might well have been raised to be a wife and co-ruler of both country and temple with him. Miriam may well have expected that they would rule together, while Moses' 40-year exile among the herding peoples gave him a different model. So it's not too surprising that Miriam was so distressed when Moses took "a Cushite woman" as his wife, rather than establishing herself as his partner.

Another clue for understanding Miriam's story may be found in her name. In the ancient Hebrew, which has no vowels, it would probably be spelled *Mrym* and the derivation of the word is interesting.

- *mr = myrrh, a bitter ointment associated with death, only handled by elders, usually women*
- *mra = master, Lord, great*
- *mrah = seeing, vision, fair, beautiful of countenance (the H makes it the feminine form of mra),*
- *mrwm = lofty, height, dignity, upward*
- *mry = rebellious, discontent*
- *yam = roaring, and by implication, sea or large river*

If we take the root syllables, we can see a whole range of interpretation, suggesting that the woman we call Miriam was a great prophetess, a "masterful seer" with dignity and "lofty vision." Even if the biblical story of Moses' adoption by the pharaoh's daughter is accurate and Miriam and Aaron were not part of his upbringing, Miriam clearly participated in various aspects of his life and could well have been included in some of his training. A woman with this background may well have become bitter and rebellious upon experiencing subjugation by the men around her. Not too surprisingly, therefore, the traditionally accepted meaning of the name Miriam is "rebellious," combining "bitter" with "roaring," describing someone who is loudly complaining about her position in life.

Through the books of Leviticus and Deuteronomy we read how the priests should now be called on, as medicine women once were, to evaluate symptoms in people and their households, and how they should act when they encounter anything contagious. The only powers remaining to the women were those related to birth and death and their own menstrual cycles; at those times, Moses said, they must remain apart from the men and, by implication, care for themselves (which was what they always had done, anyway, in the "Red Tent" —the place where they gathered during menstruation). So while Miriam, if her family had remained in Egypt, could well have been a powerful priestess as well as political leader—part of the inner circle of decision-makers, with significant influence among the people—the Semitic tradition of separation relegated her leadership to the world of women.

In all probability, Miriam would have expressed great distress and even rage in the face of such a shift. Her disagreement with Moses about his Cushite wife, with her subsequent week-long banishment from the community, might have been "the straw that broke the camel's back." Then, recognizing the futility of her raging, she would have done what she always had done: used her skills to teach the Hebrew women the secrets of mind and body control that she had learned in Egypt, as well as the use of herbs and oils, including the myrrh with which her title associated her, in healing and promoting health among the Hebrew households. She would lead the ancient women's rituals and ceremonies around the seasons and phases of the moon, as well as menstruation, weddings, births and death. She would have been a respected and revered teacher, mentor and guide—totally unrecognized by the men in their patriarchy, but nonetheless a major contributor to the wellbeing of the nation.

She would also have trained her successors. She would have met with women in the "Red Tent" and, through story and example, helped them to discover and develop their own gifts and powers. Whenever a young woman or a new widow appeared ready to learn more, Miriam undoubtedly took her on as an apprentice, giving her increasing responsibility with increasing skill.

Then, when the Israelites arrived in Canaan, the women Miriam had trained during those years in the wilderness took their leave from each other as the people spread out and populated various villages, farms, and grazing lands. We can imagine them promising to stay in touch, to find some way to visit and share and learn from each other—even to foster one another's daughters and sisters—as a way to keep the wisdom alive. (The New Testament story of Mary the mother of Jesus going to live with her older cousin Elizabeth for a few months might be an illustration of this tradition.) Over the generations, they would marry and move and explore other ideas and forget and remember, until their connection with the original Miriam was all but forgotten—certainly among the men, if not the women.

David, Solomon, an Ark, and a Temple Filled with Women

Centuries of empire building and conquest followed the Hebrews' return to Canaan. A reading of the books of Judges and Chronicles far exceeds modern television in terms of violence and bloodshed as, following the guidance of their

New Understandings of the Hebrews

prophets, Hebrew military leaders wiped out virtually everyone occupying the land they felt was theirs. From the fall of Jericho to the conquest of the valley now called Jerusalem, over and over again, they used their military training, along with the power of the Ark, the home of their God and also their "secret weapon." Again and again, they would carry it into battle, where it would flash and thunder and thousands of men, women, and children would die, leaving only young "virgins" to provide wives for their warriors.

> Many modern scientists are fascinated with the Ark of the Covenant and what it might have been. Its construction makes it a receiver-amplifier, but receiving and amplifying what? Clearly, a huge amount of static electricity would be generated by the fabric cover rubbing on the metal, but that only explains some of the deaths it caused. Possibly, the stone tablets that it held generated an electrical field known as "geoplasma" that would glow in and around the area, but again that only explains some of the events associated with it. A number of people have reconstructed the Ark using the detailed directions in Exodus, but accurate replication is impossible without the tablets that were in it.

Periodically, the people would settle into a life of balance, forming villages in which farming and herding were equally accepted and profitable. The story of Naomi and her daughter-in-law Ruth give us a lovely picture of Hebrew village life that is remarkably similar to rural life in the region thousands of years before, and still, today.

But it was not until the reign of Ruth's great-grandson, David, that the Hebrew people settled into the life of a city-state empire, and in the reign of David's son Solomon the city-state of Jerusalem, with its temple, became a model spiritual and political center, still studied today.

The story of David gives us a number of insights into the workings of Hebrew culture. During his childhood, he tended the sheep, as did the sons of Abraham and Israel, and as young boys continue today, throughout the region. As a young man, David's skill as a sling-shooter brought him to the attention of the military leaders who gave him the opportunity to use that skill in the famous battle against the "giant" Goliath. David's adventures as he and Saul vied for the kingship would sell any action movie today[31]. Once he became king, his love affair with a married woman and the death of their first child is the stuff of modern romance novels. He was also a famous musician, and is traditionally considered the author of most of the verses included in of the book of Psalms—even though many were written several hundred years later. These "songs of praise" have long provided spiritual seekers with a clear model for moving from despair to hope, from bitterness to delight, from fear to joy. Through them, we see the world from the perspective of a man whose heart and dearest memories are in the meadows and along the creeks of his youth, and whose "help" comes from recalling those memories, looking "to the hills" and singing the praises of the nurturing, loving, creative Source that created them. In the Jewish mystical tradition of the Qabalah, David is the model for one who has worked through the process of "ascending" through the Sabbath process of prayer, study, and song, into union with the divine.

The story of David also explains how the city of Jerusalem and its suburban neighbor, Zion, were founded on land that had long been occupied by Anatolian-style villages. David purchased the piece of land that he envisioned—the village threshing floor. This was a large, relatively flat stone and, following Anatolian tradition, was probably already a sacred site, attached to the Moon house and a communal storage facility (as illustrated on p. 39 of this book). This site would become the new home for the Ark of the Covenant. But David was not to build the temple he had envisioned; he

---

[31] In fact, the film "David the King" established Richard Gere's career as an actor.

had done too many things that defied the commandments that Moses had laid down and so was considered unworthy.

It was David's son Solomon who built the temple. And Solomon's temple, as noted above, supported not only the worship of God as dictated by Moses, but also housed a variety of rituals practiced by Solomon's many "foreign" wives, honoring the Goddess under her various names. So, in his story, we see the balance of masculine and feminine at work, described in detail in the "Song of Solomon," (which almost exactly duplicates the ancient Egyptian texts of the spring rites of Isis). We also find out with whom the king shared power and authority.

> Now Adonijah the son of Haggith came to Bathsheba the mother of Solomon. ... "Please speak to Solomon the king, for he will not refuse you, ..." And the king arose to meet her, bowed before her, and sat on his throne, then he had a throne set for the king's mother, and she sat on his right... And the king said to her, "Ask, my mother, for I will not refuse you" [1Kings 2: 13-20].

As biblical scholar Scott Hahn says,

> In most Near Eastern cultures, the woman ordinarily honored as queen was not the wife for the king, but the mother of the king. ...it was often the persuasive (or seductive) power of the mother that won the throne for her son. The custom also served as a stabilizing factor... the queen mother embodied the continuity of dynastic succession...*Gebirah* was more than a title; it was an office with real authority.[32]

So the mother of the king, the Queen Mother, clearly, had much power in the country—as is fitting, since she was the one who represented the Source, as would her daughter-in-law when she died and her grandson

This is only one of several references to the power and importance of the king's mother. In 2Kings we read of the king and his mother being carried into Babylon, in 2Chronicles we learn that Maacah was removed from "the position of queen mother" for making an Asherah, or image of the Goddess.

---

[32] Hahn, Scott, *Hail Holy Queen*, p.78-80

would be in power. It's not too surprising, therefore, that the women in Solomon's household, housed as they were within the Temple walls, practiced ceremonies and rituals associated with the Goddess—after all they were her representatives in their homelands, and their whole lives were focused on maintaining the balance through ritual and tradition.

Yet, still today, Solomon's temple is seen as the heart and soul of the patriarchal Hebrew religion. There, in the Holy of Holies, only the select few could enter and survive—and then only if they had removed all wool, cleansed all sweat, and wore only linen garments. There, where the gold-covered Ark of the Covenant, with its "mercy seat" and cherubim, resided beneath its copper roof and lightning rods, behind the veil of the Holy of Holies, the name, or *shem*, of the Lord Almighty dwelled. There, the name of the Lord must never be spoken, but—as some scholars suggest, it must be intoned, allowing each syllable of the name its own sound and resonance.[33] And there, day after day, and especially on the high holy days, the endless round of burnt sacrifice, for atonement and for forgiveness of the people of Israel, was maintained, depositing thick layers of carbon-rich ash all around the sacred power-source.

For the Hebrew people, the destruction of Solomon's temple in 596BCE was the end of their glory years. It was also the beginning of a new form of religious practice. The temple was destroyed as the residents of Judea were hauled off to Babylon to serve their new emperor. With neither Moses' Ark nor the altar on which to burn their sacrifices, they were compelled to maintain their religious life through telling the stories that described the history of their people and their laws. They kept Sabbath by listening to and reflecting on these sacred tales.

---

[33] Gregg Braden has popularized this idea in his book and lecture series, *The God Code*.

New Understandings of the Hebrews

Over the years that they were exiled in Babylon, those stories shifted and changed, taking on some of the even more ancient tales of their Babylonian captors. As a result, what we read in the biblical scriptures today often includes almost exactly the same language and characters as the much older Chaldean and Sumerian texts of the Mesopotamian region.

When the Persians conquered the Babylonians, the new emperor, Cyrus, was a Zoroastrian, a monotheist who was tolerant of Hebrew religious ideas. He introduced Aramaic as the primary language of his empire. It quickly became the language used in regular life for virtually all peoples of the Middle East, and remains so in many places today. The books of Daniel, describing the life of a Hebrew prophet who became second-in-command for all of Babylonia, and of Esther, describing the heroism of a Hebrew woman who convinced her emperor to stop a plan to destroy the Hebrew people and instead, put them in power throughout the entire Persian empire ("from India to Ethiopia"), were at least partially written in Aramaic.

It was as a result of these events that, in 536BCE, the prophet Nehemiah, cupbearer to the Persian emperor Xerxes, was appointed governor of Judah and rebuilt Jerusalem. So, in 520BCE, the people were returned to their homeland. There, their new prophets, Ezra and Nehemiah, proclaimed a renewed vision of the Hebrew people and the new temple that they must build. While they remained subject to the Persian emperor, they were living on their ancestral lands and worshipping the one God on the Temple Mount, once again.

But about 200 years later, in 330BCE, Alexander the Great conquered the Persian Empire and the Greeks took over the region around Jerusalem. Again, the Temple was the focus of concern. In all the Greek states, the local temples were modified to include the Greek gods and goddesses as well as the local ones, so the plan was to do the same in Jerusalem.

> This miracle is the explanation for the Jewish winter festival of lights, *Chanukah*.

The "hard-headed Jews," however, had different ideas. The struggle continued till 165BCE, when the Maccabees revolted against the Greek governor and cleansed their Temple of the Greek gods and goddesses that had been placed there. A miraculous period followed: the sacred menorah lights that had only enough oil for one day remained lit for eight days and nights. Sadly, though, the Temple was lost again, and this time utterly destroyed by the Greeks.

In 65BCE the Romans, having conquered the Greek empire, took over Jerusalem. They, however, had a different system. Rather than try to manage all the various peoples of their empire themselves, they worked through a sympathetic king, and simply occupied the territory with troops and a caretaker, or "procurator," to enforce Roman law, support Roman citizens in the area, and squelch any uprisings. A wealthy Hebrew merchant named Herod convinced the emperor that he could do the job and the Temple mount was under Hebrew control, once more.

I come to the garden alone, when the dew is still on the roses ...
And He walks with me and He talks with me...[34]

THE LIFE AND TIMES OF JESUS THE NAZARENE

Understanding the role of Nazarenes, women, and the priesthood in Hebrew culture under Roman control sheds a whole new light on the life of Jesus and the stories handed down to us in the New Testament.

Overlapping Cultures

At least four cultures overlapped along the eastern coast of the Mediterranean, in the area now called Israel, Jordan, and Palestine.

The most visible, though most recent, was that of the Romans. By 27BCE, they controlled everything from the English Channel to the Red Sea. Roman culture was essentially Hellenistic: they revered Greek scholarship, imitated Greek art, etc. Yet there was a distinct Roman presence in the provinces, with an emphasis on virility, discipline and hierarchy among warriors and governors, and chastity for matrons, a practical rather than philosophical or spiritual mindset, and an insistence on treating the emperor as divine. The Romans appointed Herod as king of the Judean province, who, in turn, appointed Caiaphas (not the rightful inheritor) as high priest. Herod lived the Roman life in his kingdom, having as little to do with Hebrew law or tradition as possible. Roman soldiers, some with families, were stationed in every market town and along the borders, and were

---

[34] "In the Garden," traditional Christian hymn.

often seen patrolling the roads and streets. Roman law was the ultimate authority.

Greek culture, with its literature, philosophy, and myth, was the next cultural layer. Throughout the countries conquered by Alexander around 340BCE, Greeks were the preferred tutors, most literature was written in Greek, and each of the Greek schools of philosophy were well known among the nobles and intelligentsia. The writings of Plato and Aristotle, of Homer and Euripides, were the standard. The Greek philosophies of Pythagoras, the Gnostics, and the Stoics were visibly expressed by wandering teachers, who established local schools in many cities and towns across the region. The Greek idea that only men had souls and that the ideal love was between men was part of the undercurrent of the time.

The Hebrew culture, with its traditions, tales, and laws, was the next layer. The temple in Jerusalem was the center of Judaic religious life—as preached and practiced by the elders (*Sanhedrin*) of the tribe of Judah, who were the primary residents of the region. The neighboring land of Samaria was populated by people who had not been exiled to Babylon, and Samaritans practiced what they believed was a purer form of the religion, which the residents of Judea wouldn't tolerate. And, in the wilderness at the edges of the Empire, other groups, notably the Essenes, lived and practiced what they believed to be the true religion, and would not tolerate contact with either of the other groups. In all these regions, the laws of Moses, as documented in *Torah* (the first 5 books of the Old Testament) set the pattern for all aspects of life, and all disputes affecting the community were settled according to them.

> The modern term, Judaism, from which we get the word "Jew," derives from the name of the land, Judea and the tribe of Judah; one title of the messiah is "lion of Judah."

Beneath all these layers the ancient way of life was maintained in the rural areas and among the lower, "uneducated" classes. It was the Anatolian way—a way of life centered on the seasons of planting and harvest, rains and drought. Some families had lived in the Jordan valley since before Moses and were not dragged off to Babylon. Some families had returned from Babylon more Chaldean than Hebrew. Some women had kept the ancient traditions, passed on from mother to daughter, for thousands of years, since the times before the raiders had driven their herds from the mountainous plains into the valleys and upset the balance that had been in place for thousands of years before.

Add to these layers the ongoing presence of Persians, Egyptians, Assyrians, and even Hindus and Buddhists—traders from the silk road, bringing products and ideas into the Roman empire—and it becomes clear that the culture of Palestine/Israel under the Romans was on the edge of chaos—with high potential for transformation.

Herod's Temple

As indicated above, the Jerusalem temple had been destroyed several times. Then, under the Roman occupation Herod was appointed "king." Determined to win the support of the people (and show his power to Rome) Herod built a lavish structure, even larger than Solomon's, atop the Temple Mount.

It had all the necessary courts: one for the gentiles, where anyone could go and exchange goods or coins from all over the world for purified temple-money to purchase pure animals for sacrifices, one for the Jewish men to discuss the finer points of *Torah*, one for priests' families and the women who served the temple and for the performance of sacrifices, and one for the Holy of Holies. There were the necessary baths for purification outside the walls, and passageways to the priests' homes.

Herod's temple as records suggest it looked.

There were great gold cherubim and lavishly decorated walls and columns. It was most impressive, a remarkable facility that had only two big flaws: the Holy of Holies, which should have housed the Ark of the Covenant, through which the presence of God could be experienced, was empty, and

> Money, as coins with imprints, was invented for use in temples and originally minted by the temple staff for people from outside the temple to buy those things allowed within its sacred walls. Bernard Lietauer's *The Future of Money* has a nice summary of the history.

the walls of the structure were patrolled by Roman soldiers who were garrisoned next door.

In order to maintain complete control of his glorious Temple, Herod selected his own High Priest to govern it—one not accepted by many orthodox believers because he wasn't raised into this service through the hereditary system initiated by Moses. So it was that the inadequately prepared but politically cunning Anas and Caiaphas ran the temple during the time of Jesus.

Women in the Temple

It's popular in our day to look at the ancient Hebrew culture as one in which women were hated and banned from all that was considered holy—especially the Temple at Jerusalem. We've taken our ideas from writings based in the Greek ideal of an all-male society, in which women were relegated to household management and childbearing—which is not too surprising since, after all, that was the culture in which Saul/Paul of Tarsus was raised and in which Christianity evolved.

> There are 7 prophetesses described in the Christian Bible: 6 in the Old Testament and Anna in the gospels. Deborah is the first so called, and years later the great prophet Isaiah, under God's direction, "approached the prophetess, and she conceived and gave birth to a son..." [Isaiah 8:3].

A close examination of the gospels, however, reveals a very different picture. Women were hardly excluded from religious life. First of all

> There was a prophetess, Anna (*Hannah* in Hebrew*)* the daughter of Phanuel, of the tribe of Ascher. She was advanced in years, having lived with a husband seven years after marriage, and then as a widow to the age of eighty-four. And she never left the temple, serving night and day with fastings and prayers. [Luke 2:36-38]

She never left the temple! This woman, whose name means "Gift (or Grace) of God," had lived as a widow since some time in her teens and was not only recognized as a prophetess (*n'biyah*)—a position of considerable standing in Hebrew culture—she clearly slept, ate, and

> This is the only biblical reference to a woman named Anna, although the Christian church maintains a tradition that Mary, mother of Jesus, had a mother by that name, called *Sancta Anna* or "Saint Anne." Most scholars agree that the name derives from *Inanna,* the goddess who preferred the farmer over the shepherd in the ancient Sumerian texts.

prayed in the temple, "serving" the temple with her daily spiritual practice. More important for this exploration, however, is the fact that it was not considered unusual for her to be there.

Then there was the court called "the women's court," where the families of the serving priests and the women who were devoted to the temple, like Hannah, lived and worked and shared the food offered by the people of Israel. There was also a tower, called the "Magdal" tower, because it was taller than the rest of the temple and some scholars have suggested that "the Magdalene" was the title given the woman who occupied that tower.

Beyond that, there are specific rituals reserved strictly for women: e.g., lighting the Sabbath lamps (candles, today) and preparing bodies for burial. And, while women sat apart from the men in synagogue, they were present and, as the New Testament confirms, spoke during the service. Historians have even found documentation that women actually led some synagogues during the Roman period.

Qumran and the Essenes

When Herod built his temple and appointed his favorites as priests, it was too much for many of the conservative, orthodox Jews. Convinced that the new temple was an abomination that was being defiled even further by these upstarts, they withdrew into the wilderness, away from the polluting effect of the city and its temple. There they prepared for the coming of the Messiah—and, it seems from the writings of 1st-century historian Josephus and the documents that have been found at Qumran near the Dead Sea, that some of them did what they could to move things along.

These men and women followed the Mosaic laws to the letter, living in an isolated community and as vegetarians to ensure that they didn't break any of those laws. They were absolutely determined that their goodness would be sufficient to persuade the Lord of Hosts to bring forth his kingdom, his will, on earth.

They lived communally, with no private property, and were very careful in choosing whom they admitted into their community. They also had a very clearly defined set of rules for their community, dictating when and how prayers would be said, what work would be done, and how each individual should live. One thing that intrigues scholars is that, unlike other Jewish sects, the Qumran residents ate communally and the priest blessed a single cup which all shared.

> Josephus, the Roman Jewish historian, tells us of a community of Essenes who lived in the wilderness during the early years of the 1st century. Edgar Cayce also describes a group, in very similar terms, called the Essenes. The Dead Sea Scrolls, however, never name the people who lived at what we call Qumran. For centuries it was believed to have been an abandoned Roman fort and only recently have archeologists begun to interpret the artifacts remaining there.

The Dead Sea Scrolls also tell us that they were very concerned about evil in the world and were preparing themselves for a major battle against its influence. The scrolls tell us that a "Teacher of Righteousness" was being undermined by a "Wicked Priest" who twisted the law—and the community's Rule—for his own purposes. While the scrolls never clearly define who is who, scholars have speculated that Jesus may have been the Righteous one and the High Priest the Wicked one, or that Paul, with his releasing gentiles from Mosaic law was the Wicked One, or even that John the Baptist may have been the Righteous Teacher who followed the strict interpretation of the Law and Jesus the Wicked One, introducing a new covenant.

Some researchers believe that the Essenes were involved in a sort of eugenics program—carefully training their children and selecting who would marry whom so that the right match would bring forth the Messiah. These scholars suggest that Joseph and Mary were selected to be part of this program and that both John the Baptist and Jesus the Christ were offspring of this program, and that both were potential candidates for the role of Messiah when they were born.[35]

The Marys: strong, independent women of power

Although differing traditions suggest there may be some overlap, Strong's *Concordance* lists six different Marys in the New Testament:

1. Mother of Jesus
2. The Magdalene
3. Sister of Lazarus and Martha, in Bethany
4. Mother of James the lesser & Joses/Barnabas
5. Wife of Cleophas, Jesus' "mother's sister"
6. Mother of John Mark, the man traditionally considered the author of the Gospel of Mark

> A Concordance is a listing of the location of words and terms in a text. For the Bible, it lists all the books, chapters, and verses in which a word appears, with the phrase it appears in. Strong's also indicates which Hebrew or Greek form the word is translated from and provides a limited dictionary of each language.

Strong's makes these distinctions because there is no clear text in the gospels stating that these are not different women. Nor is there any indication the Mary called the Magdalene is anyone other than a woman who begins to show up at the end of Jesus' time on earth or that Mary the wife of Cleophas could also be the mother of John Mark or James and Joses. To suggest anything else, based on the text, is pure conjecture.

---

[35] Edgar Cayce promoted this idea in his trance-state readings and several modern writers suggest it.

Interestingly, the name Mary is totally absent from the Old Testament, and yet there are up to six of them in the New Testament gospels—and some scholars suggest that as many as 1 in 25 women bore that name in first-century Palestine! What happened between the two periods of history?

Our first clue is that Mary is the anglicized version of *Maryamme*, which is the Greek form for the Hebrew name Miriam, or *Mrym*. So now at least we have a connection with the Old Testament. But there was only one Miriam in the Old Testament: Moses' and Aaron's sister who led the celebratory singing after the Hebrews' safe crossing of the Sea of Reeds[36] and then participated in some of the conversations with God; she who was clearly the spiritual leader among the women at that time.

The only other place in the Old Testament that we encounter a name like Mary is when the widow Naomi, with her widowed daughter-in-law Ruth, returns home from Moab and says "call me now no more Naomi, call me Mara," which Strong's *Concordance* says is the same word as Miriam, but which, based on her actions in the story and our derivation of the name in the previous chapter, is clearly a title: Naomi was declaring herself to be *Mara*, which, as we have seen, means "master". Clearly, she was the headwoman of the town of Bethlehem at that time.

Who are these women? How do they come to be called Mara or Miriam? One possible clue is that the six Marys are described in the gospels as coming from different parts of Hebrew territory:
- Mary, mother of Jesus, is described as a descendent of the tribe of Judah, living in Nazareth, south of the Sea of Galilee;

---

[28] Strong's *Concordance* is the most popular of several available. It may be found in most large bookstores.

- Mary, sister of Lazarus and Martha, comes from Bethany, outside of Jerusalem, which is associated with the tribe of Benjamin;
- Mary, the Magdalene, is variously described as coming from Magdala, on the north shore of the Sea of Galilee, and other places;
- Mary, the mother of John Mark, lived in Jerusalem itself and hosted the early church.

They are all women of independent means, with all but the Magdalene connected to, but not dependent upon, the men in their families. The gospels tell us they "support" the disciples both financially and through their assistance with menial tasks, and they travel with them freely. They are the ones with the courage and tenacity to stand at the foot of the cross during the crucifixion and the ones who care for the body as it is removed from the cross. They have the myrrh and other ointments necessary to treat the body during and after its temporary burial in the cave, and are going to give it the final anointing on the morning after the Sabbath.

If we step outside the usual way of thinking to consider all of this, it seems a very real possibility that "Miriam/Mary" is not a name, but a title, and that each of the Marys in the gospels comes from a separate community because each was the *Mrym,* the "Mara" for that community—the spiritual leader for the women at least, the anointer with myrrh, and probably, given the biblical references to prophetesses and documentation of women managing synagogues, providers of wisdom among the men in their villages, as well.

It's interesting to note that Mary, mother of Jesus, is provided with the only genealogy, or line of descent, in the whole Bible that includes women. Specifically, her ancestors include (in historical sequence among the men):

- Tamar, a Canaanite woman who, having been widowed, "wrapped herself in her veil and sat by the gate," was perceived as a "harlot" by, then had sexual relations with, her father-in-law, Judah, whose wife

and sons had died—and so became the mother of all the tribe of Judah;
- Rahab, a pagan Canaanite 'prostitute' who let the Israelite spies into her city, Jericho, and was saved, with her family, by Joshua when that city was destroyed "and she has lived in the midst of Israel to this day..."
- Ruth, a pagan Moabitess, widow of a Hebrew, who followed her mother-in-law Naomi back to the land of Judah, where Naomi renamed herself Mara and instructed Ruth to lay with Boaz, a wealthy relative, on the threshing floor at the harvest celebration, and so became his wife—taking on all of Naomi/Mara's possessions in the process;
- Bathsheba, wife of an Israelite general who was adulteress with, then wife of, David and bore Solomon, sitting "at his right hand" while he ruled over Israel and built the great temple in Jerusalem.

So Jesus' mother is described in Matthew's gospel as a direct descendent of most of the women who played a significant role in Hebrew history. Now, if we follow the honored tradition using literal meanings of the Hebrew words used as names, we find even more fascinating bits of information.

- Tamar, which is a root-word meaning "to be erect; upright, like a palm tree," gave her widowed father-in-law a son to replace those he had lost, whom she named Perez (or Pharez), meaning "to break out, breach" as his was a breach birth, and also meaning "to increase, scatter" as his descendants became the core of the mighty tribe of Judah; her name is also the last word of the title of the last song sung by Jewish mystics as they "descend from the heights" of the Sabbath union with God on Saturday evening.
- Rahab, also written as *Rachab* or *Rchowb*, is a primitive Hebrew root, meaning "proud, at liberty" and can be used as a verb, "to enlarge, make room" and the

word describing her as a "harlot" means "temple devotee" in its masculine form;

- Ruth (*Rowth*), interestingly, is not even a name—it means "female companion, mate," suggesting that whatever her Moabite name was, it was not used by her new neighbors and family—she was simply Naomi/Mara's and then Boaz' "companion;" she called herself his "maidservant" and gave birth to a son, *Obed* (worker, bondservant), who was the father of Jesse (or *Yeshe*, "I stand out," or "I exist") and grandfather to David (*Dawviyd*, meaning "loving");
- Bathsheba (*Bathshowah*) is another descriptor, meaning "daughter of freedom, of a noble, of wealth," and it's interesting to note that she is a daughter of "Sheba" which is one of the earliest names in the Bible (a son of Cush and grandson of Noah) and the title of Solomon's (her son's) lover, the "Queen of Sheba"—making her the "daughter of her son's lover," while being Queen Mother, which relationship is part of the Goddess tradition of the region.

What we have in this list, then, is a group of women who are described, not really named, whose positions relate to the Goddess tradition, and who are, as a group, independent, wealthy, noble, upright, powerful, and proud. More, most of them are described as being, or acting like, "harlots" based on a word that is translated as "temple devotees" when written in the masculine form. And to this list some medieval and modern Christians might add the prophetess "who never left" the temple, Anna (an ancient name of the goddess), calling her Mary's mother.

So the mother of Jesus descends from a lineage of women elders who function as healers, spiritual leaders, and teachers of the ancient wisdom in their communities—women who are, in all likelihood, the successors of the original myrrh-bearer, Miriam, Moses' sister. And many of them may have been associated with the Temple. We have no such record of the other Marys, but can only surmise from their independent means and actions that they, too, draw from such a lineage.

The Anointing

In her now classic *Woman with the Alabaster Jar*, the devout Christian author Margaret Starbird rocked the church by using strictly biblical references to establish the idea that Mary the Magdalene was not the adulterous prostitute described by Pope Gregory the Great, but Jesus' leading apostle. In a later work, *The Goddess in the Gospels*, Starbird describes her own journey from a pious Catholic taking an introductory course in religious studies to a world-renown leader of a movement to reinstate Mary Magdalene's role and reputation in Christian tradition. Starbird starts with the obvious:

> Christians are quick to claim that Jesus was the promised Messiah of Israel ... but they almost universally fail to mention the woman who anointed Jesus—the woman with the alabaster jar who knelt before him, poured her fragrant unguent over his head, and dried her tears from his feet with strands of her hair. And yet the Hebrew word *messiah* literally means "the Anointed One." [37]

Starbird goes on to explain what she has come to believe was really going on at that time:

> ...in the ancient rites of the Near East it was a royal bride who anointed the king. Together, they embodied the Divine in a life-sustaining partnership—the *hieros gamous*.
>
> ...
>
> The anointing of Jesus in the Gospels is ... the anointing of the chosen Bridegroom/King by the royal representative of the Great Goddess!
>
> Jesus recognized and acknowledged this rite himself, in the context of his role as sacrificial king: 'She has anointed me in preparation for burial' [Mk 14:8]. [38]

---

[37] Starbird, Margaret, *The Goddess in the Gospels*, Rochester, VT: Bear & Co., 1998, p. 23.
[38] ibid, p. 24.

We've seen that the anointing of a sacrificial God-King by the representative of the Goddess is as old as the most ancient tales of Egypt and Sumer. The language is present in the rites of Isis in Egypt and repeated in the *Song of Solomon*. As Starbird points out

> Highlights of this story ... are reminiscent of myths celebrated in ... the Middle East, those of Tammuz, Dumuzi, and Adonis. In the pagan rituals surrounding the ancient myths, the Goddess (the Sister-Bride) goes to the tomb in the garden to lament the death of her Bridegroom and rejoices to find him resurrected. 'Love is stronger than death' is the poignant promise in the Song of Songs ... celebrating these ancient rites of the Sacred Marriage.[39]

Anointing is associated with marriage as part of declaring a contract: anointing the feet with oil as a means of establishing a new covenant with someone was included in the earliest Hebrew laws attributed to Moses. Since the Hebrews had no spiritual or even legal ceremony associated with marriage, this means of creating a sacred contract, in which the new bride publicly demonstrates her willingness to care for her new husband, made some sense. The use of the unbound hair to do so also fits the cultural norms of the time, since it will be the last time her hair is unbound outside of the bedchamber or bath.

The name Mara, derived, or at least associated with, myrrh, may well be the title of "the woman who anoints." And in fact, in the Eastern church, Mary the Magdalene is called "the Myrrophore," which means "the one who carries the myrrh." This may be why Mary Magdalene isn't named in the gospels until after the anointing story.

The Nazarenes

Then there is the other descriptor applied to Jesus and his early church, translated variously as Nazarene, Nazarite, Nazarean, or "of Nazareth." The traditional interpretation,

---

[39] ibid, p. 24.

based on some of the gospel stories, has been that the man we know as Jesus grew up in the town of Nazareth and so was known by that place. According to the evidence, however, it appears that the town of Nazareth that tourists visit today did not exist during the Roman Empire—it doesn't show up on any official documents, nor have any archeological remains of a village with a synagogue been discovered in the described location. (Though there is a village being excavated that is four miles from Herod's city, Caesarea, that some are calling Nazareth.) Also of interest is the fact that among speakers of Aramaic around the Red Sea, the word "Nasorean" means "fish" and is used to refer to Christians—who, in Greece and Rome, used the sign of the fish as a secret code to identify themselves during the years of persecution.

> It's important to remember that the earliest gospel stories are dated sometime after 60 CE—almost 30 years after the crucifixion. To put this in perspective, if you were alive when Martin Luther King, Jr. or even Mother Teresa was working and heard him speak, try writing down, now, what you heard either of them say then.

There are several possible explanations. The easiest is that everyone was aware that Jesus came at the time of the shift from the age of Aries, the ram, to the age of Pisces, the fish. Zodiacs were ubiquitous at the time—even in the floors of Hebrew synagogues—and the cycle of the stars was as important as the cycle of the seasons in planning one's life and work—which we saw in the doors at Chartres, built a thousand years later! So identifying the new religion with the "New Age" made sense.

The second is more complex: the Law of Moses required that the first-born, or "womb opener," belonged to God and must be dedicated at the Temple. This dedication of a first-born child had significant implications. It meant that he or she was a Nazarene (also spelled Nasorean or Nazirite) until the vow of dedication was undone. Normally, it was undone as a boy achieved manhood, through the ceremony we now know as *bar mitzvah*.

Sometimes, though, the vow was held well into adulthood, usually because the child displayed a special, divine gift. Such a man could

> Boys and girls who were so dedicated were "God's children" and so addressed each other as "brother" and "sister," which may explain why Jesus had "brothers" and how this title became the norm in the early Christian church.

not cut his hair, drink any form of grape juice or wine, nor could he touch a woman without destroying the integrity that his power depended on.

As described in the book of Numbers:

> When either a man or a woman makes a special vow, the vow of the Nazirite, to separate himself to the LORD, he shall separate himself from wine and strong drink; he shall drink no vinegar made from wine and strong drink, and shall not drink of the juice of grapes or eat grapes, fresh or dried. All the days of his separation he shall eat nothing that is produced by the grapevine, not even the seeds or the skins.
>
> All the days of his vow of separation no razor shall come upon his head. Until the time is completed for which he separates himself to the LORD, he shall be holy; he shall let the locks of his head grow long.
>
> All the days that he separates himself to the LORD, he shall not go near a dead body. Neither for his father nor for his mother, nor for brother or sister if they die, shall he make himself unclean because his separation to God is upon his head. All the days of his separation, he is holy to the LORD. ...
>
> And this is the law for the Nazirite, when the time of his separation has been completed: he shall be brought to the door of the tent of meeting, and he shall offer his gift to the LORD, one male lamb...without blemish ...and a basket of unleavened bread ...and their drink offerings ... And the priest shall present them before the Lord ... [Numbers 6:1-21]

We can recognize immediately in this description the famous Hebrew hero, Samson, who lost his strength when he was seduced into drinking wine and, while passed out, was shorn of his never-cut hair and so lost his power. We may also recognize John the Baptist, who was miraculously born of Elizabeth and her priest-husband well after child-bearing years, and who lived in the wilderness so as not to defile himself.

Of course, if the first-born gifted one were a woman, she too, would be subject to the same vows. It's very likely that this was the "vow" that Mary the mother of Jesus was accused of breaking when it was clear that she was pregnant.

So, as we read in the gospel stories, Jesus, with his special birth, as well as being the first-born, or "womb opener," for his mother, was dedicated to God, both shortly after his birth and very likely again at age twelve, when he "astonished the priests" while remaining in the temple instead of returning home with his family.

This would explain why all the icons—even from the earliest days, when it was not at all the Roman fashion—represent Jesus as having long hair. If his disciples were also Nazirites, it would explain their iconic images with long hair as well, and why he told them not to bury their dead and also why they didn't attend the burial of their beloved Teacher.

> A 1990s *Time* magazine cover illustrated "the face of Jesus" from a forensic reconstruction of the remains of 1st century residents of Jerusalem, with the artist insisting that, based on the norms of the time, Jesus must have had short hair.

The need to document a completion of his separation would also explain why it was important to describe Jesus' Last Supper in the New Testament. The Passover ritual requires an "unblemished lamb," which he could be using to "complete the time of separation," as he created the "new covenant" with a basket of unleavened bread and a "drink offering" of wine during the Passover *seder*, on the night before his crucifixion.

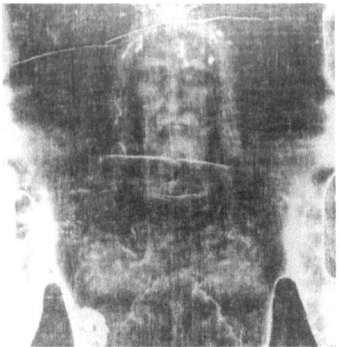

Negative of the image on the Shroud of Turin dated 1st century Palestine

Although there is much controversy around the Shroud and its origin, tests of the fabric by scientists and engineers in the late 1980s and, again, early 2000s, have demonstrated that the fabric dates from the 1st century, that the bits of pollen and leaves embedded in the fabric come from the area around Jerusalem, and that there is no evidence of paint or other chemicals making the image.

Jesus' Teachings Regarding Women

Over the past two millennia, thousands, if not millions, of scholars and clergy have explored and interpreted the various versions we have of the few words that are attributed to Jesus. Here, all that will be done is to point out a few of the sayings and actions reported in the gospels pertaining to his attitude—and the attitude he encouraged in his followers—regarding women.

First of all, he called all of them "Woman." Even his mother. While he rarely referred to anybody by name, this simple act may have profound significance. Some scholars suggest that, in a culture of male-dominance, he may have been establishing himself as part of the dominant majority and distancing himself from those who were "lesser" or outside the norm. But this doesn't fit with his other actions, in which he consistently identified himself with the outsiders and downtrodden. Another possibility is that he was honoring his Nazarite vow. A final explanation, and one that fits with the ideas being presented here, is that he was honoring the divine feminine represented by each of the women he encountered.

Another characteristic of Jesus' work was that he included women when he was teaching, as we see in the story of Martha and Mary in Bethany. In the Greco-Roman world, only men would be considered capable of learning, and in the Hebrew culture, they would have been taught separately from the men. But Jesus apparently didn't make that distinction. In fact, when confronted with the issue, he pointed out that there is no difference between male and female in "the Father's kingdom".

In the story of the woman at the Samaritan well, Jesus mystified his disciples by talking to a woman in public, as if she had value in her own right. And when given the problem of whether to stone a woman caught in adultery, he simply told her to "go, and sin no more," acknowledging her value as a human being and her responsibility for her own life.

> While traditional interpreters of the gospels assume that John was referring to himself when he used the phrase "beloved disciple," some scholars, based on the way it is phrased, believe that John was referring to someone else, and the gospels found in Egypt suggest that the "beloved disciple" was actually Mary Magdalene.

At the cross, he entrusted the care of his mother to the "beloved disciple," demonstrating that he was the leader of his family and took responsibility for her welfare rather than leaving her without means.

Then, after the Resurrection, he made sure that Mary the Magdalene saw him and knew not only who he was, but what was happening to him. Then he told her to go and "tell the others" what she had seen and heard—which instruction is the basis for her title of "Apostle to the Apostles." Clearly, the official canon shows Jesus including at least one woman among his disciples and as part of his ministry.

Then, if we are to believe the 2nd century Gnostic scriptures discovered at *Nag Hammadi* in Egypt, the ascended Jesus included several women in his advanced teachings—even praising the Magdalene extensively as one who truly understands both his words and the work.[40] As we shall see later in some detail, he encouraged mystical union with the divine feminine and denied that gender made a difference in spiritual life.

In the context of the ideas being presented here, one significant quality of the gospels stands out: *Jesus' life was about restoring balance to the lives of the Hebrew people.* His teachings encouraged the kind of life that the old Anatolian-style horticulturalists embraced. His respect for women, as well as for the diseased and other outcasts of the "perfect ideal" male-dominated hierarchy of Greco-Roman Judea, was noticeable. His recognition that each individual's life was of value, and that violence only encouraged more violence was in direct contrast with the Aryan-based "civilized" norms of his time.

Jesus' Role in his Culture

The name Jesus, which is also translated as Joshua or Justus, from the Hebrew *Yeshuwa,* or *Yhowshua,* means "He will save," or "deliverer," from the root *y'showah,* "deliverance by God." It also means "Savior." The man who was Moses' military leader, who led the people across into Canaan and "fit the battle of Jericho," was called by the same name. How-

> The 1st Joshua led the Hebrews into the Promised Land, the 2nd Joshua, usually written as "Jeshua," served as a priest with the great prophet Elijah, and the 3rd was the high priest who, with Nehemiah, rebuilt the Temple after the Hebrews returned from the Babylonian exile. The man we call Jesus is the 4th to appear in biblical texts.

---

[40] In the *Pistis Sophia,* the "Acts of Philip," and the "Gospel of Mary."

ever, only three others in biblical Hebrew history were called Joshua, suggesting that, like Mara/Miriam, it may be a title as much as a name.

In the vernacular of his people, Aramaic, he was probably called Y'shuh, or Y'sheh, which, in the Roman tongue, Latin, would be written *Iesu*, and is pronounced "Yaizoo." This then was translated into German and English as Jesus about 1500 years later.

Jesus, like his predecessors, was also called "rabbi," meaning "wise teacher" by his followers. This placed him in a role that, even today, is expected to act as investigator, mediator, and arbitrator as well as expounder and explainer of the scriptures and Law.[41] At the same time, he was a Nazarene and a miracle-worker, making him qualify among the people as at least a prophet—someone who, according to scriptural tradition—was particularly blessed by and in direct communication with the Almighty God, and so able to do God's work among His people.

> The fact that the man we call "Jesus Christ" never heard those words raises the issue of how Christians are to truly "pray in his name."
> One direction to look for a solution is that the Hebrew and Aramaic word for "name" is *shem*, as it was as far back as Sumerian times. *Shem* literally means "character, nature, authority."

There are as many interpretations of Jesus' life as there are students of his teachings, and each of them has something to contribute to our understanding of the man and his era. Virtually all of them, however, assume that the culture he lived in was the same as that of the urbanized, literate, Greco-Roman authors of the New Testament—particularly Paul—when in fact, all indications are that he was not part of that world at all. A few assume that his culture was the

---

[41] A wonderful look at the life of a (relatively) modern rabbi is in the "Rabbi Small" mysteries by Harry Kemelman.

one defined in the *Torah*, which, as we have seen, is not likely.

Jesus' world, as described in the gospels, was that of the "rural conservatives" described earlier in this book, those who hung on to the ancient traditions while empires and kingdoms and temples and priesthoods rose and fell around them. That means that the people he grew up with and walked among went through the motions of the temple-oriented religion but were, in fact, far more in touch with and concerned about their relationship with the forces of nature than with the rules and dogma of the priesthood. According to the gospel stories, they were people who spent the Sabbath listening to the ancient stories and reflecting on them, as had their ancestors before them, in Babylon. They honored the passing of the seasons with festivals and sacrifices, as had their ancestors from time immemorial, and they went to the Temple to do so only because they felt they had to. It's clear also that they had little faith in the men of the Temple: the scribes and Pharisees who ran it were not trusted, and the *Sanhedrin*, the council of elders that met in the Temple was not considered a safe place for a just trial.

> David Ovason in *The Two Children*, has gone so far as to suggest that the two versions of the birth are actually describing two different births, of two different boys who are called Jesus, born of two different sets of parents.

If we look at Jesus' birth as described in the gospel stories, we actually have two very different accounts. One focuses on the conservative, rural nature of the culture in which he was born, with stable animals and shepherds with their sheep. The other points to all the signs and portents associated with the birth, including the star and the wise men seeking the child whose birth has been prophesied for years, if not centuries. The commonality between them is the presence of the young mother, named Mary/*Mrha*/*Mrym* and her patient, protective fiancé, Joseph/*Y'shef.*

Life & Times of Jesus

    Then we read about the flight into Egypt, with the possibility that Jesus' earliest years were spent in a place totally unlike the one he was born in. The time lived in Egypt has been explored by a number of researchers, and some of the *Apocrypha* (meaning "lost" or "left out" scriptures) suggest that Jesus and his family made quite an impact on the area. It seems that he and they are remembered as having worked a number of miracles during that period.[42] A few have suggested that he and his parents were given special training there by "the magi" (that is, the "wise men," from the same root as "magic") to prepare them for the kind of skills and abilities he would develop as an adult.

    The story of Jesus' reception when he gets up to speak at the synagogue in his home town of "Nazareth" is a wonderful indicator of the duality of his role. On the one hand, he was "just one of the guys" who grew up in the region, spoke the local language, and participated in all the local activities. On the other hand, he could recite scripture extensively from memory—to the point where the priests of the temple "were astonished" at his ability when he went for what we call today his *bar mitzvah*. More, he was willing to let people know that God was present in and through him. He was part of the culture and yet able to stand outside of it. As the story goes, this contrast was too great for the neighbors of his childhood and they ran him out of town—even threatening to stone him for suggesting that in him, Isaiah's prophecy was fulfilled.

    The language used to describe Jesus gives us a clearer understanding of his role. The Greek word, *Christos,* translated as "Christ" in English, is derived from a root word that means "to furnish, touch, give, be useful." It is, in fact, a combination of two words: *chrio,* "to rub with oil," and *chrestos,* "goodness, gracious, kind." Not too surprisingly, the

---

[42] Paul Perry, *Jesus in Egypt: Discovering the Secrets of Christ's Childhood Years.* New York: Ballantine, 2003.

term *chresis*, from the same root, is translated as "sexual intercourse."

The term "messiah," applies to the successor of King David and is usually defined as one who is anticipated by the Hebrews to restore Jerusalem to their dominion and put their enemies to route. It actually means, as Starbird points out in her several books, "anointed one," and in ancient times referred to the man who was chosen to be consort to the Goddess, who would be anointed by her representative as part of their *heiros gamos*, or sacred marriage—even as David and Solomon had been (by Bathsheba and Sheba, respectively)—and through this sacred act, be given power to rule.

The term "Son of God" was traditionally a reference to the son resulting from that sacred marriage, and sometimes applied to the bridegroom himself, since the stories say that the Goddess' consort was also her son by her now-dead consort. In the gospel stories, Jesus often referred to himself as "the bridegroom." "Lamb of God" is another descriptor applied to Jesus, and, again, this is the term traditionally used for the Goddess' consort who is about to be sacrificed so that balance and harmony may be restored in the land.

> The dove is an ancient symbol of the presence of the Goddess, appearing nowhere else as a sign of the Hebrew Lord of hosts. This phrase is used in the annual Isis rites in Egypt.

Even in the story of his baptism at the river by John (which is the English version of the Greek *Johannon*, *Yehohanan* in Hebrew, "God has shown favor"), we see this duality. On the one hand, he shows up, just like any other pious Jew, seeking the unique super-purification that John offers. On the other hand, John himself questions why he would do so, saying "I have need to be baptized by you." Jesus basically says, don't worry about all that; just do it. The issue is resolved when, after they have completed the ritual, the "Spirit of God" descends in the form of a dove, and many of those present hear a voice saying, "This is my Son, the beloved."

Life & Times of Jesus 139

In short, nearly every title given to Jesus in the gospels is associated with the ancient Goddess tradition of *heiros gamos*. Consider the possibility:

> The new Mara, a Nazarene raised as one set apart for God as the representative of the Goddess, is ready to be wed, but it's not yet clear who will be the Anointed One, the Messiah, the Nazarene man she is to marry. The signs and portents are not yet clear, though they point to a man called Y'shuh, son of the elder Mara and her now-deceased consort, called Y'sher.
>
> Advised that the time for the sacred marriage is at hand, the new Mara collects her retinue, other women with similar training, and sets out to meet the man.
>
> Along the way she comes to the river Jordan, where another Nazarene, called Yehonan, whom she had met in the Temple, is preaching repentance and offering a new kind of ritual cleansing that he calls "baptism." While there, she observes dozens of men acknowledging their sins and, instead of making offerings in the temple, simply immerse themselves in the river as a means of atonement. Her heart sings as she witnesses this return to a less destructive approach to restoring balance with the divine—free of the bloodshed and burning. As she continues to watch, she sees that John is giving special honors to the man in front of him, and with an inner vision trained to see beyond the surface presentation of a person, she can see why. This man needs no spiritual cleansing—his heart is in total union with the divine, already. He is simply acknowledging the rightness of what John is doing. As he steps into the water, Mara can feel the power of the spirit moving through all three of them, so she is not surprised when it becomes manifest in the form of a dove, sign of the Goddess, descending on the scene, and the silent voice whispering in all who could hear, "This is my son in whom I am well pleased."
>
> In that moment, Mara knows that this man must be the one who will be her husband, the Anointed One, consort to the Goddess, through the sacred marriage.
>
> She has seen him and so returns to Jerusalem, to the Magdal tower that she calls home, but stops on the way to visit family in Bethany. There, in the house of her uncle Simon, called the Leper but now healed, she meets

with her Nazarene "sister and brother," Martha and Lazarus. Being of the same age-group, these three have grown up together as brother and sister in the Temple, dedicated to God and maintaining their vows. She tells them of her decision regarding Y'shuh and encourages them to invite him into their home. Then she meets with her uncle to plan the wedding feast that will precede the *heiros gamos*, itself.

Some weeks later, Mara learns that Y'shuh will be visiting and teaching at Martha's home, so she again gathers some of her women and makes the journey to Bethany. There she sits among the listeners, delighted to hear what he is saying—he has found a way to express the wisdom of the Goddess within the scriptural traditions! She's aware that this is an unusual pairing: the Anointed One is typically a well-established, highly respected man in the community, while Y'shuh preferred the company of outcasts and rebels. Yet, the signs and portents, along with his clear understanding, tell her that she is right: he is the One, the Son, the Dayspring, her Tammuz.

From that day forward her life revolves around his. Yet, in the tradition of the region, a man's life often involves many days spent away from home with other men, and Jesus' life is no different. Mara understands this and actually appreciates it as she uses her time alone to manage the many lands and people she is responsible for in her role as the representative of the Goddess. Like countless generations of women before her, she balances her time between her management and training duties, her spiritual practices, and her relationships with friends and family. She is a powerful presence in her world and she is proud to be part of what all the signs indicate is a major transformation for humanity. The time is at hand.

Finally, the perfect night arrives. The sun, stars, and planets have all traveled to their appointed places. Y'shuh, following the age-old tradition, arrives at Simon's house with his retinue of followers and family. Mara is already there, resplendent in her scarlet gown, her long light-colored hair hanging free as is customary only on one's wedding night. The wedding banquet proceeds and she enters with her jar of ointment, the fine alabaster jar that has been used for generations of Maras before her to declare and ordain the next Messiah, the next Chosen One. In accordance with the ancient tradition, she washes his feet with her hair and anoints his head, reciting the ancient verses as she proceeds: "My beloved is to me a pouch of myrrh which lies all night between my breasts ... I am the rose of Sharon, the lily of the valleys...The time has arrived for pruning the vines ... my beloved is mine and I am his ... Go forth, O daughters of Zion and gaze on King Solomon with the crown with which his mother has crowned him on the day of his wedding ... This is my beloved and this is my friend ... I am my beloved's and my beloved is mine" Y'shuh responds with his lines: "I have come into my garden, my sister, my bride; I have gathered my myrrh ...Thou preparest a table before me...Thou anointest my head with oil; my cup overflows..." The night is perfect. Their birth-vows as Nazarenes are fulfilled in the sacred coming-together.

As a result of the sacred wedding, Y'shuh now is consort to the Goddess and has access to all the riches that Mara and her women can make available to him. Nonetheless, he chooses to continue wandering and teaching around the country. Mara and her group join him whenever possible, learning from him but also teaching him some of the secrets they've learned as healers and representatives of the Goddess. She and her associates make sure that all that is needed is supplied. Trained to listen and absorb information and to integrate it into their own experience, they have no problem comprehending what he is saying, and always look forward to his unique integration of their two traditions, even when it appears that the "twelve" the chosen male disciples often don't understand either his words or his actions.

As the weeks go by, Y'shuh's power as a healer increases. He begins to feel, not only in love with God, but, through his relationship with Mara, at one with the Creative force of the universe. Recognizing that his father, Joseph, had achieved this same experience of union, Y'shuh identifies the loving Presence within and around him as the same loving, protective energy that he felt with Joseph, and he begins to call it by the same term of endearment, *Abba*.

Mara is pleased and proud that Y'shuh has stepped into the power of his position. She revels in the miracles that happen around him. At the same time, she is fascinated with his way of teaching; he seems to have discovered a totally new way to interpret the ancient truths, using the experience of the country-folk as metaphors for the spiritual life. Yet she knows that this time of teaching and healing is only a stepping-stone on his path. There is far greater power available to him, if he is willing to take it. The stars continue in their journey and the portents are clear. Y'shuh's time comes all too quickly. The two of them spend as many hours together as possible, deepening their spiritual understanding and power—and the bond between them—as they plan the next steps in their journey.

Then the day comes. Mara gives Y'shuh the seamless scarlet cloak of his office and arranges for a white donkey colt to be tethered where he will need it, as has been done so many times before. All through Jerusalem the word is sent out: "He is here! The Anointed One has come!" And, as they have for millennia, the people line the streets, shouting praises, and singing "Hosanna! Tammuz is arrived; David is reborn: Jerusalem and all of Judea is saved!"

All goes well, with no interference from the ever-present military. Y'shuh's triumphant entry is understood by the Romans to be just what it is: a sacred celebration; an ancient ritual. The people are allowed to rejoice in peace.

Now events start to accelerate. The timing is crucial. In order for the Anointed One to achieve his true power and status, he must die and be reborn. And the stars and planets must be in exactly the right place for the fullest power to support the process. Jesus explains all this to his disciples, but, unwilling or unable to step outside their old thought patterns, they don't seem to hear. Only one of them understands: Judas called the Iscariot, Y'shuh's trusted lieutenant. He knows the tradition and hates it; yet he feels the intensity of his teacher's desire, so for love of his teacher and what may come of it, he goes along with the plan.

Y'shuh, full of power and authority, makes one last visit to Herod's Temple. It has always bothered him to see how mercenary profiteers take so much advantage of the people who are trying to fulfill God's Law as they understand it. Now, though, feeling the power of the Spirit working through him, he explodes: tables are overturned, moneychangers cower behind them, caged birds and rabbits are freed, and people scurry out of the courtyard as all present feel the wrath of God descend upon them. And even as he observes and participates in this unexpected happening, Y'shuh knows that it, too, is part of the unfolding of his Sonship—and a step along the path toward fulfillment of his lifework.

The days proceed. It is the Passover. Again, Mara has arranged for the perfect location for their feast: a quiet upper room where they will not be disturbed in this, which may be the final act Y'shuh makes in his present form. He begins the feast by washing the feet of his disciples, reinforcing his role as the bridegroom by paralleling her washing of his feet at their wedding, and starting a new covenant with his disciples by anointing their feet. Mara stays as close to him as she can, resting her head on her beloved's chest as he offers the bread and wine and announces the new covenant. Then she feels a stab of pain, as if a knife had entered her heart, when he gives Judas the signal to go do what he must do. Their time together in this form is almost done.

The feast over, Mara stays close as they adjourn to the garden to pray and prepare themselves for the ordeal ahead. The Anointed One must now become the Lamb of God. The Messiah must now give up his earthly life that he might have eternal life. The Savior of Israel must become one with the Creator of the Universe. Her beloved student-teacher-husband-son must leave her. All through the long night they pray, and, though Y'shuh occasionally calls some of the men to join them, only she and her well-trained healer-priestesses have the discipline to stay with him.

A couple of hours before dawn, she hears them coming: Judas and the temple guard, coming to take Y'shuh before the Sanhedrin. It's going like clockwork, but her heart aches every step of the way. As a woman, Mara is not allowed into the trial. Even though its convening is the result of her efforts, it is located in a part of the temple women may not enter, so she is barred from the proceedings. There's only one thing to do, then, so she retreats to her tower to pray.

Dawn comes and still no word. Then her helpers come to tell her Y'shuh is being taken to Pilate to be punished as a revolutionary. Mara is concerned; they have only a narrow window to work with. A helper returns: Pilate has sent him to Herod! This will not do—a dungeon term would harm, rather than help their cause. Mara sends word to her Nazarene "sister" Salome to keep her stepfather Herod on track. Again she prays. She is so filled with the Presence that she already knows what her helper will say when he returns, so she begins to prepare herself for the next phase of the ordeal, drawing the crimson cloak of her office over her shoulders. As she leaves the tower she can hear the voices of the crowd in the distance: "Crucify him!" Dreamlike, she walks the streets of Jerusalem, headed for the fearful site, feeling the love of the Goddess even as she feels in her own body the weight of the cross on Y'shuh's lacerated back. Her joy and pain are so intermixed, she can barely stay upright along the road.

Soon she is joined by the elder Mara, her teacher and mother-in-law. Both in the trance of the Presence, they support each other along the way, and, as they do so, they feel divine energy moving through them, sustaining them, as well as the focus of their shared love, Y'shuh. They arrive at the Place of Skulls shortly after the Romans have begun to fix their beloved to the cross. The energy is so intense in this place that all is silent except the sound of the hammer. As the cross is raised, Mara notices that Pilate really does understand what's going on: he's arranged for a sign on Y'shuh's cross saying *Iesu Nazarenu, Rex Iudei* ("Jesus the Nazarene, King of Judea"). Then, as she gazes upon the face of her beloved, she feels the intensity of the bond between them, and recognizes that love is the only thing he is feeling—love for her, for his mother, for his followers, for the men being crucified with him, even for the Romans who are doing this terrible deed. And in this love, Mara knows, lies his salvation. Hand in hand with his mother she stands there, feeding his love and life with her own sense of the Presence. She barely hears the words he speaks, only that he is being uplifted by this overwhelming sense of love. She hears him call on his *Abba*. She hears him proclaim *Lama Sabachthani*, "for this was I brought forth from you!" Then the part of her that feels along with him knows that it's time to give him the bitter herb she has brought for this moment. She checks the sky above to ensure that, in fact, the time is right, and gives a wet sponge to the guard, silently compelling him to let Jesus taste it, and, miraculously, the soldier does so, placing the sponge on the tip of his lance and lifting it to her beloved's mouth.

Within moments, Y'shuh declares clearly, triumphantly, "It is finished!" Immediately, she feels the release as his spirit lets go of the body—and at the same instant, the sun is darkened by the moon's circle. A full eclipse, long anticipated as an essential part of this process, is occurring. In the darkness, she lets out a shout of exhilaration: It is done! All that they had dreamed and planned has come to pass! Then, still holding on to the elder Mara's hand, she braces herself for what she knows must come next: the shaking of the earth, imbalanced by the eclipse; the response of the Mother to the loss of her Daystar, her Son.

Then it's over. The two women begin to prepare for the entombment. Their elder "brother" Nazarene, Y'sef of Arimathea, has prepared the perfect cave for the unfolding of the drama and they have brought a shroud. Jesus' body hangs limp on the cross and the Romans are unsure what to do. Crucifixion is designed to be a long, slow, process, and this has gone much too quickly. More, they are disturbed by the eclipse and the subsequent earthquake; even in their tradition these are substantial omens and signs. Finally, one of them decides to make sure of the matter, and, unaware that he is fulfilling an ancient prophecy, he pierces Y'shuh's side with his spear. Blood and a clear fluid flow profusely. Mara and her mother-in-law breathe deeply, determined not to lose sight of their intention in the face of any evidence to the contrary: Y'shuh is the Anointed One, born to eternal life, and their job is to make it so.

Their "brother" Y'sef comes with one of Pilate's stewards, giving them permission to receive the body and entomb it before nightfall, as long as Pilate's men can guard the tomb. The guards grudgingly lower the cross. Lovingly, the two women embrace the body of their beloved. Well-trained and long-accustomed to preparing the dead for burial, they work quickly and efficiently, determined to complete the process before sunset's onset of the Sabbath. They lay the body on a long strip of linen fabric spread over a stretcher, scattering dried and fresh herbs around and over it. Prayerfully, they place their hands over the open wounds, sealing them with their healing touch. Then they fold the rest of the fabric over the body and signal to the men to lift the stretcher and carry it to the nearby cave. As the sun begins to set, they watch while the men lift the covered body from the stretcher. Lovingly, holding their intention, they bless the body of their beloved and leave the cave.

Finally, with the last rays of sunlight leaving the sky, they watch as a huge stone is rolled over the opening and the guards take their position on either side. Then they rush to the Magdal tower to light the Sabbath lamps.

That Sabbath is spent in deep prayer. The power of the Presence is strong. Her beloved has fulfilled all her expectations. Both Miriams are confident that all is well. Still, the drama must unfold. So, in the early pre-dawn of the next morning, Mara of the Magdal Tower gathers her ointments to further anoint her beloved. It is the third day. The time has been fulfilled and the representative of the Goddess has always gone to the cave to weep for her beloved on this day. And so, in accordance with tradition, Mara does the same. Once there, however, the drama overwhelms her — the stone has been rolled away! The tomb is empty!

Automatically, the ritual words are spoken, "They have taken away my Lord!" And, automatically, Mara finds herself reenacting the ancient ritual of crying before the empty tomb. All the strain of the past week seeks release in tears. It is over. He is gone. Then, through her tears and wails, she hears a voice calling her name—it's unfamiliar, hoarse, and barely audible through the sound of her own crying. Again she hears it, and this time she turns. Through the bushes, across the path from where she sits, a man stands, looking at her. It's hard to focus through her tears in the semi-darkness, but she realizes that the drama is still unfolding, and repeats the ritual words, 'Where have they taken my Lord?" She stands as she speaks, and, with her vision no longer impeded by the bushes between them, she sees that the man is Y'shuh, fully alive! Joyfully she runs to him, ready to embrace him, but he puts out his hand to stop her, "Don't try to hold me; I've not yet completed my journey."

Too worn out by the whole thing to argue, she simply collapses at his feet, her tears flowing for joy now, as well as release. As she has so often, she sits at his feet

> and listens to him tell her about his experience and what she is to share with the other disciples. As he talks, the sun comes up. And as the light increases, his appearance begins to fade, but his final words ring in her heart: "I ascend to my God and your Goddess."
> In the silence of his absence, Mara rests a while, simply breathing and taking it all in. It worked! The ancient process worked, and her beloved lives! The transformation of the world is begun! It's almost too good to be true, but the empty tomb with its rolled-away stone remains mute testimony to her experience.
> Once refreshed, she rises and hurries to the upper room where the Passover feast was held and some of the disciples are hiding. At first they don't believe her, but man-like must go see for themselves. Finally, they understand, and in that moment, though the door is locked, Y'shuh appears in the room with them! He nods to Mara and she knows that now the "journey" is done and he can come and go as he pleases. She sits back and watches as the men digest the reality of this miracle, her heart silently thanking the Source and loving Presence for the balance and harmony restored to her people and the new life about to be born.

Consider the possibility.

Initiates from Egypt to India have been entombed for three days and arisen to a new level of wisdom and power. Druids and Yogis have done the same. Ancient documents describe a process by which the dying Pharaoh may achieve eternal life and exit his tomb—and the great pyramid had no body, only a coating of "white powder" over everything when opened. A number of texts describe Hindu and Buddhist monks disappearing in a cloud of light, leaving only hair and fingernails (the parts of our bodies that are not living tissue) where they had been meditating and, among at least one group of Tibetans, it is through relationship with

> Some believe this powder is a form of gold called "shewbread" and used to help the spirit transform the body; David Hudson is the best known presenter of this idea, in a number of videotapes made in the 1990s.

the divine feminine that this is possible. Healing touch is taught in nursing schools and hospitals across the country. And thousands of people have seen and heard Mary the Mother, or Jesus the Christ, in dozens of places around the world, some of them experiencing the "visions" as solid bodies.

Modern science makes it clear that matter is not solid, but is instead overlapping fields of energy taking form as guided by observers' thought and feeling. Perhaps we've been taught to read the Bible through a filter of limiting ideas that prevent us, just like Jesus' disciples, from perceiving what's really being said—and offered—to the discerning reader.

A Continued Ministry?

Traditional gospel stories provide descriptions of a few visits and teachings by Jesus after his death and resurrection, then describe his "ascending into heaven" and leaving the scene. The New Testament continues with stories of the disciples attempting to make sense of what he had taught them and this new Spirit-filled life he had left them. Jesus' ministry, according to traditional sources, ended with his ascension and was picked up forty days later, at Pentecost, by his disciples.

The New Testament is not the only documentation we have, however, of Jesus and his ongoing teachings. In the late 1940s, an Egyptian farmer discovered some jars filled with leather-covered, parchment and papyrus codices (books bound like scrapbooks or old-fashioned photo albums). He took them home and dumped them in the trash heap, from which several pages were taken for kindling—before an expert took a look and hauled them off to a museum. They became known as the "*Nag Hammadi* Library."

It's taken over fifty years for these books to be made accessible to the public, in part because of changing international relations and in part because of academic egos and the demands of rigorous scholarship, but many remarkable texts have been translated into various European languages and English from the original Coptic (a mixture of Greek and Egyptian).[43] Among these are:

- *The Gospel of Thomas*
- *The Acts of Philip*
- *The Pistis Sophia ("Faith Wisdom")*
- *The Dialogue of the Savior*

In addition, other scholars have found similar texts, one in an antiquities' shop in Cairo in 1895, called *The Gospel of Mary*, and the more recently discovered *Gospel of Judas*. All of them offer radical alternatives to traditional understandings of what occurred during the time of the crucifixion and resurrection—and afterward. These texts suggest that Jesus continued teaching for years following the crucifixion,[44] providing deeper and deeper insights into the nature of God, the universe, and humanity—and the processes by which his students might come into their own power.

---

[43] For translations of many of these works, as well as many of the Dead Sea Scrolls, see *The Other Bible*.

[44] Another source describing a continued ministry by Jesus, from a much later date and source, is *The Book of Mormon*.

*There were those who came to power,
through domination.
They were bonded in their worship
of a dead man on a cross...*[45]

CHURCH AS ROMAN/ARYAN EMPIRE

The 2,000-year history of the Roman church is replete with tales of intrigue, personal vanity, murder, and political maneuvering, as well as a heartfelt effort to make the blessings of Christianity available to the greatest possible number of people. Traditional scholarship has focused on the relationship between the Church and the nations of Europe, describing the complexities of constantly changing control over lands and the wealth generated thereon. Questions of which pope and which king were working together or in conflict tend to be the focus of academic research.

To look at the historical record from that perspective, however, is to ignore the pattern. From the day when Constantine declared Christianity to be the religion that would preserve his failing Roman empire, it's clear that the church fathers had one goal: to build a universal empire based on a universal Church. In true Aryan fashion, the value of "more is better" took hold, even among those who had vowed to maintain "poverty, chastity, and obedience," and they did everything they could to control as much land and as many people as possible, "for the glory of God."

---

[45] Title tune from the record album, "Burning Times," by Charlie Murphy.

The Canon—Foundation for an Empire

One example of this thought process is the formation of what we call The Bible. There were hundreds of "gospels" and related texts before the Council of Nicea, in 325CE, when the emperor Constantine requested a copy of the sacred scripture on which this strange religion he was adopting for the Empire was based. Some scholars estimate that as many as a thousand documents were being used by members of the Christian movement to teach the "good news" of Jesus Christ at that time. The leaders gathered at Nicea were faced with a monumental task: how to select a coherent set for the emperor?

Fortunately for them, they were not the first to try. Several bishops and historians had suggested collections of what they thought were the "true" teachings, and some had even edited some of the documents they had, leaving out the parts that they felt were not consistent with what they believed Jesus had in mind—or made sense to them in the moment. This gave the Council members a working list. The books considered for inclusion in the New Testament at the Council of Nicea were:

> This practice was not limited to the early church leaders. Many Masonic lodges encourage their members to write their own versions of the Bible, and Thomas Jefferson's personal version has been published.

- Four gospels: Mathew, Mark, Luke, John
- Acts of the Apostles, attributed to Luke
- 14 letters attributed to Paul
- 2 letters attributed to Peter
- 3 letters attributed to John
- 1 letter attributed to Jude
- Revelation of John
- The Shepherd, attributed to Hermas Didache
- Revelation of Peter

What was needed was a set of writings that would make sense to urbanized Greco-Romans of the 4th century, whose homeland, Italy, had been taken over by barbarians and whose empire was now managed out of Asia Minor, in the city known variously as Byzantium, Constantinople, and Istanbul. What they sought to create was a set of stories and teachings and doctrines that would unify the people under one church, established by the government as the official religion of all people, regardless of previous religious background or preference.

What they did was to decide on a common creed (the "Nicene (sometimes spelled Nicean Creed" and later modified and called the "Apostles' Creed"). It was a set of statements that define what it means to be Christian:

> This creed, with only slight modification is still recited in almost every Christian church in the world—especially at baptisms.

> We believe in one God, the Father Almighty, maker of Heaven and earth and of all things visible and invisible.
> And in one Lord Jesus Christ, the only-begotten Son of God, begotten of the Father before all worlds, God of God, Light of Light, true God of true God, begotten, not made, one in being with the Father by whom all things were made, who for us men and for our salvation came down from Heaven. He was incarnate by the Holy Spirit of the Virgin Mary, was crucified under Pontius Pilate and was buried. On the third day He rose again in fulfillment of the scriptures and ascended into Heaven. He sits at the right hand of the Father and, with the Father, is adored and glorified. He will come again in glory to judge the living and the dead and his kingdom will have no end.
> We believe in the Holy Spirit, the Lord and Giver of Life, who proceeds from the Father and the Son and with the Father and the Son is adored and glorified and who spoke through the prophets.
> We believe in one holy, catholic, and apostolic church, We acknowledge one baptism for the forgiveness of sins and look for the resurrection of the dead and the life of the world to come. Amen.

Roman Church as Empire

Then, based on that clear statement, and the determined negotiations of one bishop, Iraneus, the group chose the set of stories and letters that we now call the New Testament, as printed in the Roman Catholic or New Jerusalem Bible. These contain a few more "books" (*Biblia* means "books" in Latin) than the Protestant King James, Revised Standard, or New International Version, but the essence remains the same.

So the task was done. The doctrine and supporting scripture for the movement was defined. Christianity, as the holy catholic (meaning "universal") church, was established. All the accepted texts were written in Greek—ignoring the fact that the events had taken place in the Aramaic-speaking region they called Palestine. Nearly half of the accepted stories were written by a Greek physician, a visitor to Jerusalem sometime in the late 60s, writing to a man named *Theophilus*, which means "God-lover." Luke had become involved in this movement through the enthusiasm of one of his patients, Saul, a Greek of Jewish heritage from the town of Tarsus in what we now call Asia Minor. Most of the rest of what became the New Testament were letters written by that same Saul after he changed his name to Paul--or they are at least purported to be, and addressed to Greeks and Romans around the empire who were beginning to take on this new religion.

These writings made far more sense to urbanized Greco-Roman citizens than the highly mystical, wild stories and sayings found in some of the other gospels and documents available for them to choose from. In fact, those others were so strange and so dangerous that the leaders at Nicea decided they should be destroyed, to ensure the fulfillment of Constantine's desire that one set of scriptures would define the established church of the Empire.

Historians of the period recorded how various bishops went about "cleansing" the churches and monasteries in their regions of those dangerous, heretical works. They burned whole libraries of books and imprisoned or whipped scholars and monks for reading or copying them. For centuries since, the only way we've known they existed was by way of these churchmen's derogatory references to them in letters and pronouncements (at least until the discovery of the *Nag Hamadi* codices, which had been buried in Egypt during that time).

Immediately upon establishment by Constantine, the Roman church sought to fill all the corners of the Empire. As Augustine documented a few decades later, missionary priests and monks were sent as far north as they were willing to go to convert the pagan (rural) villagers and kings in the Celtic and Gothic tribes of Germany, France, England, Ireland and Scotland. Others went eastward, into the Orient, to convert the heathens (people of the heath, or plains).

As they went, they were encouraged to build working farms as monasteries, and to replace existing temples with Christian churches. In this way, the Roman church began to acquire a fair amount of property across the various kingdoms of Europe. The bishops justified their expansionist activities with scriptural references that exhorted the disciples to "go forth and preach the gospel," drawing on texts from the Bible that encouraged the reader to believe that God's ultimate plan was for all people, everywhere, to be followers of Christ. They convinced themselves that the important thing was the salvation of souls, and that any means to this end was justifiable.

The early Christian bishops saw themselves as "holding the center" by maintaining the cultural standards of Rome. In the past they had worn normal dress for gatherings and celebrations. Now they adopted the dress and behaviors of the Roman priesthood—which, in turn, had been adopted from the Etruscans (who were, it seems, refugees from Anatolia). Like their Etruscan predecessors, they wore white robes and conical hats, carried a shepherd's crook or cross as a sign of authority, and blessed the land and its people by pointing to the heavens, then to the earth, then to the eastern sea and the western sea. The leader of both Etruscans and Christians, called "the pontiff," mounted the steps of the capitol with the Vestal Virgins (now called "Holy Sisters"), to maintain the eternal flame of divine presence and blessing for the city and empire of Rome.

For the first few hundred years, it was touch-and-go: marauding tribes, plague, and mutinous bishops all took their toll on the power and authority of the Roman pontiff. To restore order and ensure that Rome, the "Eternal City," would become Augustine's "City of God," clear lines of authority had to be set. Power had to be institutionalized and centralized, and the means was church doctrine, combined with carefully crafted alliances.

The alliances were relatively easy, a matter of constant negotiation and renegotiation, until, in 799, church and state were united when the pope crowned Charlemagne (meaning "Charles the Great") as the first Holy Roman Emperor. Charlemagne conquered the various local kings across Europe and divided his empire into bishoprics, each with their own monasteries. He also established harsh laws against the old, "pagan" religions. His empire flourished and faded, and was restored again 200 years later, by Otto the Great.

The doctrine of the Roman church was very specific about the nature of error, or sin, and its punishment—both on earth and in heaven. It was a doctrine designed to control the population by fear. A whole body of "Canon Law" was developed over the centuries to address the various issues that came up. By the time of Henry VIII, in the late 1500s, this law was often used to prevent kings and nations from prosecuting anyone associated with the church for any wrongdoing. Needless to say, this was an erosion of power the royals did not take lightly, and, in fact, was probably a greater contribution to England's breaking off from the Roman church than Henry's famous need to be able to divorce his wives.

Over the years, the power inherent in their positions as final authority, as well as judge and jury, for millions of people did what power always has done: corrupted those who wielded it. So, following the ancient pattern, several papacies and bishoprics became dynasties, and murder and intrigue became as common in the Vatican as in any Egyptian harem. Italian nobles fought for the Papacy through the early Middle Ages, with children of popes actually inheriting the position, until a Benedictine monk from Cluny was elected as Gregory VII. Secure in his support from the monasteries, he challenged both the Italian nobles and the Holy Roman Emperor, establishing the papacy as a position of authority over the nobility and even the royalty of Europe. Now, through his bishops and monasteries, the pope could influence life in all its aspects, throughout Europe.

From then on, until World War II, the issue was no longer how to attain power, but how to keep it and support the system necessary to maintain it.

The Crusades—seeking control of the Holy Land, too

A major feature in every history of the Roman church is the series of Crusades launched between the years 1095 and 1250. The target was the Muslim Saracens who controlled the Holy Land—along with much of Asia, northern Africa, and the coast of Spain. The stated goal was to reclaim the Holy Sepulcher and other sacred sites from "the hands of the Infidel."

These Crusades affected every aspect of European life and ultimately led to major changes in both the economic structure and the intellectual traditions of the Age. Millions of people participated directly in the battles and millions more were involved in producing and transporting the necessary supplies.

They were begun, at least in part, as an attempt to give the people of Christendom something to focus on besides how difficult life was. There were many young, hotheaded warrior-knights, first-born sons of warrior princes, who had no real battles to fight under the Holy Empire and so were marauding the countryside. They needed something less destructive to do. So, although the Saracens in no way limited access by Christians to the Holy Land, their control of the region was a nagging irritant. If the Roman church had control over these important pilgrimage sites, it would mean more souls and economic gain for the institution and would open up new trade opportunities for the merchants who supported the war effort. It was the perfect solution. So, in 1095, on the steps of Vezelay Cathedral (which was then dedicated to Mary Magdalene), all the knights of the Empire were called to the holy task of invading and controlling Jerusalem.

The First Crusade was, surprisingly, successful. In the name of Christendom, European knights walked and rode their horses across Turkey and Syria, and took control of Jerusalem and the sacred sites within it, including the Temple Mount—which by then was also a sacred site for the Muslims. It was a bloodbath: men, women, children were slaughtered without mercy; as one monk wrote, "the streets were ankle-deep in blood."

The Crusaders then set up a new king and nobility and proceeded to occupy Jerusalem and surrounding territories, creating a whole new tradition of ex-patriot warriors. Dozens of knights built castles and either brought their wives or married local girls and set up whole new dynasties. Much like the British in India during the "Raj" period, they lived their values and norms within the context of the local climate and culture.

For some of these first Crusaders, the goal was not so much to give the Church control of the Holy Land as it was to re-establish the lineage of David on the throne of Jerusalem. They were living at the beginning of the second millennium after Christ and they believed that the prophecy of *Revelation* was about to come true—so it was their Christian duty to help it along (not unlike many Christians, today!). The king they appointed to occupy the throne at Jerusalem was neither a great warrior nor statesman, but he was descended from the Merovingian kings of southern France, who, most of them believed, were descendants of David through the daughter of Jesus and Mary Magdalene (details about that in the next chapter). The knights were there to help him fight for God at Armageddon.

A few decades later, however, the Saracens decided to recover their losses, and in spite of repeated Crusades, depleting many royal and personal treasuries and siphoning off Europe's strongest warriors, the Holy Land was turned over to the Saracens in 1244 and never returned to Roman control again.

With the final loss of the Holy Land and the declared end of the Crusades, discouraged warrior-knights returned once more to European soil—some of them after generations of living and fighting among the Arab peoples.

The Church was once more faced with a problem: what do you do with a

> The "Stations of the Cross," a series of images that follow the final hours of Jesus' life and crucifixion, were created to permit those who could not make the pilgrimage to the Holy Land and walk the *Via Dolorosa* in Jerusalem to have the experience at home.

standing army when there's no apparent enemy? Initially, like the military reservists in the U.S., the knights were put to good use restoring order in the countryside and taking on major rescue and construction projects. Over time, however, even these were insufficient to keep the growing supply of warrior-trained sons of nobles occupied.

Eliminating the Cathars--protection of doctrine at any cost

Students of European history may have a vague recollection of one last, tiny Crusade. There may be a faint memory that it was, strangely, waged against some people in France, bordering on Spain—some group of heretics, perhaps influenced by the Moors. In fact, the Albigensian Crusade of 1209-1244 wiped out the richest, most highly cultured region of France, the Languedoc—an event from which that area still has not recovered, economically or spiritually.

During the early Medieval period, the region of France known as Languedoc was a flourishing, cosmopolitan culture, nominally Christian, but not particularly concerned with the expectations of the Roman church. Many of the ruling nobles and over a hundred thousand of the residents of the region followed a version of Christianity that was far more Gnostic than Roman—and in fact, like the Essenes in Palestine before them, abhorred the opulence and power of the Roman hierarchy.

They were a secretive group and, in the Church's determination to exterminate them, their homes and churches were burned. So, as with the Gnostics, most of what we know of the Cathars comes from writings deploring their beliefs, supplemented by letters, journals and diaries of their neighbors from the period. According to one researcher:

> Cathars led very simple lives. They preferred to meet in the open air or in ordinary houses rather than in churches, and although they had an administrative hierarchy that included bishops, all baptized members were spiritually equal and regarded as priests. [There was] equality of the sexes... They were fish-eating vegetarians and pacifists, and they believed in a form of reincarnation. They were also itinerant preachers, traveling in pairs, living in the utmost poverty and simplicity, stopping to help and to heal wherever they could. ...
> They were vociferously antagonistic towards the symbol of the cross, seeing it as a gruesome and sick reminder

of the instrument that tortured Jesus to death. They were also haters of the whole cult of the dead and ... relic[s]...
The Cathars were pacifists, who so despised 'the filthy envelope of the flesh' that they were eager to shed it, even if the means of doing so meant martyrdom...[46]

They were prepared to die rather than give up their way of believing and practicing Christianity. The Roman church sent in envoys and missionaries to try to turn them around, including the famous Bernard of Clairvaux (whose report to the Pope attempted to divert destruction, pointing out the Cathars' exemplary way of life). Finally, the church declared the Cathars incorrigible and sent an army of mercenary knights in to destroy the "heretics."

> One legend has it that the Cathars were the keepers of the vessel known as "the Holy Grail" and that a few people got away, carrying it to safety, before the last strong-hold was stormed and all the people in it were burnt.

It was one of the most horrific acts of the age: over 100,000 people, known to their neighbors as *Les bonhommes* ("goodmen"), were systematically chased down, rounded up, and, when they did not recant their heresies, burned where they stood—whole villages at once.

It began, notably, on the feast day of the Magdalene, July 22, 1209. According to a monk writing four years later, the whole town of Beziers gathered in the local church, with their Cathar neighbors, hoping to function as a human shield. It didn't work. The knights of the Roman church had been so riled up about the "abomination" of this heresy that they simply burned them all. For the Cathars, it was the ultimate transfiguration, death. Their preparation for death was such that they were able to face their inevitable defeat at the

---

[46] Lynn Picknett and Clive Prince, *The Templar Revelation.* New York: Simon & Schuster, 1997. pp. 89-91.

hands of the Roman church with relative ease, compared to their less-prepared neighbors.

By 1244, it was all over, and the Languedoc province in which the Cathars had thrived, only recently a richly endowed garden region with a highly cultured society in which women were honored equally with men, the birthplace of the troubadour movement with its remarkable music and poetry praising courtly love, was a barren wasteland. Nor has it yet recovered.

It was, the Roman church leaders hoped, the last step in wiping out the belief that Jesus, and all of life, was empowered through his union with the divine feminine.

Redefining Religious Experience

Up until about 1200CE, it was pretty universally accepted that the religious experience was a deeply emotional one, in which some connection with the divine was experienced and expressed. For the 200 years that the school at Chartres had been training religious philosophers, noble households and monasteries all over Europe had access to training in a mode of thought that built on rational understanding to achieve mystical insight. Prior to that, memories and tales of the great mystery schools of Greece, Syria, and Rome kept the awareness alive.

The years between 1200 and 1225, however, saw a remarkable shift in accepted thought. During those years, the University of Paris grew tremendously, under the leadership of Thomas Aquinas, who held Aristotle's reasoning in great esteem and found Plato's science, on which the Chartres curriculum was based, to be lacking. In those same years, the Dominican order was replacing the Cistercian order as the route to power within the Roman church—the black friars, with their emphasis on doctrine and hierarchy, replaced the white brothers with their emphasis on effectiveness and democracy. Finally, a strange new icon began to appear in churches: graphically detailed images of Jesus on the cross—what we call "crucifixes" today.

These changes led to a new way of thinking about being a Christian. Now it was about learning specific doctrine and being able to repeat it on demand. It was about contemplating the agony of the man rather than the victory of the Spirit. It was about control of one's own—and one's brother's—mind. And the idea of pain and agony became deeply entwined with the idea of holiness.

The Inquisition, Witch Hunts, and the resulting Plagues

The leadership of the Roman church, already controlling a significant proportion of the land across Europe and often in control of the kings, as well, wanted more—only total submission by the population would do. They created the Inquisition, under the administration of the Dominicans, to identify and eliminate any group or individual whose belief and actions might undermine the "True Faith," as mandated by the Nicene Creed. (Tangentially, the property of anyone who was declared a heretic by the Inquisition became the property of the Roman church.) The Inquisitor's concern was not for the life of the body but the salvation of the soul. He was told that, by whatever means he could convince someone to confess, he brought "more souls to Christ." [47]

The Dominicans and the Inquisition were not only responsible for the destruction of Cathars of Langedoc in the Albigensian Crusade, they also supervised the forced conversion of thousands of Jews in Spain to a professed faith in Christian doctrine. It was by means of the Inquisition that the Templars were tortured, tried, and burned in 1307. Finally, it was through the Inquisition that, some estimates say, up

---

[47] Many books have been written about the horrors of this period, but one remarkably insightful piece of fiction is Piers Anthony's *For Love of Evil*.

Roman Church as Empire

> Any activity that was abnormal was fair game. Even for a woman to be able to read was potential cause for trial, as is effectively illustrated in the film, *Dangerous Beauty*.

to 9 million women were tortured, tried, and burned or hanged as witches in Europe between 1200 and 1650CE.

Although many women who used the ancient methods to draw on the power of the divine feminine in their work as healers, teachers, and midwives were killed during the Crusade years, not until the 1300s, after the elimination of the Templars, was the existence of a definite sect of witches finally accepted by the Roman church as a dangerous movement. According to the last and clearest explication of the logic, *Malleus Malificorum*, (usually translated as "The Hammer of Witchcraft" but more accurately, "Hammer of Evildoings") written in the late 1480s, "A witch is one who has made a pact with the devil to effect his purposes on earth. The worshipper of the devil is a heretic..."

And so the Roman church began to systematically remove from every parish and bishopric any woman or man who was perceived by anyone in the region as having made "a pact with the devil." Everyone got into the act. If crops were bad or a cow's milk went sour, a local widow or enviably beautiful woman would be blamed. If one farmer did better than another, their family would be accused of witchcraft. If a midwife was extraordinarily successful—or failed to bring forth a healthy child—she would be brought to trial. Through horrifyingly devious and painful means, the accused would generally be made to agree to whatever the Inquisitor wished them to say, and would then be burned or hanged or "drawn and quartered" to expiate their guilt—and so "save their souls."

One totally unexpected consequence of the battle against witchcraft is that virtually all of the healers and teachers were killed—leaving whole generations without healthcare or instruction in hygiene. The men of the church didn't realize

the important role that the women they feared and killed had played in their communities. As a result, large portions of the population were defenseless against the ravaging effects of disease and vermin. The impact was dramatic:
> By the end of 1348 the Black Death was decimating the Mediterranean islands, Italy, Spain, France, the south of England; by the end of 1349 Germany, central Europe, Flanders, and the north of England; and by the end of 1350 the Baltic ... [48]

In many places, as many as half the population succumbed to the plague, leaving empty houses and farms—in some places, whole villages—and creating a huge labor shortage. In short, disease and death completely transformed the social and economic structure of Europe.

The Transformation

The Renaissance emerged out of this dramatic and tragic decimation of the population and subsequent restructuring of the economy. Almost as if to turn their backs on the horrific memories of the plague, and partly because the wisdom held by the murdered women and men was gone, young Europeans plunged into the study of the Greek and Roman scholars. The new (ancient Chinese) art of block printing made it possible for these classic books to become part of private libraries, stimulating the intellectual life of scholars in such ports as Amsterdam, Venice, and Naples, and soon spreading inland.

The new generation believed that they were the first to discover the works of Plato, Aristotle, Cicero, and the many other classical scholars whose work has formed the basis for much of European thought. Totally ignoring the presence of the great cathedrals and castles, they believed—and taught their children and grandchildren to believe—that Europe

---

[48] Gimpel, Jean. *Medieval Machine: The Industrial Revolution of the Middle Ages.* New York: Barnes & Noble, 2003.p. 209.

Roman Church as Empire

prior to their generation was a dark, static, backward world, in which little had been achieved beyond the preservation of the works of the ancient culture in dark corners. The preceding centuries were called the "Dark Ages," out of which seeds of the past flowered in the Renaissance (meaning "rebirth") of intellectual culture. (This metaphor referred to the creative darkness of womb and soil long associated with the Goddess, but the connection had been lost to the intellectual community through the deaths of their teachers and elders).

Partly because the nobility had been decimated, new civic leaders arose from the merchant class. London had its Mayor; Venice its *Duce;* Florence had the Medici family. Guilds, formed in the Medieval period to support the highly mobile artisans, became important institutions in the renewed urban centers. Guildhalls became political, as well as social structures. Coffee from the Americas, with its stimulating effects on the intellect, was rapidly replacing beer as the beverage of choice among tradesmen, and as it did so, hours once spent in "boozy boisterousness" were now occupied with spirited debates and creative problem-solving, often focused on civic affairs.

Then, in 1498, Gutenberg replaced hand block-printing with the mechanical printing press, and books were no longer a luxury. Suddenly, anybody who could put together a few extra coins could have a book. This, combined with the effects of drinking coffee instead of beer, and the importance of accounting to guild members, meant that reading was now a fashionable, rather than frightening (as it had been during the years of the Inquisition), skill.

With an increasingly literate population, the church could no longer rule by sim-

> During the Middle Ages and early Renaissance, the church calendar included as many as 160 holy days each year (including Sundays)—on which shops were closed and people stopped working to go to church.

ple doctrines and decrees proclaimed in pulpits on Sundays

and holy days. The Roman church had to find new methods to maintain its hold over the people and its lands. A whole new system of management was needed—and it emerged in the form of an old, but little-used idea: "indulgences."

In Florence, a fiery monk named Savanarola demonstrated the potential for controlling the populace with fear of damnation. Through his sermons and street-preaching, a whole population were convinced of their sinfulness and the dangers of going to an everlasting torture called "Hell." Soon priests and other leaders in the church were literally selling masses to people who hoped that having someone dedicate this sacrificial ritual to them would save their souls from such an awful fate.

Another, totally non-biblical, concept that was introduced during the years of the active Inquisition was that of Purgatory—which was still taught in church schools during the 20th century. This was a state of being that one who had only small sins would endure for some tens or hundreds of years to undo the effects of their sin and so become eligible to reside with the saints in Heaven. "Indulgences" were sold to people to shorten their time in Purgatory. Priests would set the number needed and those who could afford them would find the funds. Those who couldn't were living under the constant perception that their deaths would be even more painful than their lives—unless they could, somehow, atone for their sins. And it was the priests, of course, who determined whether they had.

It was the selling of Indulgences that drove a certain German priest to transform the Christian religion. He was so infuriated as he observed clergymen becoming wealthy off these sales that he went to Rome to complain to the Pope. While there, he was given some time to "cool off" and, being a Doctor of Divinity, was given full access to the Vatican library. In that library, the story goes, the Reverend Dr. Martin Luther found a shelf of books marked "potentially heretical texts." One of them was a book he had never seen before:

Roman Church as Empire

Ta Biblia, meaning "The Books," which we know as the Bible. He pulled it down and was amazed. So much that he had been taught was wrong! So much that he found in Paul's letters made perfect sense! He went home and posted his famous "theses," or points of debate, on the doors of his church, thus launching the Protestant Reformation.

The Reformation began in Germany, but quickly found a safe haven in Switzerland, which had avoided being controlled by the Roman church. There, in relative freedom, John Calvin moved the newly reformed Christianity forward, creating what are now the Presbyterian and Lutheran churches. Protestant Christianity, emphasizing reading and understanding the Bible, rather than the simple acceptance of an authoritarian priest as the foundation for faith, became the basis for the industrial and democratic revolutions over the next 300 years.

While the Roman church continued to grow and maintain considerable power and wealth in the world, the Reformation was the death-knell of its European empire. Like the Roman empire, it fell apart under its own weight, unable to defend itself against the independent spirit of its largely Celtic subjects. Today, it struggles to maintain its role in the world, with a seriously diminished priesthood, law suits for its mishandling of pedophiles, and ongoing issues with the role of women in the church.

> Centuries of using Canon Law to address such issues left the church unprepared when nations passed laws against such behaviors that required civil or even criminal action.

Protestants have their own issues—among them highly visible scandals, bickering among denominations, etc.—but they feel justified in looking askance at the Church of Rome's sinfulness.

Still, virtually all Christian leaders see themselves as "Sons of Light" bringing "Light to the world" by imposing their hierarchical, autocratic structures on others—as have all Aryan invaders for 6,000 years.

How do you solve a problem like Maria?
How do you hold a moonbeam in your hand?[49]

WOMEN: A CONUNDRUM IN THE CHRISTIAN CHURCH

As we've seen, the recorded history of the Roman church is deeply intertwined with the history of the kings, kingdoms, and empires in and around Europe. Church leaders and secular leaders worked closely and supported—or undermined—each other in the acquisition and control of lands and wealth. Most of us who have studied this history have learned the names of kings and popes and empires and nations, when and where significant battles were fought, and what machinery made them possible. A few students of history may discover some of the underlying liaisons—through marriage, friendship, and family ties—that drove many of those surface actions. Only a very few find out the remarkable string of ideas, fears, dreams, and strategies that led to the actions recorded in the history books. But virtually no one has access to records of the feelings of the women associated with those strategies, liaisons, and actions.

Keeping that in mind, it's worth taking a new look at the history of the Christian church from the perspective of the feminine. As one scholar has described it:

> Women's leadership was a widespread phenomenon in the early Christian churches. Tensions were nevertheless generated by the disparity between the socially established fact of women's leadership and the strict Greco-Roman demarcation of gender roles. The mixed messages about Mary Magdalene's significance reflects the am-

---

[49] From *The Sound of Music* by Richard Rogers & Oscar Hammerstein, 1960.

bivalence about women's leadership as the Gospels were taking their final canonical form. ... If these accounts of women's important participation hadn't been grounded in intractable fact, they would not have survived in such a male-dominated culture. But ... these traditions were ignored and submerged as much as possible in order to conform Christian teaching and practice to social convention.[50]

Women as Leaders

Throughout the first century after Christ, women founded and maintained churches in their homes. Luke's Book of Acts and Paul's letters, both written between 60 and 90 CE, make it clear that women were the central figure and support for many of the early churches. In Paul's letters alone, several dozen women are appreciated or greeted as having played a major role in the establishment of local churches. In Jerusalem we find Mary, mother of John Mark. In Corinth, Paul met and learned to rely on Priscilla and her husband Aquila. In Tyatira, he relied on Lydia. In Rome, a dozen women are mentioned as having "labored much," including Mary, Tryphena, Tryphosa and Persis. And so on, across the Mediterranean region.

Also in Paul's early letters, it's clear that women, including Phoebe and Junia, are bishops and deacons in the early churches. "fellow-laborers," "sisters in the Lord." "... there is neither male nor female: for ye are all one in Christ Jesus."

At the same time, Paul and his associates encouraged a special role for widows in the church. They were to be cared for by the community, and, insofar as they remained sexually inactive, were to be honored for their dedication to the virtue of chastity. Many of the deaconesses and other leaders of the early communities were widows. This practice may be related to the Aryan tradition, expressed in Mosaic law, that a

---

[50] Torjesen, K. J., *When Women Were Priests; women's leadership in the Early Church and the Scandal of their Subordination in the Rise of Christianity.* HarperSan Francisco, 1995. pp. 35-37.

man would take his brother's widow as his wife, and, if she had not yet conceived a child, inseminate her in his brother's name so his brother would have an heir. Given Greco-Roman distaste for polygamy, which became part of the Pauline Christianity, this pattern could not be continued. In the Greco-Roman traditions, widows who could not support themselves would join the temple. Yet, since early Christians met in homes and avoided the temples, that was not an option. So, a new role and consideration for widows had to be developed.

1st century women blessing the bread and wine;
on the wall of the catacombs of Rome.

Disempowerment

Then, in the later "Pastoral Epistles," addressed to Titus and Timothy, women are no longer allowed to have authority over men. They are to "learn in silence with all subjection," and younger widows are to remarry, allowing their husbands to be their head, as "Christ is the head of the church," a pattern that reverts to the old, male-dominated traditions. Some scholars have said that these letters were written to new, younger congregations, without the blessing of wise, older women to provide leadership. A number of scholars now suggest that they may not have been written by the same Paul that Luke describes in his Book of Acts.

Moving forward in time, we see a continuation of this latter trend. Iranaeus, bishop of Lyon in 177CE, was shocked that women in the Gnostic sects were allowed to prophesy and to celebrate communion, saying the prayer to consecrate the host. A generation later, Tertullian, presbyter of Carthage (northern Africa) about 200 CE, wrote:

"It is not permitted for a woman to speak in the church, nor is it permitted for her to teach, nor to baptize, nor to offer [the eucharist], nor to claim for herself a share in any *masculine* function—not to mention any priestly office."

He criticized women in the Gnostic sects who were able to teach, engage in discussion, exorcise cure, and possibly baptize. At the same time, however, he makes it clear that widows have a significant role to play in the church—primarily to pray and "lay on hands."

Marriage, however, remained a conundrum in the Roman church (though not in the Byzantine, or "Eastern" church, where priests were expected to marry). In 305 CE the Council of bishops at Alvira decreed that those involved in ministry of the altar must maintain abstinence from their wives or lose their office, but full celibacy was not required. Then came the meeting at the Council of Nicea in 325 CE, where the "church fathers" selected which of the thousands of texts should be included in sacred scripture and drafted what became known as the Apostles or Nicean Creed. No women attended this meeting and the Gnostic gospels were thrown out. It was about this time that the *Nag Hammadi* library, with its copies of the *Gospel of Thomas*, the *Pistis Sophia*, and the *Gospel of Philip* was buried in the dry sands of Egypt.

Finally, the Council of Laodicea, 352 CE, forbade women from serving as priests or presiding over churches (which suggests they had been doing so up till then, at least in some areas).

The Fifth Council of Carthage, in 401, decreed that married clergy should be separated from their wives. At the same time, co-ed or double monasteries—side by side for men and women—were common. Hilda was abbess at Whiby, 614-680 and Hildegaarde led at Bingen 1100-1179. Pope Gratian issued a decree against female ordination about 1100, making it clear that it was still happening then. This was a few years after "Pope Joan," a woman who had disguised herself as a man named "Johan" to join a monastery and had been steadily elevated through the ranks, had died and finally been discovered. Their powers were slowly eroded, however, so that by 1200, women could only preach to other women.

Then Thomas Aquinas, about 1250, justified women's ineligibility for ordination based on Aristotle's *Politics*, which, following the ancient Greek (Aryan) tradition, put women in the same category as children and mental deficients, thus laying the groundwork for the work of the Inquisition. Women were now seen as evil temptresses who might draw a good Christian man away from his ascetic discipline on the "narrow path" of faith. As described in the preceding chapter, the Renaissance flowered in the ashes of the burning of so-called "witches."

A New Devotion, Mixed with Fear-based Hatred

It was during this same period that the "Cult of Mary" began. Great basilicas and cathedrals, hymns, poetry, and prayers were created in honor of the ever-Virgin Mother of God. Monastic orders were founded to find salvation through serving her. Ancient images of the Great Mother were elevated and placed in the center of new chapels, churches, and cathedrals, and called The Virgin, Madonna, and Our Lady. The ideal of "courtly love," of adoration from afar, began during this period, as well, with the first *troubadors* emerging out of the Languedoc region of southern France, where the Cathars' ideas of spiritual, rather than physical union, were increasingly popular—even as the Cathars, themselves, were being wiped out.

Nonetheless, Pope Boniface's *bull periculoso* of 1293 required women within the church to lead cloistered lives, "altogether withdrawn from public and mundane sights." At this point, screens were installed in convent chapels, separating nuns from others attending services.

The Age of the Crusades was over, but the Age of Exploration was about to begin. For the next 400 years, knights and monks boarded ships to "round the Cape" of South Africa to find India—and stopped on the way to buy a few of the local tribes' dark-skinned slaves to work the ships and provide sexual services for the sailors. Others, most famously Columbus, headed westward across the Atlantic and landed in the Americas, discovering a whole "New World" to explore—and conquer—physically by the knights and spiritually by the determined monks and priests (usually of Franciscan and Dominican orders), who traveled with them. And the adoration of the Mother of God was at the core of their mission.

Reformation & Redefinition

The whole picture shifted in 1521, when Martin Luther posted his *Theses* and launched the Reformation—soon thereafter marrying a nun. The possibility of marriage for clergy and the lack of biblical support for the elevation of Mary, Jesus' mother, to "Queen of Heaven" and "Star of the Sea" were major factors in the Protestant split off from the Roman church.

Through the Reformation and subsequent "Enlightenment" period of European history, the role of women became increasingly fuzzy. Paul's letters remained the primary source of doctrine, but Jesus' inclusivity was widely perceived as a model of appropriate behavior. Religious freedom in the Americas encouraged alternative approaches to Christian spiritual practices.

Then, in the late 19th century, several significant religious movements, launched by women, expanded across the U.S., among them the Shakers, Foursquare, Seventh Day Adventist, Christian Science, and the several denominations known as "New Thought." Primarily North American in perspective and membership, these movements are congregational rather than priestly in focus, and honor the Christ as an attainable state of being for both men and women, with Jesus as the teacher and guide. Thousands of Americans formed churches based on these ideas, many of which were led by women. Some sent missionaries to other countries, introducing these new ways around the world. They have made and impact on thousands of lives but remain, however, a very small minority of churches in the world.

The 1970s feminist movement, combined with a great reduction in applications to become priests, opened a hornet's nest regarding ordination of women to the priesthood in the Roman church. Pope John XXIII's Vatican Council II reframed many practices in the church, including letting nuns work in the public arena and not wear a habit, as well as allowing women in church to wear pants and uncovered hair, and to act as chaplains and in other leadership roles. The Council still maintained, however, that only men can perform sacraments. That position has been re-affirmed by each of his successors.

Through the 1970s and '80s, however, most Protestant denominations began ordaining women. In 1992, the Anglican high church voted to ordain women. Soon after, the Roman church agreed to accept married Anglican priests who can't stand the idea of women in the priesthood. Nonetheless, a group of Episcopalians recently broke off to form a new branch of the Anglican church rather than work under a woman as bishop.

Clearly, the ancient Aryan tradition that women are spiritually inferior remains a central theme in the Christian church. The male-dominated theology of modern Christianity, though it has little relationship to the actual life and teachings of Jesus, justifies a male-dominated institution, with a perception of the divine that includes only masculine qualities.

*You have to be taught to before it's too late,
before you are six or seven or eight...*[51]

OUTSIDE THE CHURCH: POWER-FULL TEACHINGS

Because of the papacy's determination to wipe out anything that smacked of "heresy," the doctrines of the Roman Christian church were the "only game in town" by 1500CE and so became the basis for the Protestant churches that followed.

For the first few hundred years of Christian thought, however, they weren't the only teachings out there—and traces of some of these alternatives may even be found, today. In the swamps of Iraq, a group of "Christians" study a "Bible" that focuses more on John the Baptist than Jesus, as they have since the early Roman empire. In Ethiopia, Christian priests carry replicas of the Hebrew Ark of the Covenant through the streets of the cities every year, in celebration of the miraculous powers of this sacred relic, believed to be hidden in the "holy of holies" of that country's greatest church. In the Philippines, Mexico, and several other Spanish-speaking countries, *Penitentes* parade through the streets at Passiontide (the weeks before Easter), beating themselves with whips and chains, just as their Muslim counterparts do in Iraq and Iran during *Ramadan*.

Of course, there is also the whole, huge "Eastern" church: Russian Orthodox, Greek Orthodox, and others. They, too, have had an influence on Western culture, but that influence has been felt in much the same way as have

---

[51] "You Have to be Taught" from *South Pacific* by Richard Rogers & Oscar Hammerstein.

the Protestants, Jews, and Muslims: in contrast to the norm, rather than defining the norm. So, while whole books could be written about the role of the divine feminine in these traditions, this one will focus on the Roman church in Europe and the "heresies" it fought.

Today, scholars are beginning to get a sense of what "that other half" was thinking in those early years. Thanks to the discovery of the *Nag Hammadi* texts and the Dead Sea scrolls, among other finds, archeologists and historians have been able to piece together the philosophical principles and spiritual practices that shaped the lives of the earliest Christians.

Jerusalem Christians: Jews for Jesus

The New Testament makes it clear that Saul/Paul never met Jesus (unless he happened to be present at Jesus' trial while he was training to be a Pharisee, for which we have no evidence). More, he was teaching something that Jesus' disciples and their followers in Jerusalem did not approve. They were, first of all, Jews; they might even be called "Messianic Jews." They were circumcised and required circumcision for men who wished to join them. They followed the Talmudic laws and went to Temple. They also taught, preached, healed, and prophesied "in the name of Jesus Christ." Recent scholarship tells us that, under the leadership of James and Peter

> They were called the Nazarenes, and in all their beliefs they were indistinguishable from the Pharisees, except that they believed in the resurrection of Jesus, and that Jesus was still the promised Messiah. They did not believe that Jesus was a divine person but that, by a miracle from God, he had been brought back to life after his death on the cross, and would soon come back to complete his mission of overthrowing the Romans and setting up his Messianic kingdom. ... The Nazarenes did not re-

gard themselves as setting up a new religion; their religion was Judaism.⁵²

These men were focused on Temple and *Torah* and on the return of the Golden Age of same. They knew Jesus as a well-trained rabbi, conversant with the Pharisees, conforming to Jewish law and tradition, and ready to return as the Savior of the Israelites. There was no divine atonement for sins in their experience or understanding so, when Saul/Paul began to teach otherwise, they disowned him. And, for all practical purposes, they were wiped out when the Romans smashed the Jewish revolt in 70CE. After that, only tiny pockets remained in distant villages, and these people and their descendants carefully maintained and copied whatever writings they could salvage from that time.

The Roman church, as described above, chose the Greek writings of Paul and his associates as the basis for their Christianity, instead. The Byzantine church did so, as well, but included some of the insights from other Eastern groups, among them the Egyptian Christians.

> It is these remnants and scrolls that George Lamsa depended on when, in the mid-twentieth century, he translated the gospels from the original Aramaic.

Coptic Christians in Egypt: seekers of divine union

We tend to think of Egypt and Palestine as some distance apart, but in fact, a few days of walking through the Gaza strip and a brief boat ride or wade through the "Sea of Reeds" was all it took to move from one continent to the other. As a result, much that happened in and around Jerusa-

---

⁵² Hyam Maccoby, *The Mythmaker: Paul and the Invention of Christianity*. HarperSan Francisco, 1986. p.17.

lem was rapidly included in the life of the large Jewish community in Alexandria, Egypt.

So it's not too surprising that followers of Jesus who feared Herod or the Temple priesthood would find their way to Egypt very soon after the crucifixion. In fact, the story of the Pentecost in Luke's Book of Acts tells us that visitors from that area were in Jerusalem and, witnessing the remarkable impact that "receiving the Holy Spirit" had on the Nazarenes, sought to become disciples of the risen Jesus, as well.

Egypt at that time had been controlled by Greeks (the descendants of one of Alexander's generals, Ptolemy) for over 300 years, with Cleopatra being the last of the Greek rulers, followed by a series of Roman governors. As a result, the written language of Egypt was a blend of Greek and Egyptian that's called, today, "Coptic."

The Coptic Christians were committed to a spiritual union with Jesus. Their churches have a unique style and symbolism, designed to inspire and support that union. They invented the monastery and desert hermitages, and it was not far from one of these that the leather-covered codices were found (at *Nag Hammadi*).

Although no one knows exactly when any of the *Nag Hammadi* texts were written, most scholars date them between 120 and 180CE. Based on the dates on the scrap paper used to stiffen the covers, these documents appear to have been copied and bound about 300CE. They appear to have been hidden about 340CE, shortly after Constantine's Nicene Council declared Gnostic and Coptic ideas to be heretical.

Typically written as dialogues with Jesus, rather than as stories about Jesus' life, these writings appear to be descriptions of and

> The texts were found in shallow caves that were once graves located near an ancient monastery. The Greek name for the nearest town was *Chenoboskion*, and the Egyptian name is *Es-Sayyad*, causing some confusion in early references to these texts.

quotations from Jesus' teachings to his followers during the years following the crucifixion and resurrection. They provide an image of a patient teacher, helping his disciples to understand that it's not what they do that is of greatest importance, but where they focus their attention and feelings.

From these writings, we get a rich picture of Jesus' continuing ministry, as well as of the women in his life and their roles. We learn in the "Gospel of Thomas," for example, of Jesus' continuing appearances after his crucifixion, in which he offers a distinctly mystical understanding of our relationship with God and the universe—and of the way we are to live our lives. This is a very mystical Christianity, in which human action is always considered in light of one's ongoing relationship with the divine.

The Egyptian Gnostics: uniting *animus* and *anima*

While all of these books are written in Coptic, not all of the codices are Coptic Christian in doctrine. Some are clearly from another alternative group, called the Gnostics (*gnosis* being the Greek word for "inner knowing" and gnosticism being a school of Greek philosophy). This group was founded in Syria, by Nicolas, one of the original deacons appointed by the Apostles, and two Samaritans, the best known of whom is described in the book of *Acts* as Simon of Gitta, and by Josephus and other historians of the period as "Simon Magus." He was known to do miracles and accused of practicing magic. His beloved Helen was a former "harlot" (probably the usual mistranslation of the Hebrew word for "temple devotee" when applied to a woman) and he encouraged the practice of "perfect love"—a term which was often misrepresented by his critics, and even some of his followers.

Under the persecutions of Roman emperor Hadrian around 120CE, the Gnostic movement shifted to Alexandria, Egypt where it was picked up by Basilides and his student

Valentinus, who was actually a candidate for the bishop of Rome in later years. Valentinus' teachings spread from Rome to Cyprus and into Gaul, as far as modern-day Lyons. So the Christian Gnostics, though defined today only in the Egyptian texts, were thought of then as having "infested the whole of the Mediterranean world."[53]

Prior to finding these texts, the only documents available about the Gnostics were written by Roman church leaders who sought to negate their value in the new Christian Roman empire. Reading these texts, one can see why. These people believed in a very different kind of Christianity. They described a hierarchy of divinity: a primordial Principle, the void, impersonal and ineffable Spirit, out of whom emerged two creative forces, polar opposites, called the divine mother-source and the creative masculine force. In general, they believed matter to be an abomination, created out of a misuse of spiritual power, and so they sought to experience purely spiritual lives. Even more disturbingly, union between masculine and feminine was central to their practice. Basilides acknowledged 5 aspects of reality:

Nous—Mind, from which proceeded the Word; [Logos, the Greek basis for all creation]
Reflection; and from Reflection,
Wisdom and Force; and from Wisdom and Force,
The Virtues, powers, and angels by which, from emanation to emanation, the heavens above were created ...

Basilides was followed by Carpocrates, who is generally acknowledged to be the founder of the Egyptian Gnostic tradition. He was followed by Valentinus, who carried the idea of emanation throughout the Roman world—stating that each step in the hierarchy of emanations was a pair, which in union produced another pair, from the original Mother-Father through Intelligence and Truth (the only

---

[53] Doresse, Jean, *The Secret Books of the Egyptian Gnostics.* New York: MJF Books, 1958. p. 13.

Son), producing Word and Life, and so on, to the "pleroma" or fullness, which is Wisdom, or *Sophia*.

We learn in the *Pistis Sophia* that Jesus taught the importance of union with the divine feminine in order to achieve spiritual power and authority. He speaks eloquently of the inner light and the path toward it in a series of dialogues that echo the style of Socrates. In the *Gospel of Thomas*, which is primarily a list of Jesus' sayings, we read:

> The disciples say to Jesus: "Tell us what our end will be."
> Jesus says: "Have you then deciphered the beginning that you ask about the end? For where the beginning is, there shall be the end. Blessed is the man who reaches the beginning; he will know the end and will not taste death!" [verse 19]

The dialogues often include women as well as men, and, consistently, Mary called the Magdalene shines as the star pupil. We learn in the *Acts of Philip* that the Magdalene was "Jesus' closest companion; he often kissed her…" And we learn in the *Gospel of Mary* that Jesus taught the Magdalene some things he hadn't taught his male followers and that, when they asked her about it and she began to share, Peter, in particular was most upset that "a woman" would be taught things the rest weren't. Mary not only responds intelligently to Jesus' questions, she also

> *The Da Vinci Code* and other interpreters of this passage in *Philip* have ignored the fact that there's a hole in the papyrus (called a *lacuna* by archeologists), so we don't really know where Jesus kissed the Magdalene. They've simply inserted a word that would fit into the space: "mouth." Interestingly, by doing so, they've actually weakened their argument that this is an indication that the two were lovers. As George Lamsa, the Aramaic scholar who has retranslated much of the Bible from copies of ancient Aramaic scrolls, tells us that to kiss on the mouth means to share secrets.

helps the others to understand. In the *Pistis Sophia*, Jesus tells her she is:

> ...she whose heart straineth toward the Kingdom of the heavens more than all thy brothers... happy beyond every woman who is upon the earth, because thou art she who will become the *Pleroma* of the *Pleromas* [fullness, completion, as in a bridal chamber] inheritor of the Light.

Besides suggesting that Jesus' ministry continued well after the resurrection, and establishing a very different perspective on Jesus' relationship with the Magdalene, these codices define a form of Christianity in which God could only be experienced from inside the heart. These teachings are a significant shift from the norm in a world where one's god was believed to reside in a building where an altar was. They state that Jesus was teaching that who his followers perceived themselves to be is not who they were, but that, rather than material beings living life trying to be reconciled with a God who lived in a temple, they were, in fact, spiritual beings with full capacity for total union with God—in this lifetime! The goal of "communion," these documents say, is union of the divine masculine and feminine within oneself.

The Greek word *gnosis* refers to inner knowledge, as opposed to information derived from some outside authority. In the Gnostic tradition, one learned to meditate and contemplate the nature of the divine in order to be able to experience the presence of, and ultimately total union with, God. Jesus, in this tradition, was "the way-shower" and master teacher—one who had achieved the desired union—who had embodied the totality of the divinity inherent in all humanity—and was able to help others do the same. His miracles and wisdom were a product of the state of union that he achieved.

Several conditions were necessary to achieve the desired union.
1. The desire must be for its own sake, rather than for power in the world.

2. The seeker must be willing to leave behind all other concerns, issues, responsibilities, desires, and identities for this "pearl of great price."
3. The seeker must be willing to enter into the *heiros gamos*, at least figuratively, for the union of the masculine and feminine was a critical stage in one's progress toward union with the All-power, All-love, All-wisdom.

In part this was because Wisdom is feminine in the Jewish tradition. As *Sophia, Shekinah*, or *Chokma*, she was "with God before the creation" and so must be with the seeker before the creative power can be fully experienced. To love God 'with all one's heart, mind, soul, and strength' was therefore to love the divine masculine *and* feminine, honoring "God the Father and God the Mother," and encouraging the full expression of both. On top of that were the traditions of all the ancient wisdom schools—from Sumer to Greece—that said true power could only be found in the sacred marriage.

> *Shekinah,* the focus of divine union among those who study and practice the *Qabalah*, was not described in writing until about 1000 CE, when the Jews in Spain came into contact with the Islamic Moors who occupied that nation at that time.

The Egyptian Gnostic tradition tended to focus on the spiritual life and to minimize—even deprecate—the material. Integrating the ancient wisdom schools with Egyptian teachings about the soul and Jewish teachings about divine Wisdom, these seekers turned inward, away from the world around them. Things were distractions. The body was less perfect than the soul; therefore, one might allow the body to simply waste away in pursuit of the transcendent union. Jesus had appeared in body and in spirit; therefore, one could hope to do the same.

Clearly, there's a big difference between what the Gnostic Christians believed about Jesus' ministry and what the established church taught. This form of Christian belief didn't make much sense to the urbanized, materialist Roman and Byzantine hierarchy as they were meeting in the Emperor's splendid halls as Nicea. The bishops there felt a need for a much more earthy Christ, a teacher pointing to a spiritual life, but fully focused on our physical experience. More, their Hellenistic training made it virtually impossible for them to see the use of or need for a woman's presence in any man's life.

They decided that Paul and Jesus were saying that anyone who hoped to become spiritually wise must shun sexuality altogether—and women in particular. This meant that the Gnostic tradition was seen as something to be downgraded and eliminated wherever encountered—beginning in Egypt and moving across the Mediterranean in the early centuries, then into Spain and France, culminating in the Albigensian crusade of the 1200s.

The Johannite Movement: Magic and Mystery

One New Testament character whose role has been downplayed over the centuries but who keeps emerging around the edges of the Roman church, is the man who baptized Jesus and appears to have been one of his teachers. For those of us raised in the Protestant tradition, this man, John the Baptist, is simply the "forerunner" who woke people up to Jesus' coming. In the Roman church he is venerated not only as the forerunner, but also as a saint—and from the Protestant perspective, that doesn't make much sense, since John clearly died before Jesus and therefore could not have been a Christian.

Then, when we get into the historical literature, we learn, for instance, that there were as many men calling for people to repent and prepare for the end times then as there are today. There were also many men calling themselves the Messiah—and still more being called that by others. So what made this particular John so special? And why are so many churches built in his name?

Again, the first clue is in the name: *Yehohanan*, which was translated into *Johannan* in Greek, and means "God has shown favor" or "favored by God." This suggests that John may have been more important than Christian writings would have us believe. Another clue may be found in how he is represented in the arts. And that, in turn, may be the result of an underground movement that was quietly flourishing while the Roman church looked elsewhere.

Perhaps the most famous European artist is Leonardo da Vinci. And one of the more bizarre characteristics of the life and work of this remarkable man is his attachment to John the Baptist. Many of his paintings placed John in direct opposition, and sometimes in a superior position, to Jesus.

DaVinci's images of John the Baptist: in "Virgin of the Rocks" and as a young man (both with the long cross, possibly added later), c. 1450-80CE.

As pointed out in Dan Brown's *The DaVinci Code*, his famous fresco called The Last Supper (and illustrated on p. 201 in this book), uses a woman as the model for the person whom he calls "John" in his notes (presumably the young disciple John), and dresses "him" in the colors associated with Mary Magdalene. Yet, in his painting of the Holy Family on the way to Egypt (above), he has both John and Jesus as infants sitting with the same model as the Mother Mary (with her head in very nearly the same position), and John is placed above Jesus. A young, slightly effeminate, John the Baptist, smiling and pointing upward was Leonardo's last painting, which he refused to sell and had in sight at his deathbed.

Not only art historians (and writers of detective fiction!) have noted this curious behavior. A number of other scholars have attempted to explain how a man who made his living producing art for the Church and other Christian leaders could have such a strange perspective on things—and illustrate it for all to see. Some have suggested that he was part of an ancient cult, or secret society. If so, it was truly ancient.

More than 200 years before Leonardo, in the construction of the North porch of Chartres cathedral, an unknown artisan portrayed the great men of the Bible around a statue of a woman holding a woman child—officially called "St. Anne with infant Mary." Among these men are Abraham, with his iconic images of knee-high son Isaac and a ram, and other Old Testament prophets. On the other side of the doorway are some of Jesus' disciples, and John the Baptist.

John the Baptist on the North porch, Notre Dame de Chartres, 1220CE.

We know he is John because of his camel-hair robe and the platter he carries—but the face of this man is so sweet, so dear, that he almost seems to be blushing at the attention he's receiving—and in his arms, on top of the platter that usually holds his head, is a lamb

What's going on here? Why would these people characterize this wilderness prophet in a way so different from the powerful, locust-eating preacher of repentance that modern churches describe?

It turns out that the solution to the puzzle may be found—not in the Essene texts associated with Qumran—but in those codices found at *Nag Hammadi*. They show us that the Gnostic tradition taught that neither man nor woman could achieve spiritual enlightenment without the aid of a member of the opposite gender—and that the completion of a human being was the total integration of both aspects in one person: the androgyne (*Andros* means "man" and *gyne* means "woman" in the ancient Greek).

Now the DaVinci paintings and the Chartres statue begin to make sense—John the Baptist represented the totally completed man, he who has unified *animus* and *anima*. He was the image of the balanced being: a "forerunner" of the heavenly state.

The Johannite movement involves much more, however: many chapels, all over Europe—often adjacent to ones dedicated to Mary Magdalene.

One of the more bizarre accusations placed against the Knights Templar at their Inquisition was that they spat on the cross and worshipped a head on a platter. And, of course, John the Baptist was portrayed, throughout the Middle Ages, with a platter that represented the one on which, according to the New Testament, Herod had presented John's head to his step-daughter Salome at her request.

It's usually just a small part of the biblical canon, and paid little attention to, but there's layers and layers of meaning in this story. First there's the king himself, who took the throne by marrying his brother's wife, Herodias, which is in accordance with the ancient tradition of marrying the previous king's wife as the means to attain royalty. Then there's Salome (which is Greek for the Hebrew *Shalom*, meaning "peace, wellbeing"), daughter of Herodias, the "means of power," doing the Dance of the Veils before her step-father the king. It turns out that this particular dance is associated with the *heiros gamos* and is representative of the Goddess's (originally Inanna's) journey into the underworld to fetch her deceased lover, where she is stripped of seven layers of clothing, representing the seven divine doctrines creating life. After dying and being reborn herself, the Goddess is allowed to return to the surface with her lover. Salome would have to have been a priestess to know this dance, and she would have to have been participating in a reenactment of the Sacred Marriage to perform it. It's also interesting that one of the women attending Jesus' crucifixion and burial is also called Salome—with the addition of the name/title "Mary."

The execution of John the Baptist is, in itself, intriguing. Here was a man who had been gathering crowds at a wilderness site along the lower Jordan River, and who had obviously been training disciples for years. Suddenly, he's taken to the palace and kept a prisoner—for some time, apparently. We have no idea what the nature of his imprisonment was, whether he was "under house arrest" or in chains in a dungeon, but we do know he was allowed to talk with his disciples, because the gospels describe messages going back and forth with Jesus. We don't know if Salome, or anyone else, was expecting him to be the next messiah—but apparently, being only six months older than Jesus, he was the right age and lineage and had avoided Herod's father's "massacre of the innocents." Suddenly, for no apparent reason, other than Salome's request, he is executed. Soon afterward, the people shift their attention to Jesus.

The fact of the Baptist's existence is corroborated by the Roman historian Josephus, who states that when Herod lost a battle, the local citizens thought it was because he had executed John "whose surname was the Baptist." It's further supported by the recent archeological find of Shimon Gibson, whose *The Cave of John the Baptist* provides a remarkable addition to our understanding of that time. It seems that, not far from where John was born, there is a manmade cavern, long since silted up, but which, as Gibson and his colleagues have excavated it, has turned out to be a place for ritual cleansing—first of the right foot with oil, and then of the whole body with water. Gibson's research indicates that the site was occupied for some time before John would have been using it, and continued to be used as late as 170CE.[54]

In trying to understand the significance of this find, Gibson offers an unusual perspective on John's work. Responding to those who would like to place the Baptist's work in the context of the Qumran community, he points out that, since John's father, Zacharias, was an active priest in the Jerusalem Temple, the Essenes, who abhorred all that the Temple had become, would probably have had nothing to do with him. For those who have been taught to believe that John saw himself as Jesus' "forerunner," he points out that the term "forerunner" is used only once in the New Testament, and that was applying to Jesus, as going to heaven before his disciples. Further, he points out that John's ministry had all the characteristics of one who anticipated the return of Elijah—including holding special purifications at the spot on the Jordan where Elijah was last seen—and he clearly did not stop what he was doing when Jesus began his work. In fact, Gibson states, it's clear that Jesus was baptizing others soon after having been baptized by John.

Another set of interesting bits may be found in the buildings and traditions of the Holy Land. According to Shilom Gibson,

---

[54] Gibson, S. *The Cave of John the Baptist,* New York: Doubleday, 2004.

> From the Crusader period, the traditional tomb of Zacharias [the father of John the Baptist] was placed at Sebaste, adjacent to the tomb of John the Baptist. According to an account ...of the capture by Salah ed-Din's forces, the large Crusader cathedral was described as the 'tomb" or "sanctuary" of Zacharias. Yqut, around 1225, also mentioned that the mosque contained the tombs of John the Baptist, his father Zacharias, and other prophets.[55]

So, at the same time people were building the cathedral at Chartres, with that lovely, sweet image of John the Baptist, they were maintaining a tomb for him in the Holy Land.

Gibson also points out that several other sites are said to be the tombs of these famous men, and at least two include the tomb of Elizabeth, John's mother. In the Jerusalem area, he says, "only a handful" of inscriptions date from the first few centuries refer to the Baptist, or "the forerunner" and cites an intercessory prayer that calls for the help of "Lady Mary Mother of God and Ever Virgin and of John the Forerunner and Baptist, and of all the holy saints."[56]

Then there's the head itself. In our culture, a piece of bone—especially a skull—is weird at best and horrifying at worst. However, that's not the case in many other cultures. There's a long-held tradition among the Celts—evident in archeological sites as long ago as 5,000 years, and going on even today in Alpine villages—of preserving and honoring the head

> It's possible that many of the European and British sites, called "tombs" because of the presence of dried bones, were in fact "women's houses" or goddess sanctuaries, and the bones were there to honor those who had been part of the community in years past.

(skull) of beloved and noble personages. And, interestingly, many images of Mary Magdalene include a skull.

---

[55] Gibson, S. *The Cave of John the Baptist*, New York: Doubleday, 2004. p. 135.
[56] ibid. p. 139.

These traditions may be related to the very ancient ritual of spring sacrifice: for several hundred years in Babylon, part of the spring equinox ritual was to cut the head off a bull-calf and float it down the river as an offering to the goddess, and for millennia, the head of a bull (which, with its horns being the shape of the uterus and fallopian tubes) was a sign of the goddess, whose home was always in natural flowing water. The skull could be seen as a sacrifice, cleansed by the flowing water, just as John baptized and purified with flowing water in accordance with Hebrew purification rites.

It turns out that a significant number of Eastern Christians believe that John was the Messiah. Interestingly, there is a "Christian" sect located in the marshlands of the Euphrates that has its own "Bible," stating that John, not Jesus, was the expected Messiah, that his are the teachings we read in the gospels, and that his chief disciple, Simon Magus, a well-documented miracle worker who was in Rome when Paul was there, was in Egypt when John's execution occurred so could not take the reins. In short, they say, Jesus was an upstart, supplanting the rightful "heir to the throne."

Perhaps even more relevant to the ideas being presented here, though, is the fact that the priest who took the vows of the first Templar knights in Jerusalem was one Theocletes, Patriarch of Jerusalem, and a known "Johannite."

Taken all together, these bits suggest an interesting interpretation of the story. Consider the possibility:

> Elizabeth (*Elisheva*) and Mary (*Maryam*) are both Nazarenes, bred, chosen, and trained to become the mother of the Messiah, whose prophesied birth date is fast arriving. Unfortunately, however, Elizabeth is barren—in spite of all the prayers and sacrifices she and the priest chosen as her husband have performed, there has been no child. But the stars keep moving and the time is at hand, so Mary, though almost too young to bear a child, is given a husband.
>
> As it happens, both are visited by the Holy Spirit and become pregnant—Elizabeth is a few months further along

than Mary, but she doesn't tell anyone lest she lose the child and suffer even more humiliation. When Mary comes to her with her own news, though, she feels her child leap in her womb and she knows all is well. Mary stays with Elizabeth through the birth of Elizabeth's boy, whom they call *Yehohanan* as he is destined to be a priest like his father.

Mary's child is born and the word is out that the new messiah is born. Herod has heard that he may be supplanted and plans to kill all baby boys, so both families are quickly taken out of Palestine and into Egypt, where other Nazarenes are ready to continue their training and help prepare the infant boys for their coming roles. The boys grow up in the Nazarene rule and *Yehohanan*, later to be known as John (*Iohanus* in Latin), begins his ministry. First, he spends the requisite time "in the wilderness" to complete his training with Nazarene elders. Then he sets up his school near the riverbanks of the Jordan—far enough from Jerusalem and Caesarea not to create a stir, but along the travel routes so he can reach lots of people. In fact, the site he chooses is a close as possible to the site where Elijah was last seen, before mounting to heaven in a fiery chariot. He begins to let people know that the signs and portents are in place and the messiah, or Elijah, is about to return. He tells them that they must prepare, must purify themselves, must stop letting the urban life and the false temple pollute their souls, so they can experience the new kingdom of God.

Drawing on the ancient Hebrew required ritual of cleansing for purification, John creates a new ritual. First, the man walks into the river with him, just as he would walk into the pool outside the temple. The men who respond to John's message are then invited into a cave near Jerusalem, where a natural spring provides a series of pools, going deep into the earth. John uses these pools as opportunities to teach deeper lessons about the nature of God and man and the earth. He also uses it to create a covenant. Deuteronomy says that one makes a covenant by putting oil on a foot. John's disciples are each given the opportunity to have their right foot oiled before entering the pools in the cave. As the disciple learns each lesson, he receives the next cleansing, and he becomes stronger in his faith—in himself and in the divine.

Outside the Church

In time, enough people have heard of the Baptizer and his work that hundreds, sometimes thousands, show up to hear him speak and experience his new ritual. John, himself, is in a near-constant state of ecstasy, brought on by lack of food and frequent prayerful ritual, and his words come from a source even he doesn't recognize: words that he is sure will transform his listeners' hearts and turn them to the path of right-living.

Herod's administrators become concerned. This man is saying things they think might be dangerous and lots of people are paying attention. They know the prophecies and they see that, in spite of Herod's father's efforts, the next messiah may have slipped through their fingers.

A council is held. How to proceed? Then someone realizes that it may be possible to complete the prophecy without endangering the kingdom. If John can be enticed to the palace and can complete the *heiros gamos* there, then he can be "sacrificed" as the Anointed One, letting Herod continue to serve as king (and not be killed as his brother was). They proceed to invite John to the palace, but he refuses. Again and again, they ask and he refuses, until finally, one night, an over-zealous guardsman simply drags him in.

Herod, who had married his brother's widow, the priestess Herodias, in order to attain the throne, knows that only her chosen one can fulfill the role of the Goddess in the anointing. Finally it all comes together, the sun and moon are in an appropriate alignment, the feast is established, John is anointed, and the sacred marriage is made. John is now the bridegroom and Salome the bride. Herod, determined to keep his position in safety, quickly sets up the next stage—the sacrifice. So, still in the palace, away from any outside influence that might make things difficult, Herod arranges for John's execution.

Following tradition Salome does her dance, imitating the Goddess going into the underworld for her lover. She feels the whole process deeply—so deeply that she takes the story as her own: in her heart, she *is* the Goddess and John is her lost lover.

The dance ends. In her ecstasy and grief, Salome continues a very ancient tradition and requests that she be given the head of her husband, which request her stepfather grants, and a guard presents the bloody object to her on a platter.

Salome and her mother, being daughters of the old way, treat the severed head with reverence and prepare it for permanent honor, as is due a king—of however short duration. Then Salome goes into mourning, weeping the loss of king and lover. For the rest of her life, the sacred skull is something she carries with her always.

Two years later, Salome hears from the other priestesses that a new candidate for the messiah has emerged. As the most recent representative of the Goddess, she is a leader among the women and is expected to participate in the process. As her mother did before her, she witnesses the anointing of Jesus by Mara of Bethany, as well as his crucifixion and burial. As a member of the royal household, she lends him and his disciples her protection and helps with their provisions. Among the Hebrew women she is known as a Mara, and will be described in the gospels as two different women—one the wanton step-daughter of the king who demanded the head of a prophet on a platter, and the other the loving and devoted disciple of Jesus who helped lay him in his tomb.

During the whole process, she is there beside the next representative of the Goddess, the Mara called the Magdalene, as they complete the sacred rituals and fulfill the ancient prophecies. This time, though, it becomes necessary to leave the country very soon afterward. So, with the Magdalene and a few others, she goes to Egypt where they share their stories with other Nazarites and devout Jews—until the Roman officials become inquisitive. From there, she retreats to her step-father's estate in southern France (known then as *Provincia*). With her, as always, is the treasured skull.

Generations later, Salome and her story have become the stuff of legend throughout the region, and the skull that she treasured is considered a source of power and authority. The Gauls, being of the same Anatolian heritage as Salome, understand the importance of a skull as a bearer of the power of the person who it belonged to. John was an Anointed One, a Great One according to local tradition; therefore John's skull has great power, and whoever has the skull can use that power for the good.

As family members marry and move away, chapels are built around the region honoring the skull and its source. The Johannite cult of Southern France is established.

Outside the Church

Consider the possibility.

Herod is known to have maintained a villa in Provence—and retired there when relieved of his duties in Palestine (which is to say, "went into exile"). Hundreds of chapels dedicated to John the Baptist sprinkle the countryside of southern France. Josephus and others talk about a man called Simon Magus who claimed to be a disciple of John the Baptist and worked miracles in Rome shortly after the crucifixion of Jesus (described also in the New Testament book Acts). Consider the possibility.

The Templars—opening the door to new understandings

It's popular today to consider the Knights Templar as a vast, secret brotherhood, protecting some major piece of information. It's probably more accurate to describe them as a remarkably effective international university, security system, and banking organization whose leadership sought to rise above the corruption they saw in both church and state, while dedicating themselves to being the greatest warriors they could be.

In 1118, a group of nine French noblemen who had been part of the first Crusade over twenty years before and felt more at home in the Palestinian desert than their ancestral domains, officially formed the Order of the Poor Knights of the Temple of Solomon. They studied with, and their vows were taken by, an Eastern Patriarch, by name of Theocletes, who is known to

> Nine was an important number in the education of a nobleman of those days: it is completion at the material level. It was also the cycle of the planet Venus, indicator of the time for a new *hieros gamos*.

have honored the miracle-working power and teachings of John as much as Jesus. For nine years, the nine men worked in Jerusalem under the protection of the Merovingian king placed there by the pope. Then, in 1127, their founders returned to Europe, where they shared their story and ideals and won the support of the pope during the Council of Troyes (a city controlled by several family members of the group) in 1129.

Almost immediately, their numbers and wealth grew exponentially, as the order became known to provide the perfect opportunity for second-sons with high ideals and an intense desire to live and die as spiritual warriors. In addition to the usual oaths of poverty (more correctly, holding goods in common), chastity (purity of action and intent—some were married when they joined), and obedience to the Rule and their superiors in the Order, the knights swore that they would never let themselves be taken prisoner in battle, nor take up the sword unless attacked—which is an idea that at that time only existed as one of the tenets of the *Koran*. They chose as a symbol a red, equal-sided, cross with flared ends on a white background, which they wore on cloth tunics over their armor.

Their formation and acceptance as a religious order was guided by the famous monk, Bernard of Clairvaux, an abbot of the Cistercian order and closely allied with the pope. In helping to create their order, Bernard imposed much the same rule of operation as in his own Cistercian order, including the relatively democratic decision-making processes followed in Cistercian monasteries. He added a section to their Rule that appear to be almost identical to the War Rule found among the texts in the Dead Sea Scrolls, suggesting that at least some of what the founding Templars discovered in Jerusalem were texts from that period. However, he went beyond the usual monastic oaths and the special warrior oath for the knights, insisting on their obedience "to Bethany, the keep of Mary and Martha," and, above all, to *Deo et Dama Nostra* ("God and Our Lady"). Further, according to Picknett and Prince, the prayer of absolution for sins among the

Templars was "I pray God that he will pardon your sins as he pardoned them to Mary Magdalene..."[57]

The Templars grew into a sizeable force of several thousand knights, with several hundred stationed in Jerusalem on rotations for over a hundred years, along with all the horses, grooms, pages, squires, cooks, accountants, and other supporters needed to maintain such an army for so long—as well as a huge system of supply for all of these people, coming in from all over Europe. They had strongholds, identifiable by their distinctive large, round towers where foods were stored for local farmers as well as for the knights and lay members of the Order, on properties that had been turned over to them by their supporters and members from the British Isles to Asia Minor. These were havens for travelers and locals alike, with safe-houses where "notes of credit" carried from other branches of the Order could be exchanged for cash or goods, thus establishing the first banking system in Europe.

The knights who were stationed at these centers would patrol the roads, keeping them safe for merchants and tradesmen, while other lay and ordained men and women of the order would farm, manage records, build and maintain the buildings, and undertake all the other kinds of tasks that contribute to a well-run community. In short, they provided the infrastructure for a booming economy of trade across Europe.

They worked with builders and tradesmen and food producers from northern France to the Sinai desert, and many spoke Arabic and Aramaic as well as French and Latin. We know, simply because of how long they lived there and what they did while they were there, that the founders and leaders of the Templars were well acquainted with the teachings and practice of their Arab neighbors, who included Muslims and

---

[57] Picknett, L. and Prince, C. *The Templar Revelation.* New York: Simon & Schuster, 1997, p.107

Sufis, and Persian Zoroastrians, each with their own beliefs and technologies.

That the Templars had information unavailable to "normal" people—both inside and outside of the church—is undeniable. The question is what *kind* of information they had.

Many researchers believe that Templars dug deep under the Temple Mount to find ancient objects from the time of Solomon— possibly including the lost Ark of the Covenant (it was not included in the detailed list made by the Babylonians when they had sacked the Temple 500 years before). It's even been suggested that they kept the Ark there until the Saracens retook Jerusalem, at which point the Templars, following a tradition of Solomon and Sheba's son being the rightful inheritor, took it to Ethiopia.

Lynn Picknett and Clive Prince, in *The Templar Revelation*, point out that virtually all of the founding nine came from Languedoc or Champagne, and included the Count of Provence—regions notoriously antagonistic to the Roman church and strongly influenced by the Gnostic Cathars and both the Johannite and the Magdalene cult. They state that one defining characteristic of the Order was

> their unusually strong veneration of John the Baptist. ... some have suggested that the severed head they were rumoured to have worshipped was that of the Baptist himself. ...
> Even much of their apparently orthodox symbolism hides specifically 'John' allusions ... the Lamb of God was one of their most important images ... in many places, such as the West Country of England, this symbol is taken to refer to *John* himself...[58]

They remind us that the mysterious figure of worship often referred to in Templar legends as *Bahomet* spells, when deciphered with the code used in the Holy Land since the time of the Dead Sea Scrolls, the Greek word *Sophia*, meaning the feminine embodied "wisdom," which, in the Gnostic text,

---

[58] Picknett, L. and Prince, C. *The Templar Revelation*. New York: Simon & Schuster, 1997. p. 101.

Outside the Church

Pistis Sophia, is linked directly with the Magdalene. They point out that nearly a third of Templar strongholds were located in the parts of France that its founders had come from—close to the home of the Cathars and the Magdalene legends.

Based on this and other evidence, they suggest that the Roman Church's crusade against the Cathars and the subsequent destruction of the Templar order were related. Apparently, not only was a very wealthy standing army dangerous, but their ideas about democratic rule (part of their Rule from the Cistercians—and possibly the Essenes) and a direct, individual connection with God—along with the secrecy in which they were shrouded—were not acceptable either.

The official story is that King Philip "the Fair" of France sent his men, with approval by the papacy, to every known Templar home and stronghold to arrest them all and try them for heresy. Hundreds of men were captured—with no resistance. They were tortured under the Inquisition, tried on the basis of the confessions extorted, and, in most cases killed, and so the Templars were wiped out in a single, well-planned attack on Friday, October 13, 1307. Case closed.

> Some suggest that this event is the origin of the idea that "Friday the 13th" is unlucky.

A more careful look at the events, however, suggests otherwise. The Templars had a significant merchant fleet, which bore the flag of a skull and crossed bones (part of the symbolism of the Templar initiations)—which was nowhere to be found on that dreadful morning. They were the bankers for thousands of people across Europe—yet King Philip "the Fair" found virtually no funds in the strongholds he invaded. Also, the Templars had vowed never to surrender—yet those who were captured gave themselves up without a struggle. Clearly, the organization went underground, leaving a few members, probably volunteers, as a sacrificial "cover."

Some went off to other lands. There is, for example, increasing evidence that the Templars had built colonies in the

Americas as early as 1300, and maybe earlier. The Roslyn chapel in Scotland, built by the Sinclairs in the early 1400s, includes representations of plants that are distinctly "New World" in origin. Ponce de Leon's journal refers to a castle seen along the coast of the Carolinas, and there's a round tower with the image of a medieval knight with a square cross carved into a rock in New England that apparently was already there when the Pilgrims arrived in 1620. The Templars also appear to have traveled to various ports around the Indian Ocean, including parts of India and Yemen, Bahrain, and Ethiopia—in some of which they built outposts in their own distinctive round-tower style.

Finally, it's perhaps no coincidence that a neighboring country, high in the natural fortress of the Alps, has for centuries been the banking capital of the world, refuses to participate in any war except in self-defense, yet drafts every single adult into the military, is the home of the best-known and trusted international service organization, whose symbol is a red cross on a white background and is called the Red Cross—and bears as the national flag a square white cross on a red background.

A Golden Thread?

In his remarkable piece of scholarly detective work, *The Goddess, The Grail, and the Lodge,* Alan Butler uses the idea of a golden thread to tie together all of these apparently disparate movements. He suggests that each of them is part of a larger story, a larger movement, within the culture of medieval Europe—and that we, today, have much to gain by understanding them.

A not very obvious part of that larger movement was the emergence of a landed gentry who were often much better educated than the priests who served them and who were not so sure they wanted to be controlled by the papacy. For very good reasons, these folks aren't talked about much in the history books. One must read and interpret letters, visits, decisions made at councils, and patterns of visitation and family relationships to make sense of them.

Butler focuses on what he calls "the Troyes Fraternity," those families living around the city of Troyes in France whose members, he believes, were committed to establishing the "New Jerusalem" and sought every scrap of information and every opportunity that might bring it closer. He points out that the history of Burgundy was one of independence from the Church and the Frankish crown, and under the leadership of the Merovingians, a royal house symbolized by the lily, who some believe to be descendants of Jesus and the Magdalene, descendants "of the house of David." He also notes that the Christianity practiced in the region had come by way of Celtic Ireland, with its rather more tolerant views of religious practice than those of Rome.

When the Pope let the Carolingians of northern France take over the region, Butler points out, the new "rigid autocracy made demands that some of the landed families in the region must have found difficult to swallow."[59] He suggests that the locals carefully and strategically used their influence to ensure that the right popes were elected and then encouraged the taking of Jerusalem—to place a Merovingian king on that throne and then protect him with their own warrior-sons—the men who would become the Templars.

Other researchers suggest similar motives for the formation of the Templar order. Clearly, there is a connection between whatever was going on in France at that time and what ultimately occurred in Jerusalem, and whatever it was, it didn't fit with the Roman church's ideas.

One piece of the puzzle remains a mystery: what did the Templars, also called the "white knights," find under the Temple Mount? Theories range from the Ark of the Cove-

---

[59] Butler, Alan and Stephen Dafoe, *The Knights Templar Revealed.* New York: Barnes & Noble, 1999. p. 143.

nant to the Holy Grail to an early version of the sort of writings we have in the Dead Sea Scrolls. Again, no direct descriptions have been found—all is inference, supposition, and deductive reasoning. Whatever it was, the combination of their discoveries and their dedication won over thousands of people in Europe, and many nobles and sons of nobles joined their cause, donning the white vest over their armor and adopting the monastic Rule.

Monastery as Cultural Transformer

The monastic order emerged in the Medieval period as a response to the lack of options for orphans and adult men in the culture A number of orders were established between 1000 and 1300CE that are well-known today, including the Franciscans, the Dominicans, the monks of Cluny ("Cluniacs"), the Carmelites, and the most famous, monastic Rule-establishing, Order of St. Benedict. Schools as well as retreats, many offered teachings that were contrary to the village churches.

At one time, the fastest-growing, best-known system of monasteries were the integrated agricultural-manufacturing operations that made up the Cistercian Order, defined in large part by the incredible work of Bernard of Clairvaux. The Cistercians, called the "white brothers," were originally herders of sheep and producers of wool and became an order of engineers and agriculturalists that trained hundreds of technicians in the art and science of building and maintaining healthy communities. Their buildings and machines were remarkable in their efficiency and utility, and many of them form the basis for our life today. One historian describes their waterworks:

> The Cistercians may have modeled themselves after the Essenes, (including the wearing of white) and documents found by the Templars—like the Dead Sea Scrolls—were part of the reason they were so unique in their time.

Cistercian monastery waterwheel in Belgium.

A twelfth-century report on the use of waterpower in a Cistercian monastery (that of Clairvaux in France) ... could be written 742 times over for the... number of Cistercian monasteries ... built in ...Portugal, Sweden, Scotland, Hungary—all had very similar water-powered systems within almost universally similar plans for the monasteries themselves. It has been said that a blind Cistercian monk moving into any of the monasteries would instantly have known where he was. ...

In the Clairvaux report, four distinct industrial operations are mentioned that required waterpower: crushing wheat, sieving flour, fulling cloth, and tanning. ... Running water was used for domestic purposes, as well as for industrial ones. It was carried in lead or wooden pipes to the kitchen for cooking and washing and to the gardens for watering. It was also used to clean out the drains, presumably situated under the lavatories, or *necessaria*, and to carry away the waste so as to "leave everywhere spotless."[60]

The Cistercians built relatively isolated but remarkably successful monasteries on the marginal land no one else wanted and offered an example of sustainable horticulture and democratic management that could not be ignored. Each

---

[60]Gimpel, Jean. *Medieval Machine: The Industrial Revolution of the Middle Ages*. New York: Barnes & Noble, 2003. pp. 3-4

abbey was formed by an abbot and twelve lay brethren. They would build a chapel and huts and farm the land, and, over a five-year period, bring in masons, choir-monks (those who had taken vows), and other helpers to complete the compound, beginning with the abbey church. Daily, pre-dawn meetings of choir monks would be held in the chapter house, following St. Benedict's Rule and other local rules that the order and monastery had established through democratic vote. Self-government was the norm in these monasteries, in stark contrast to the feudal system of the surrounding regions. And the inclusion of "lay" brothers and contracting with tradesmen from the region meant that this "new" way of life and decision-making were known to the local public.

Clairvaux, where Bernard remained as abbot for nearly 30 years, was one of the earlier monasteries built in this way. From it, dozens of "daughter-houses" were created, and many of them had "granges:" factories, mines, herding cabins, and farms located some distance from the chapter-house monastery.

Since choir monks had to be at the chapter-house each night for their meeting, uneducated lay brethren were brought into the order to maintain the various extensions of the monastery. This meant that a given monastery might involve dozens more than the actual brothers and produce many times more usable and sellable product than could otherwise be expected, making them a significant part of the economic system. These lay monks often far outnumbered the choir monks, and many men were attracted to the life as far better than the life of a serf. As a result, far more people were influenced by the Cistercians than the official membership rolls might suggest.

Bernard, however, was more than a masterful builder of monastic communities. He wrote nearly 90 sermons on the "Song of Songs" alone, often equating the Bride of that poem with Mary of Bethany, who, at that time, was considered to be the Magdalene. He was particularly devoted to the Black Madonna of his childhood church, from whose breast he reported having received several drops of milk while in prayer and with whom he felt a spiritual union. He was instrumental in the election of Pope Innocent II, whose earliest acts included conferring the titles "Mother of God" and "Queen of Heaven" on the Virgin Mary. Moreover, he was born near a site called "Is," which the Romans identified as Isis, and at least one historian has suggested that the "s" at the end of the names of so many gothic cathedral cities would have been, at the time the cathedrals were built, "Is." Clearly, he was committed to a spiritual life that honored both masculine and feminine divinity.

Bernard was also committed to the mystical experience. His education in the *trivium* and *quadrivium* of the Liberal Arts, followed by the practice of alchemy, had taken him beyond the rational, analytical mindset into a sense of union with divine wisdom and intelligence. Like the American transcendentalists, half a millennium later, he saw in nature, in trees and stones, a wisdom that could not be found in books and lectures, and he sought to introduce his brothers—and the world—to that wisdom.

As the architect of many abbeys as well as of the Templar organization, Bernard's influence was felt across Europe and into the Holy Land. He taught thousands of monks and created a remarkable library that included, curiously, many texts in old Hebrew, for which he brought in Hebrew scholars and masters of the Qabalah from all over Europe—a process which some modern researchers see as a sign of the Templars' having discovered ancient texts.

Clearly, this is not a man who followed the traditional doctrine of the Roman church. Just exactly what he was doing, and with what resources, however, is not fully understood. What we do know is that, through the efforts of the Cistercians, integrated manufacturing mills and waterwheels and the practice of democratic "common law" were disseminated across Europe. More, the legend of the Holy Grail was made acceptable to the Roman church.

The Holy Grail — or Cauldron

Around 1190 CE, someone who called himself *Chretien de Troyes* (meaning "Christian from Troyes") published an unfinished story called *Le Conte du Graal* ("The Tale of the Grail"). In it a young man finds himself wandering in a wasted land, meeting very strange people and ending up in a processional entering a castle, with, among other gruesome symbols, a spear dripping blood and a head on a platter. His fate—and that of the wasteland he is in—depends on his asking the correct question—in this case, "whose is the head?" The tale was as wildly popular in its day as *The DaVinci Code* was in the early 2000s, and for much the same reason: it dealt with the heretical ideas of the underground resistance to the cultural and religious norms of its day.

The "quest for the Holy Grail" almost immediately became the subject of hundreds of stories, poems, and plays, some of which were written by Cistercian monks using Christian theology. Many of them were written in the newly popular style called *troubadour*, spreading rapidly across Europe by wandering minstrels whose songs and stories emphasized the importance of chaste, courtly love, in which the feminine is seen as divinely virginal: absolutely pure and desirable and totally unattainable.

In most of these tales, the Grail is never even seen. In a few it is described as a chalice—the one that Jesus used to bless the wine at the Last Supper—and by association and inference, capable of ensuring eternal life.

Historically, *Graal* is a Celtic term referring to a mythical cauldron big enough for a wounded warrior to be immersed in and come out healed. The Irish and Britons have several tales describing the process. According to historian Carol Lee Flinders, "Ceridwen is one of the forms of the Celtic Goddess, and her cauldron is the womb-cauldron of rebirth and inspiration... In early Celtic myth, the cauldron restored slain warriors to life. ...[61]

Flinders suggests that there may be some truth in these ancient legends and that the *Graal* may have been a real object to which magical powers have been ascribed. She points out that

> ...a mysteriously beautiful object was found, in pieces, in a bog in Jutland. Assembled, its thirteen silver plates form a deep bowl, sixty-nine centimeters [29"] across and forty-two [15"] deep. Each of the plates is decorated... with a great many wild creatures: elephants, a dolphin, lions, a hyena... and a man with antlers ... made in Eastern Europe in the second century A.D. ... the Gundestrup Cauldron was taken apart deliberately so that the pieces could be buried separately ... one of the outer pieces has never been found. Whoever possessed the cauldron, and had to hide it, wanted to make very certain that its power didn't fall into the wrong hands...[62]

Symbolically, as Riane Eisler made clear in her book, *The Chalice and the Blade*, a chalice, or cup, stands for the receptive feminine, while the sword, spear, or knife stands for the penetrating masculine.

Lynn Picknett and Clive Prince, in their *The Holy Blood and the Holy Grail*, suggest that the Holy Grail is the womb of Mary Magdalene, which, they say, carried the "holy blood" of Jesus in the form of a child. As depicted in Dan Brown's *DaVinci Code*, they saw the close relationship between the old French term *San Graal* ("Holy Grail") and *Sang Raal* ("royal blood') and began deducing possible connections. They draw on traditions that the Merovingian line of royalty (including the king that was placed on the throne in Jerusalem) were descendents of Jesus the Christ and Mary the Magdalene

---

[61] Flinders, Carol Lee, *Rebalancing the World, why women belong and men compete and how to restore the ancient equilibrium*. New York: HarperCollins, 2002Pp. 83-84

[62] Flinders, Carol Lee, *Rebalancing the World, why women belong and men compete and how to restore the ancient equilibrium*. New York: HarperCollins, 2002, p. 146-7

through her daughter Sarah, the girl who reportedly arrived in France with *La Madeleine*. They also note that the family known "St. Clair" in France or "Sinclair" in England have a tradition of the same understanding.

Another possible interpretation of the Celtic *San Graal* is a large silver or gold platter—not unlike the one usually depicted as part of the iconography of John the Baptist (see the statue from Notre Dame de Chartes, p. 188).

The first printed story of King Arthur and his round table is derived from early Celtic tales, so it's not too surprising that the most famous stories about this Celtic icon are those associated with Arthur and his knights. One of the great commentators on Grail stories, Malcolm Godwin, points out in his book, *The Holy Grail,* that all these tales describe the alchemical process by which a mere human is transformed into an immortal—usually symbolized by lead becoming gold. Which brings us back to the work of Fulbert at Chartres, introducing the study of alchemy into the noble families of Medieval Europe through his school. It also points ahead to Isaac Newton, who wrote far more about alchemical processes than he did about physics.

That the idea of a Holy Grail was first made popular by a nobleman from the city that launched the Templars, that it was Bernard's order of Cistercian monks who translated the tale into Christian terms, that the Templars were leaders in the construction of the many cathedrals and chapels honoring Notre Dame and John the Baptist—together suggest that there is, indeed, a "golden thread" linking them all. At the very least, they managed to keep alive the idea of the divine feminine through the period when leaders steeped in Greco-Roman misogyny threatened to eliminate it completely.

Sleep and I shall soothe you, calm you and anoint you—
myrrh for your hot forehead—
Oh, don't you know? Everything's all right now; everything's fine... [63]

THE CULT OF THE MAGDALENE

From the texts discovered at *Nag Hammadi*, we can see that Mary Magdalene has played a much larger role in some Christians' experience than the modern Roman church, with its emphasis on Paul's texts over the Gospels, has allowed us to believe. Over the centuries, she's received a lot of attention, however, and her location and perceived role have shifted and changed, to the point where at least three churches, in three different countries, claim to have her remains buried in them, and at least three different interpretations of her life have been popularized at different times in history.

The Magdalene in Ephesus

Gregory of Tours, c. 584 CE, said that Mary Magdalene went from Jerusalem to Ephesus, where tradition had it that John, as "the beloved disciple," had taken Jesus' mother after the crucifixion. Gregory said that the Magdalene's tomb was at the grotto known as the Cave of the Seven Sleepers (a Christian mausoleum that was first documented in 449), where she "rests, with nothing to cover her." Many tourists, today, are shown this site as the tomb of St. Mary Magdalene.

---

[63] "Try Not to Get Worried" from *Jesus Christ, Superstar* by Tim Rice & Andrew Lloyd Weber, Decca, 1970.

Modestus, patriarch of Jerusalem to 634 CE, wrote: "it was there that the *myrrhophore* ("myrrh carrier") ended her apostolic career through her martyrdom..." He claimed she remained a virgin and a teacher of other holy women, appearing to her executioners as "a pure crystal." Her feast day, 22 July, was set by Bede, abbot of Jarrow (eastern England) about 710, based on this martyr story.

Emperor Leo IV announced having moved her remains to Constantinople, placing them there next to the long-established tomb of Lazarus, shortly before 900CE, and again, tourists today are shown this site as the tomb of Mary Magdalene.

The Magdalene in England

One popular version of the Holy Grail story is that Joseph of Arimathea, the wealthy man who provided Jesus' tomb in the garden, also provided the cup that was used during the Last Supper and used it to catch the last drops of Jesus' blood as the body was removed from the cross. Tradition has it that this Joseph was a tin merchant, and that one of his main sources of supply was the area now known as Cornwall, in England.

There are several versions of this story, but one has it that out of concern for the Magdalene's safety, he whisked her off to his property in Cornwall, leaving her there with the chalice, at the place that is known today as Glastonbury. In the process he thrust his staff into the ground, which miraculously took root and blossomed, becoming "Glastonbury thorn" or Hawthorne—which is the flower used to crown statues of the Virgin Mary all over the world on May 1st, May Day or Mary's Day (called *Beltane* in the Celtic calendar). At the site, a spring (everywhere associated with the Goddess) erupted, which turns red at certain times, so legend associates it with the blood of Jesus and the Holy Grail.

The Magdalene as Hermit

In Northumbria, England, about 850 CE, a monk copied a Latin manuscript dated about 100 years earlier. It was a description of Mary Magdalene going into the desert and fasting for thirty years, being lifted into heaven by angels every day "to be with her beloved, the Christ," and then returned to her cave in the rocks—where she was found and, at her death, was given mass and buried by the local priest. Susan Haskins, in her *Mary Magdalen, Myth and Metaphor*, notes the similarity of this story to a 5th-century story of a "St. Mary," a "harlot" from Alexandria who plied her trade to earn her way to Palestine and spent the last 47 years of her life in the desert, living in a cave, clad only in her hair and fed by angels—then finally, at her death, given communion and buried by the local bishop, Zosimus.

Around 1160 the *Vita eremitica beatae Mariae Magdelenae* ("the hermit's life of the blessed Mary Magdalene"), then believed to have been written by the 1st century Jewish historian Flavius Josephus, was adopted at Vezelay as the official story of the Magdalene's life after the resurrection. It's essentially the same as the Northumbria/St, Mary of Egypt story except that the cavern was identified as the grotto of *Sainte Baume* ("holy grotto") northeast of Marseille, which had been a major Diana temple during the Roman period and was converted to a Christian site in about 240CE. It was managed by Capetian (the word *capet* means "head" in Latin) monks until about 1170, when the Benedictines took over. Also, rather than working her way out of Egypt as a prostitute, in this story Saint Mary is "set adrift" with her friends in a boat that miraculously floats to the coast of France. The priest/bishop in this version of the story is named as either one *Maximinus* (meaning "Greatest") or the resurrected Lazarus of the gospels. A young, dark Egyptian "maid" named Sarah (which, you may recall, means "princess") as well as Martha and Lazarus, as her brother and sister, are said to have come with her, with Martha going on to Tarascon, where legends about her power are still part of local lore and her bones were announced as having been discovered in 1187CE.

The Magdalene in France: La Madeleine

The earliest reference to the Magdalene's presence in France is a history by the King of Arles that describes a son of the King of Italy coming to visit Ste Baume, "the place where she lived and died," in 935. References to Mary of Bethany, widely assumed to be the same person, along with her sister Martha, abound throughout the region from the early 1000s. The cathedral at Vezelay, in Burgundy, several hundred miles northward, was begun at the site of a small monastery in 1037, managed by Goeffrey, a monk from Cluny who seems to have had well-placed connections: he attended the Council of Reims in 1049 and was with Pope Leo in 1050 when Leo confirmed the Magdalene's patronage (or "spiritual presence") at Vezelay. The numerous miracles ascribed to her there became famous. The monastery's possession of the Magdalene's body was confirmed by several popes over the next centuries.

The first images of the Magdalene's arrival with her friends in a boat appeared in stained glass windows at Chartres (1200CE) and Auxerre (1230CE). At the same time appeared the first images of her (or any woman, ever) preaching the Good News of the resurrection—to the men and women of a coastal city in France. Today, such images are to be found all over Provence.

After a few decades of evading the subject, new stories were needed to explain how her body came to be at Vezelay (the first written stories of her arrival in France with Martha, Lazarus, and Maximinus appeared about 1200 CE), and why the crypt couldn't be opened so the body could be seen. One widely published explanation was that the body was moved to Aix-en-Provence to protect it from the Saracens and then the elderly keeper of that ruined tomb had called the monks at Vezelay to come rescue it, which they did, finding it uncorrupted (as if still alive, not decomposed), and sealed it into a crypt at the abbey. The monks told dire tales of the consequences associated with attempts to unseal it, but finally arranged for the pious king Louis IX (St. Louis) to confirm (and take some of) the now-skeletal remains—very publicly and with much ceremony in 1267.

(left) Disembarking, taken from the Marie Madeleine window, Notre Dame de Chartres (photo on back cover). (right) Speaking to the residents of Marseilles, from a manuscript.

But Louis' nephew was not convinced, and continued to support efforts to discover the remains of this beloved saint, not to mention possible grandmother of French royalty. Just 12 years later, in 1279, the monastery at St. Maximin in Provence announced that the bones of *La Madeleine* had been found in their crypt, with an ancient inscription, and a document reporting the transfer of her body from its original alabaster tomb in Vezelay to this marble sarcophagus to protect it from a Saracen invasion in the 700s—which document "dissolved into dust when touched." In 1295, Pope Boniface VIII declared these to be the rightful remains and shifted control of the monastery from the Benedictines to the Dominicans.

At that point Mary Magdalene became the patron of the Dominican order and her feast is still celebrated there, today, with thousands of devotees singing her praise as an enshrined skull is removed from its home in the crypt below St. Maximin's basilica and paraded around the town (photo of the skull on p. 197 of this text).

In 1276, Jocapo de Voragine, Dominican archbishop of Genoa, Italy, published his version of her story in his encyclopedic *Lives of the Saints*. The encyclopedia was extremely popular and the story quickly made its way into Italian art, with a panel in Florence depicting it fully in 1280, and many variations created over the years.

To paraphrase:

> The resurrected Jesus had sent the disciples to many countries to teach and the Magdalene went to Egypt, but "the heathens" set her and her companions (Martha, Lazarus, Maximinus, the other Marys, Joseph of Arimathea, Sarah the Egyptian, and others) adrift to be drowned. They drifted across the sea in a rudderless boat. On land, they sought refuge under a "porch" of a "temple of the people of that country," pagans, to whom Mary is inspired to preach. The rulers of the land ask her to pray for them to have a child; she does and they do, and they are converted.
>
> After other dramas, Lazarus is appointed bishop and the region is declared a Christian state. The Magdalene retires to a cave and gives up everything, clad only in her hair, praying and fasting. Angels come every day to take her to heaven to be with Jesus, her *bien-ami,* "best-beloved."
>
> One day, thirty years later, another hermit sees her levitating, visits her and hears her life story—after which she asks him to tell the bishop (now Maximinus) that she will appear in his chapel. Soon thereafter, angels carry her there, Maximinus gives her communion, and she dies. The angels come to take her soul heavenward,

which is seen as a glowing light, and the bishop places her body in a simple sarcophagus in the crypt of the church he has built.

Italian illustration of Voragine's tale: 1280 CE.

In the introduction and throughout the story, Voragine emphasizes the Magdalene's role as *Illuminata et Illuminatrix*, "illuminated one and illuminator of others"—as does the Gnostic text, *Pistis Sophia*. Like many other titles of saints adopted by the Roman church, this one happens to be one of the common titles for the pagan embodiment of the divine feminine known as Diana, who was the occupant of *Sainte Baume* during the Roman occupation of *Provincia* (the Latin name of Provence)

Ste Baume, or the Holy Grotto, described as a hermit's retreat in all the literature, is now a church, managed by the brothers who live in the monastery built against the walls of the cliff surrounding it. On a quiet Sunday, a dozen or so locals and tourists and an equal number of monks celebrate the mass there. On Christmas Eve and *Lammas* (August 1), however, hundreds make the pilgrimage through the ancient forest, past the holy spring, and up the steep trail to the cavern.

Sainte Baume **(Holy Grotto) in the hills above St. Maximim in Provence.**

Sainte Baume is not now, nor has it ever been a hermitage. Rather, it's a magnificent natural amphitheater, in which the faithful have worshipped the divine feminine for millennia.

The rocky ledge behind the marble altar structure near the center has a wonderful larger-than-life statue of a voluptuous woman reclining in contemplation. This area is said to have been where the Magdalene slept, and stairs lead up to a gateway where the statue may be viewed and a candle lit. Below this is a pool of water, from a spring, *source* in French, which is another indication of a site sacred to the divine feminine, as at Chartres and hundreds of others around Europe.

La Madeleine reclining behind the altar at Ste Baume.

Having stood at the edge of the grotto, I could very easily see how the story of the saint's being "carried to heaven by angels" each day could develop. A sweeping view of the valley and distant hills, reminiscent of the area around the Grand Canyon in Arizona, calls the spirit to soar. A near-constant light wind along the cliff face seems to lift the body—I almost felt as if I had to hang on to prevent floating away! If one were in an ecstatic trance state, the sensation would undoubtedly have been overwhelming.

The Magdalene as a Model for Repentant Sinners

In a sermon to the people of Rome, Pope Gregory I, on September 14, 591CE, declared that the "repentant sinner" in the gospels was the same as "the adulterous woman" and that "Mary, called the Magdalene" was that woman. She was portrayed as the blessed penitent, whose love for the Christ and willingness to submit to his healing (the Gospels say he "cast out seven demons" from her) allowed her to overcome her sinful nature and become holy. This sermon was included in a book of sermons provided to priests and abbots for the next several hundred years and so became the accepted teaching of the Church.

Around 1250, Thomas Aquinas, a Dominican leading the University of Paris, set her colors: the deep blue of compunction and charity and the red fire of love. This was while Vezelay was under pressure to prove their Magdalene relics to be real. About the same time, between 1200 and 1278, 32 new convents and monasteries were founded as the Order of the Penitents of St. Mary Magdalene, starting in Italy, through France, and into Germany. Many of these were homes for repentant prostitutes and adulteresses (and far too many women who had been denounced as such without evidence). Passion plays and poetry, along with annual sermons on her feast day, kept her humanness and love for Christ in full view—she was the model of both mystic and reformed whore. Soon the prostitutes of Paris organized a guild under her patronage. This practice continued over the centuries, so that by the mid-1900s, halfway houses for repentant prostitutes (and sexually abused girls), called Magdalene houses, dotted the English and Irish countryside and provided a source of labor for the laundry and catering needs of the churches that supported them.

Marie Madeleine, by Reni, with the long flowing hair and skull that are her icons and the long cross that is the symbol of John the Baptist.

For most of us, this is the familiar Magdalene image: half-dressed, lots of flowing, usually red hair, an anguished look, clearly wishing things were very different. Thousands of paintings and drawings have given us this depiction, and hundreds of sermons have reinforced it. This version of the Magdalene has won the hearts of millions of women over the years—women who found the Virgin a bit cold and the Madonna unapproachable. In this sinful yet devoted woman, who was so close to the Christ, there was someone they could relate to, could even identify with. Quietly, with little fanfare, they adopted the "dark" (though often red-haired) Magdalene as their patron saint, turning their backs on the "white" Virgin Mother. Only lately have we been shown other possibilities.

A Female Apostle

The Magdalene has long been recognized as the one whom Jesus sent to tell his disciples about his resurrection—and as such is now called *Apostola Apostolorum*, "Apostle to the Apostles." But it turns out that there's much more to her apostolate than those few moments.

With the discovery and recent translation into English of the ancient codices at *Nag Hammadi* in Egypt, the traditional priorities are shifting. According to these documents, along with one or two others found in different places, Mary Magdalene's role in Jesus life and teachings was far greater than even the greatest feminists has ever considered. In them Mary is described as

> "The happy one, beautiful in her speaking," "pure spiritual Mariham," quoted as leading the others in asking questions and understanding Jesus' teachings... *Pistis Sophia*
>
> ...one of the followers; Jesus promises to "make her male" in order for her to be a living spirit in heaven. (to the Gnostics, like Plato, man is made up of spirit, soul and matter, with the spirit *(pneuma)* enveloped in a "fleshly garment," the female principle, which must be discarded to regain the spiritual self—primordial androgyny) *Gospel of Thomas*
>
> ..."the apostle who excels the rest ... the woman who knew the All ... [who reveals] the greatness of the revealer" and brings understanding to the other disciples. *Dialogue of the Saviour*

These new "scriptures" completely reframe the Magdalene's role among the disciples—and for all women who follow the way of the Christ. Her unique capacity to grasp the mystical and esoteric teachings that Jesus offered made her "teacher's pet," and her responses to his questions give us a significantly different theology from that which Christians have been taught for the past 1700 years. Clearly, for Jesus, unlike the later writers of epistles (meaning "letters") who called themselves "Paul," women were not required to "sit silently" while the men taught scripture.

As a result of these "new" scriptures, many women who have all their lives accepted the church's interpretation of the New Testament and quietly accepted the behind-the-scenes roles that the Roman (and Protestant) church has handed them, have started to reinterpret the biblical texts for themselves; they're beginning to use the Magdalene as an icon for their right to speak publicly about their spiritual lives.

The Church's Response

It was 35 years, one full generation, after the end of the Crusades—both in the Holy Land and in Languedoc—that the Dominican bishop of Genoa published his story of Mary Magdalene in his encyclopedia of the saints, *The Golden Legend*. That same year a new sepulcher bearing her remains was "discovered" outside of Marseille. Seeming to honor the Magdalene's wisdom and contribution, the story had the effect of moving her out of the mainstream of religious life into the backwaters—from the great Cathedral at Vezelay in Burgundy into the tiny, never-finished (to this day!) basilica of St. Maximin on a backroad in Provence—and, in the process, completely diverting the world's attention from any unusual ideas, or "pagan" power, she might represent.

Commenting on this whole process Lynn Picknett states, "The Church made strenuous efforts to suppress the Magdalene cult—which were largely successful..." Picknett asserts that the 1279 "discovery" of the sepulcher at St. Maximin with what she calls a "falsified document" explaining its presence there, combined with the placing of its basilica in the hands of the Dominicans and their later declaration of the Magdalene as their patron saint (hence controlling her veneration) was clearly an effort to regain control over the ongoing Mary Magdalene movement.[64]

The Root of the Matter

In her *Mary Magdalen, Myth and Metaphor,* Susan Haskins points out that, at each stage of the history of Europe, the Magdalene has been reshaped to address the most pressing needs of the moment. Penitent, Prostitute, Leading Apostle,

---

[64] Picknett, Lynn. *Mary Magdalene.* New York: Carroll & Graf, 2003, p. 99.

Bride, Mother of kings—all of these images are but partial glimpses of the complex and powerful being we call Mary Magdalene. All of them are seen through the limiting filter of the Hellenistic misogyny that was the essence of the Roman empire and dominates the Roman church. Even the Gnostic texts are essentially Greek in origin, with the same underlying assumption that women are, by nature, less capable and intelligent than men, so must be taught and led by them.

To understand the amazingly powerful hold that both the Virgin Mother and the Magdalene have on the people who adore them, it's essential to "step outside the box" of Aryan/Hellenistic thought. It became clear across Europe very early on that the Roman church placed little or no value on that which the rural pagans valued most highly—powerful, knowledgeable women, trained in the skills of healing, prophesy, ministering to the needs of others, and teaching. And when empire builders (religious or political) move into a territory and impose their values on the locals, the locals inevitably take their precious belief systems "underground."

So, to understand the role of the Marys in European-based Western culture, we must return to the mindset that was the norm throughout the world prior to the series of invasions out of the Caucasus and Taurus mountains that began 6000 years ago. This way of thinking remained the norm among the rural conservatives, the "pagans," who occupied the vast majority of Asia and Europe until well into the final years of the Inquisition—and still does in many places.

Hard as it is for us to accept, to the Asian and European pagan, it is not the woman who must be taught, but the man. Women, outside of the Aryan hegemony, are recognized as having a special kind of intelligence, a direct "knowing" of the essentials of philosophy, ecology, anatomy, and psychology, which a man must study and learn to understand. In western culture this is called "women's intuition," but in culture areas where the ancient Neolithic model of the universe

The Magdalene

is still alive (though sometimes buried beneath a veneer of patriarchy), it's simply a matter of women being made in the form of the creative source of all that is: embodying the dark womb-source, the life-giving breasts that flow with "milk and honey," and the loving, cradling arms and hips of the universe.

In short, for people raised outside the Aryan/Hellenistic tradition of Western culture, woman is honored as the representative of the divine. And for those people it's assumed that women are the ones who teach men how to heal and love and develop their creative capacity. It's understood that no man can achieve his full potential without the assistance—or mentorship—of a powerfully self-aware woman. Whether a shaman or a Sufi or even a Buddhist lama, the guidance and wisdom of the feminine is understood to be essential for fulfillment in all aspects of being.

We see this understanding expressed when we analyze the Arthurian stories, or pay attention to the words of the poems and songs of the *troubadors*. The Grail legends are, with virtually all "hero's journeys," very clear—the path to fulfillment requires the mystical/intuitive power, intelligence, and emotional support of a power-full woman. We see it also in the veneration of Tara and other female figures, including the *kundalini*, among Buddhists and Hindus.

Three Aspects, or forms of power, of the feminine

The reality of woman is that, unlike man, she has distinctly different stages in her life. While men simply move from being weak to strong to weak again, women go from being individual, almost genderless, virgins/maidens to being deeply female, bonded mothers/matriarchs to being individual, often isolated, elders/crones, with elevated testosterone levels and many masculine characteristics.

Each of these age/stages has significantly different powers and potentials associated with them. The maiden attracts, the mother creates and nurtures, and the elder teaches, heals, and prophesies.

In the herding-based Aryan/Hellenistic culture, the woman with greatest value is a virgin; her "unspoiled" nature makes her a "blank slate" for the man to impress his particular style upon. Hence, the Virgin has the highest status in the Roman church. The next most important is a mother: as long as the man's son needs her for food. The Roman church therefore honors the Madonna, the "Great Mother" who is virtually always seen holding an infant son, and often is breast-feeding him. In the Aryan/Hellenistic mindset, the elderly woman has no value and, as such, is totally dispensable—hence the ease with which widows and crones were burned as witches during the Inquisition.

In many ways, the combined stories of Mary Magdalene embody all the qualities of the divine feminine. As Mary of Bethany, she is the unmarried, but strong and independent woman who "goes with her heart," sitting at Jesus' feet, instead of following the cultural norms that her sister Martha (whose name means "householder") focuses on. As the beloved of Jesus, she is the Bride, anointing her beloved, walking with and supporting him in his work, weeping over his maimed body, and glorying

> These functions—healing, prophesying, ministering, and teaching—are described as "gifts of the Holy Spirit" in Paul's *Letter to the Romans*.

in his miraculous return. As the "Grail" or "Chalice" she fulfills her destiny as a woman, bearing a child, creating life where none existed before. As the beloved Teacher of Provence, she is the Matriarch, the *Pistis Sophia*: "faith and wisdom" embodied. As the reflective mystic hermit, ascending daily to be with her *bien-ami* (her "best-beloved"), she embodies the royal elder, or Crone, who walks the 2 worlds—this and the next.

She is also the Matriarch: her usual name in France, *La Madeleine*, becomes, with only the common shift from *r* to *l* over time, in the old Latin-French, *La Mader Reine,* or the Queen Mother, the one through whom, in ancient cultures, the king's power flowed.

For these "pagan" people, therefore, to eliminate the divine feminine from the story of the Son is to remove the source of his power. He cannot achieve his kingship, union with the godhead, without the feminine—hence the need for the women's presence in the garden at Gethsemane, at the foot of the cross, and in the sepulcher. This could be why the cathedral at Vezelay was so important for so many years—The Kingmaker resided there!

The Magdalene's Ubiquitous Image

So it's not too surprising that, somehow, no matter how her story is twisted, the Magdalene always emerges among the people as a woman embodying the power and potential of the current age. The very minimal descriptions of her in the New Testament leave a great deal to the imagination, and each generation has applied their own needs and standards to her image. She has been the darling of artists for generations, and her images abound—but there are far more images of her than most museum or cathedral catalogs admit.

While, like most women, I've always been curious about and drawn to this character in the gospels, it wasn't until I saw the many statues called "the Virgin," "the Madonna," "Our Lady," or even "Ste Anne" in France that I really felt the need to clarify and share a deeper understanding of the Magdalene and her role in our culture. She's everywhere! And usually mis-labeled.

To realize how ubiquitous the Magdalene's image is, it helps to know how to recognize her. Like all the other biblical characters occupying the many buildings of Europe, she has a particular iconography. John the Baptist has his platter; Jesus has his cross or his throne. Abraham has a boy and a ram; Moses has the tablets (and sometimes, horns on his head!) The symbols associated with images of Mary Magdalene include:

- <u>Height</u>—from early on, the Magdalene has been depicted as taller than, or set above, the men and women around her.
- <u>Unbound Hair</u>—Mary Magdalene has long been assumed to be the woman who washed Jesus' feet with her tears and dried them with her unbound hair. Since "proper women" would never let their hair down in public, this act is significant. The traditional assumption is that she must have been a prostitute, but some commentators suggest that, in fact, this act was part of the wedding ceremonies of the period—the beginning of intimacy between bride and groom. Unbound hair is also a sign of unmarried status in the Mediterranean region—while women wouldn't show their hair, young girls did. Often her hair is portrayed as red, in contrast with the Virgin Mary's, whose hair is typically portrayed as blond and tied back or well-hidden under a veil. The traditional assumption has been that red hair is associated with "naughtiness," but the fact that most of the mummies of Egyptian pharaohs, as well as the leaders of most Celtic tribes and the Mycenean and Cretan royalty were redheads suggests another hypothesis: red and blond hair, being typical of Aryans, were (and in many places still are) the sign of high-class, even royal, ancestry.
- <u>Book</u>—The book was, well into the Middle Ages, a common symbol for Wisdom, meaning comprehending the Word. Jesus is often portrayed as reading from a book, and Mary Magdalene is frequently portrayed reading, as the model for "la vie contemplative," the contemplative life (see p. 21). Interestingly, however, it was very unusual for a woman to be able to read prior to the Reformation—and in most of Europe, only courtesans did so.

The Magdalene's skull reliquary in St. Maximin, encased in golden, unbound hair.

- <u>Tower</u>—The Hebrew word *mgd* means, "to be eminent or distinguished, valued." The word for tower adds l, a reference to the heights, or God: *mgdl*. *Migdaleder* is the term used by the prophet Micah to describe the "tower of the flock." Magdalah was the name of the taller tower on the Temple at Jerusalem built by Herod a few years before Jesus' birth and today is the name of a village in Palestine. It's clear from both Old and New Testament that women lived in the Temple, and some commentators believe that Mary the Magdalene could have resided in the Magdalah. Also, *Migdol*, again meaning, "tower" is the name of a town in Egypt near the border with Palestine and stories about her life always include a trip to Egypt.
- <u>Chalice, jar, or urn</u>—Most images of the Magdalene include a covered jar or urn, presumably containing the oil of Jesus' anointing. Many show her with a cup

or chalice, which was usually associated with the covenant made by Jesus at the Last Supper, but sometimes with the cup that legends say Joseph of Arimathea used to collect the drops of Jesus' blood while he was on the cross—known by many as the Holy Grail.

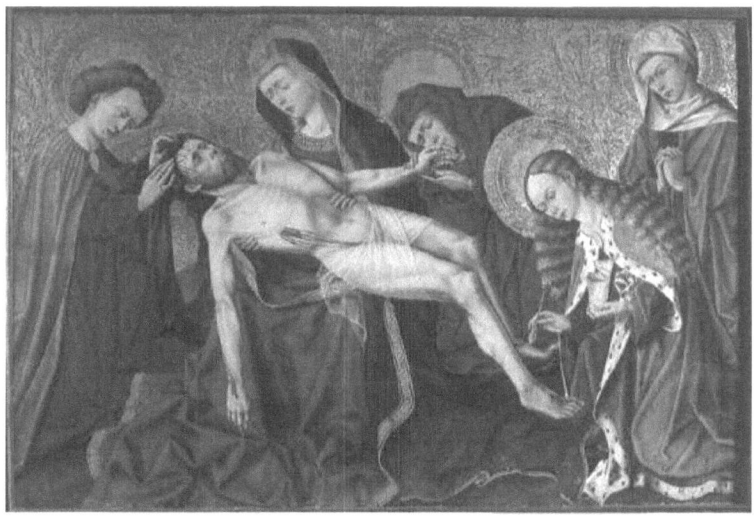

One of many images of The Magdalene Anointing the Crucified Jesus.

- Deep blue & red. Thomas Aquinas, great theologian and Doctor of the Church, declared these to be the Magdalene's colors about the year 1250. By contrast, the mother of Jesus was declared to wear pale blue and white, honoring her purity and her title of "Queen of Heaven"
- Skull—In addition to the enshrining of what was believed to be the Magdalene's skull in the Basilica of St. Maximin in Provence, she was often depicted with a skull. Some scholars believe the skull to be a reference to the Magdalene's relationship with John the Baptist.

And, as we have seen, Celtic peoples have enshrined the skulls of honored men and women since time immemorial.

- <u>Xs</u>—A common, but not often obvious, symbol associated with the Magdalene is the X, which may also be a +. Usually, there are several on the ground at her feet.

When these iconographic clues are taken into account, then the world of religious art takes a whole new spin—and the Magdalene is, truly, everywhere. Thousands of paintings and sculptures have two or more of these iconographic clues.

"The Virgin" with blond, unbound hair, a deep blue cloak, and an open book at the Musée de Cluny, Paris.

Two of my favorites are the "Twelve Apostles" with its central figure with flowing hair in her scarlet gown holding a chalice, and "The Assumption of the Virgin" wearing deep blue and scarlet, with flowing hair, rising above a city that is clearly the port of Marseille—both of them on display at the *Musee de Moyen Age* in Paris.

Then there are:
- Dozens of depictions called "Virgin and child" and "Assumption of the Virgin" where the central figure has long, unbound red or reddish-blond hair and is wearing red or deep blue (and some of the children being held are girls!)
- Dozens of statues of "the Virgin" with long, unbound hair, reading a book
- And, of course, the unrestored "Last Supper" by Leonardo Da Vinci, in which "John," the person by Jesus' right hand, is very feminine, wearing scarlet and deep blue, with no beard, a broach, and unbound reddish-blond hair—and is the same model as the mother Mary in the "Virgin of the Rocks" (p. 187, above). The restored version of the Last Supper has clothed him/her in the Virgin's colors of pale blue and white!

The central portion of DaVinci's *Last Supper* before restoration. "John" is to the viewer's left of Jesus (His right), with Peter's hand across the throat.

The Magdalene

Clearly, a significant number of paintings and statues that have been labeled "The Virgin" or "Madonna" turn out to be images that fit the iconography of the Magdalene, rather than of Jesus' mother. As Margaret Starbird has suggested, Jesus' mother has carried the burden of both Marys for a very long time.

An Explanatory Story

Many books have been written with alternative interpretations of the Magdalene's life and role in the story of Jesus, some of which are listed in the Resources section at the back of this book. All of them contain elements of what probably actually happened, but perhaps it's worth considering another possibility:

> For the first few days after Y'shuh's resurrection, Mara lives in an ecstatic "high." It worked! All the training and traveling and planning and arranging came together and her beloved lives! Surely now balance will be restored in the land; surely now all will see that it's not the *things* that matter but our relationship with Spirit/Mother, or, as Y'shuh called it *Abba*/Father.
>
> It isn't long, though, before she realizes that, while the Romans were willing to put up with the familiar ritual, they aren't about to let the reality of the resurrection become known. She also sees, to her great dismay, that the men who've been following her beloved and listening to him all these years don't believe her own power and worse, don't have the vaguest notion of the importance of what has happened—they're simply overwhelmed by it all. She also sees that, as always happen when people grieve, they want to lash out—and Peter, especially has done so toward Mara who, he seems to feel, is somehow responsible for their loss.
>
> So Mara spends a lot of time with the other women who've been part of this whole process. The elder Mara, her mother-in-law, is a great help. She, too, has been left behind, when her beloved Y'shef ascended. And she, too, knows the love and strength of She-who-Is-from-all-time. Her "sister" Salome continues to be a great source of strength—and information. Salome's mother, Herodias, maintains her role as priestess while living in Herod's

palace and knows the importance of what has just been completed; she keeps them up to date on Roman and Herod's plans. With the other Miriams they all continue to pray and hold the beloved Anointed One, with all the people they are connected with, in the love of the Mother, as is their duty and joy.

Whenever Y'shuh appears, Mara feels as if the whole world has lit up. She wants to know what it's like on "the other side" and listens raptly as he tells her about his experiences since that morning at the sepulcher. Everything that she's always loved about him is enhanced: where before he was loving, now he embodies love, even radiates it! Where before, he spoke words of wisdom, now he has, clearly, united with Universal Wisdom, so that not only his words, but every action, every moment he is present, is filled with the deep understanding of one who Knows. Where before, she found him attractive and alluring, now he is Beauty incarnate—totally desirable and wonderfully uplifting, just to see.

His visits are wonderful, filled with the excitement of new experiences and discoveries. But when the men are gathered, the tone is more subdued, as if their fear and awe somehow dampens his impact.

She listens as he explains to them what has happened and what will happen—and what they need to do to grow in the power and their ability to share what he's taught them. And she sees how confused they are: theirs is the world of the Temple and its laws. They don't understand how the Way is woven into the Law, so they don't even hear what he's telling them.

Finally, Y'shuh realizes that, as long as they can see and hear him they will not take on their own power or grow in their own understanding and capacity. Reluctantly, he accepts the fact that he must leave them on their own, and he tells them so. Again, they don't seem to understand, but he wastes no further effort explaining.

In their private time together, Mara and Y'shuh work things out, as they always have. There will be two events: the first will be his very visible Ascension, to give the disciples a sense of closure. The second will be a felt experience of the power of his Spirit—at the Pentecost, the celebration of the "new offering" fifty days after Passover, when many observant Hebrews will be in Jerusalem. In the meantime, Mara, too, will depart, so the men will be truly on their own.

Mara contacts their Nazarene "brother" Y'shef, the tin merchant from Arimathea, and the three of them plan out the details. While Y'shuh's disciples are gathering for Pentecost, she will leave the country as part of Y'shef's caravan into Egypt. There, she'll connect with family members in Alexandria, and maybe take a few months to study at the library there. At the beginning of the year, when Y'shef's ship heads north, she'll go along with him and visit some of the places that Y'shuh enjoyed visiting during his training and now enjoys in his new form.

When Mara shares this plan with the other women, they agree. Some, including her "sisters" Salome and Martha, ask to join her. Her mother-in-law, however, says she's been to all those places and feels drawn to join the priestesses in the great temple at Ephesus.

As they always have, they set up the arrangements for the disciples' meetings, planning meals and sleeping arrangements and making sure everyone's needs are met. With Mara the Magdalene leaving the area, a new Mara must support the group, and the mother of John Mark volunteers; her home in Jerusalem will be more than adequate to meet their needs. The other women provide her with a purse full of talents and make their own servants available to her to help.

The days turn into weeks and Mara realizes that she has not yet visited the Women's House. She checks her moon chart and realizes that, yes, it's true—she is, indeed, carrying the seed of her beloved. When she tells Y'shuh, he looks at her with that look that says, "Of course you are! How could you not be?" And she realizes he has known about it all along.

The plans go without a hitch. Y'shuh's public ascension is glorious and his disciples finally begin to see the parallels between his work and that of Elijah and Moses before him. Mara leaves soon after, riding a donkey across Gaza into Egypt with Y'shef and his caravan, while Y'shuh's mother prepares for the Pentecost event, to be followed by her journey to Ephesus. The event at Pentecost is spectacular: hundreds of people bear witness to the transformation of Y'shuh's disciples into men of power, and hundreds more are attracted to the teachings by the gifts that Y'shuh's *shem*, or Spirit, has given them.

Dozens of others also have the experience of being in Y'shuh's Spirit and experiencing the same gifts. They become curious and start asking questions; now the disciples are required to become teachers.

The trip to Egypt is uneventful. Y'shef and his helpers are most respectful, aware that their guest is true royalty. Mara spends most of the journey in a semi-trance state, sometimes supporting the other women as they hold the power for the Pentecost event, and sometimes communing with Y'shuh and the child within.

Alexandria in Egypt is everything wonderful about Jerusalem multiplied a thousand times. The library is overwhelmingly huge. The Hebrew community is delightfully welcoming. The sun is unbearably hot. The synagogues are fascinatingly alive with intellectual explorations of *Torah* and *Talmud*. The temples to the Goddess are filled with strange images and languages, but fortunately, they follow the same ritual sequence and bear witness to the same loving, nurturing Power.

Mara spends the remaining months of her pregnancy taking it all in, studying in the library, and building relationships with her spiritual "sisters." When the time comes for the child to be born, she is ready. Using the ancient methods of breathing, visualization, and empathic rapport, she becomes a mother with ease. Nor does it surprise her a bit when, as the child emerges from her body, she looks up and there is Y'shuh, smiling, loving her.

The time comes when Y'shef is ready to leave. Mara, however, decides to remain in Egypt to study and teach and raise the child. Y'shef promises to check in on her each year as he makes his annual journey to the mines and merchants in the area.

Mara settles into a routine of visiting with her "sisters" in the garden while the child sleeps or plays with one of the other women. During these times she shares the lessons of her own training and, with some, expands on them with the ideas she has developed from traveling and communing with Y'shuh. Each morning, just before dawn, she goes to a quiet place, an "upper room" where, when she can still her mind and body, she experiences the deep peace that she felt in Y'shuh's presence. And sometimes he appears in the room with her and shares his new experiences and wisdom. On rare occasions, he even joins her as she teaches in the garden.

In a matter of weeks, the word is out. The Magdalene is teaching! Sometimes the Anointed One teaches, too! Scores of women and a few men start to show up in the garden where Mara shares the wisdom that she has to offer.

Then, one day, Mara looks up and sees Judas the Twin (called Thomas Didymus by the Greeks and Romans)—the disciple who needed to see and touch Y'shuh's wounds before he could believe who it was. She is delighted! She ends class for the day and invites him in. He, however, is troubled. The disciples have decided to split up and spread the word, but he doesn't feel as if he's really understood what Y'shuh was teaching. Mara, clearly, understands the teachings; would she help him? Mara laughs gently and suggests that he spend the night in her meditation space, the "upper room."

The next morning, he comes into the garden so excited that he can hardly contain himself! "He's here! He came to me! The master came to me and taught me!" Mara smiles and encourages him to tell her all about it, indicating to her scribe to write down everything her guest says. And so begins the Twin's own private instruction in the philosophy of the Savior—and the text that will later be known as *The Gospel of Thomas the Twin*.

The process goes on for some weeks and then, once more, he walks into her garden—a changed man. Where before stood an uncertain, frustrated, fearful being, now stood an upright, powerful man, sure of himself and of his gifts. Mara acknowledges him and invites him to share some of what he has learned with the group. He does so and is transformed once more: love, like light, seems to radiate from him. The listeners are totally enraptured by his words, and some of them inch forward, wanting to be closer, to feel the presence of this master teacher.

When the sun has set and the last seeker has left the garden, Mara hands Thomas a papyrus scroll, telling him that these are the words he has shared with her each morning. It's a copy of the one that the scribe wrote as he was talking and he may take it with him on his journey, for, clearly, he is ready. They embrace as brother and sister, knowing that he will be leaving the next morning to find a ship to India, where he has been called to teach.

The years pass and Mara realizes that she will be in Egypt for a full cycle of Tammuz, the Daystar. Then her daughter, the *Sarah* or "Princess," will be old enough to travel. One more cycle after that and she will be old enough for the *heiros gamos*, herself. Mara, Salome, and Martha settle into their lives, developing their power in this strange country.

Each year, as promised, Y'shef, her "brother" from Arimathea, comes by to meet with her. They talk of his travels as a tin merchant and of the events in Jerusalem. Mara learns that a man named Saul, a Greek Jew raised in Tarsus, has been working with the Romans and the temple, trying to wipe out the disciples' community there. She is concerned. Later, during one of their visits in her "upper room," she mentions it to Y'shuh: surely there's some way to stop this persecution? Surely this is a good but misguided man! Again, they work out a plan. Saul will be headed out to Damascus soon; Y'shuh will appear before him, out in the open, where he can't run away from the experience, somewhere along the road. There he will show Saul the consequences of his actions and the possibility of a new direction. Mara, in the meantime, will hold the vision of a conversion to contribute her own power to the event.

Time takes its course and finally the child is old enough to travel. Mara looks her over carefully and realizes that she's nearly black from playing in the sun her whole life! No one would recognize either parent in this "dark but comely" child. With Martha and Salome, she prepares for the journey. Y'shef normally arrives near the summer solstice, spending some weeks trading up and down the river of Egypt, then ships out northward at high summer, to arrive in Britain at the fall equinox. She wants to be ready when he is.

Y'shef arrives on schedule and is expecting them to join him. When all is prepared, they board the ship. How cunningly arranged everything is! There's very little space for people, with all the cargo and their household belongings, but what's there is just right to meet their needs. The first day out of port is glorious! The brilliant blue of the sky, the many-colored buildings of the city, the other ships and boats on the water, all make a wonderful scene. Mara and her daughter and friends stand on the back deck, watching, until it all disappears behind the horizon.

The first days at sea are very pleasant, indeed. They stop at a couple of ports and exchange cargo, then go on. Mara realizes, as she watches the dolphins playing and senses the life all around her, that it's no accident that the words for "mother" and "sea" are virtually the same. She tastes the sea water and realizes that the salt in it is almost the same as in blood. She sees the men catch and cook fish and realizes that these men are very much like the men Y'shuh chose to follow him along the Sea of Galilee.

Then the storm hits. At first she revels in it, the power of the wind, the mixture of rain and splashes from the waves, but soon she realizes she's in the crew's way and goes below. There she and the other women form a circle of power for the safety of the ship and all aboard. Even Sarah, who has been observing their rituals in these tight quarters, joins this time. In the circle, they feel the peace of the Goddess and the protection of Y'shuh's Spirit. Soon they are totally unaware of what's going on around them; all are simply aware that all is well, and Sarah goes to sleep.

The next morning, the storm has ended, and all aboard the ship are safe, but the hull has been damaged and the cargo is in danger. Y'shef informs them that they'll have to pull in to shore to repair the ship, but they've lost their rudder, so will have to guide the ship with the sails and the distribution of weight, heading north to the first landfall they see.

Immediately Mara and her companions go to work. First, they make sure that anything not absolutely essential is discarded. Then they re-organize their quarters so that everything is as close to the center of the ship as possible. Finally, again, they form their circle. As they had at the foot of the cross and during the Sabbath following; as their "sisters" had in Jerusalem during the Pentecost; they set their intention and hold it: a good landing in a supportive community; easy repairs for the ship; safety for all. Little Sarah comes and goes as they hold the circle, her curiosity about what's happening overcoming her desire to be part of the women's effort.

Suddenly there's a shout on the deck. Sarah runs up to see; the lookout has seen a figure out in front of the ship, seeming to guide it. Sarah looks and giggles—she's seen this one before: *"Abba!"* she calls, and the figure waves. She runs up to the prow of the ship watching her father skimming across the water in front, feeling the ship following as if on a rope. Part of her wants to be out there with him, but mostly she just enjoys watching. After a while she's aware that she's not alone—just about every man on the ship is watching, amazed at what's happening. The women break up their circle and join them.

Soon, rocks appear in front of them. The figure begins to fade away as the ship comes to rest in a quiet little cove. Then, looking up, beyond the rocks they see distant hills and wisps of smoke from chimneys; they realize they are safe. Prayers of gratitude in many languages are expressed—and Mara and Sarah say a silent thanks to Y'shuh for his help.

A few of the men climb off the ship and onto the rocks. They realize that they're on a small island in a large harbor, and that a good-sized town, with a temple, straddles the mouth of the river across the bay. When they return, Y'shef holds a council with the crew and the women to decide what to do. There's a landing-boat on board that could take a few at a time into the harbor-town. He thinks it's one he's stopped at before, along the southern coast of Provincia, on the border of the empire. If so, then truly, all is well, because these are friendly people with good hearts and a strong awareness of the divine working in their lives.

Then they hear a shout from across the water—even as they've been deliberating about what to do, the harbormaster has been coming out to check on their ship. And yes, he remembers Y'shef and is glad to be of service to this honorable trader in trouble. He offers to take Y'shef in to shore to arrange for repairs to his ship and send boats out to collect his passengers and cargo.

Mara, Salome, Martha, and Sarah get their remaining belongings together in preparation for the boat ride across the harbor. As she clambers down the ship's ladder into the boat, Mara says a little prayer of thanksgiving for this gallant vessel that has carried them safely through the storm—and for her beloved Y'shuh who guided them into this welcoming spot. Soon, they are being rowed across the water by strong-armed sailors who speak a language they don't recognize.

Y'shef and the harbormaster have arranged for the local temple priestesses to meet the women and provide shelter for them. The women are gracious, and, in spite of the language differences—they limp along in what little they all know of Roman Latin—they recognize one another as kindred spirits. Soon they are comfortably housed in apartments around the temple—much as they had been when they stayed in Jerusalem and again at Alexandria—and, after a warm meal, the whole group sleeps.

For several days they have no contact with Y'shef, but they can see the boats going back and forth across the harbor to the little island, so they relax and settle into the routine of this new temple. At first, it feels strange: this is a temple to the Mother, alone, without the ongoing sacrifices to Yahweh demanded under Mosaic law. Yet it's clear that the men in the community honor the temple and its priestesses even more than they did in Jerusalem—and the daily and weekly prayer cycle is much the same.

One of the temple women has become their guide and sponsor. Using the little bit of Latin that they have in common, she teaches them words in the language of this region, *Provincia*. She shows them a map, pointing to where this harbor is located, and Salome quickly recognizes that Herod's villa is only a day or so away. This is both welcome and disturbing news: Herod was no friend of the Nazarenes, yet Salome, as part of his family, will have rights to at least visit the villa. It also means that there is a Hebrew community in the area—with its familiar language and customs. The women feel their bodies relax with this realization, as if they'd been carrying a burden and were now relieved of it.

At first, it's hard for Mara to find a place where she can be alone long enough to settle her thoughts and invite Y'shuh's presence. After several days, however, she finds a corner of the temple garden, against a rock wall, that feels very like the garden in which Y'shef's sepulcher had been located. There, in the first light of day, she can feel the deep quiet and peace that allows her to connect with him and, with the sun's rays low on the horizon, see him when he responds.

While she is preparing to meet with him, she reflects on this strange relationship in which she may see her beloved only now and then, and yet never feels separated from him. He's always with her, always guiding and supporting her every action. It's as if the loving, nurturing Presence of the Goddess has taken form in the love of her Anointed beloved.

Finally, he arrives, and, as she had at their first encounter in that garden so far away, she rushes to embrace this man who has become so much more than a man; this beloved who is so much more than a lover. And again, he warns her away—"Don't hold on to me; I am not part of this place, your own place, now." Mara falls to the ground at his feet, confused: will she not see him again? Is he abandoning her in this strange place?

Y'shuh reaches out and draws her up to his eye level. Gently, he reminds her of how they worked to make it possible for the men who had followed him to continue to work in his nature, through the event at the Pentecost. He repeats some of the words of praise he's used in years past when she was able to express a difficult idea clearly. He encourages her to go on teaching, healing, and ministering to the people around her, as they had done together in Judea and Galilee. Finally, he tells her that here is her ministry; here in this new country. Here she and their daughter will found a new nation—a place where God is honored as Mother and Father, where men and women respect each other as equals, and where the "2-law" of Moses, along with the Golden Rule, will be the basis for all interaction, where *Torah* and *Talmud* would be less important than the mystical texts of the Essenes, and praise and gratitude would replace suffering and sacrifice, as the Kingdom of Heaven becomes manifest in each person, household, village, and temple.

Mara listens, letting tears fall where they may. All kinds of feelings fill her: joy in his presence, fear of the task before her, pride in his faith in her, wonder that such a thing could be, and more. She can hardly take in his words, but the disciplined mind is remembering every detail, even as the heart overflows with emotion.

They talk for a timeless hour, then, as the sun rises in the sky, the bright light seems to envelop him in a glowing cloud. Again, she leans toward him; this time to be met by a touch so intense, so penetrating that her forehead will remember it for years to come. She looks down, then up again—Y'shuh is disappearing into the cloud. This visit, perhaps the last, is over.

Mara closes her eyes and breathes for a while, processing what she has heard, and storing the memory. When she opens them, she sees that she is not alone—several of the temple novices have wandered into the garden and are clearly in shock at what they have seen. When they see her see them, they start chattering like squirrels in a mixture of the Provincial language and Latin. Try as she might, though, the only word she can understand is *Maximinus*, "the Greatest." She realizes they are asking if this is the Anointed, consort to the Goddess, and she nods, smiling, "yes; it is he." The novices, clearly awed by the possibility, immediately drop to their knees in obeisance as they realize that, in Mara, they are seeing the power of the Goddess, embodied.

Suddenly everything at the temple has changed. That day Mara and her "sisters" and daughter are immediately moved from the transient quarters into what can only be the rooms of the high priestess. No objection or question is considered. The simple gowns they'd been offered while their travel-worn garments were cleaned and repaired are replaced with fine linens and soft woolens. Mara is astonished at the transformation, but begins to realize it was meant to be when she sees that they are dyed in the colors of her robes back home: the bright red of the Nazarene and the deep blue of the Mother.

So Mara becomes the high priestess; the representative of the Goddess and the *Myrrophore* for her new home. At first her duties are focused on learning the language and the rituals of this new temple and town. She is given a secretary and shown a well-stocked library in the temple grounds, with scrolls in every known language, describing the history of the place and the names that the Lady has borne, here. These are a great help as she "learns the ropes" of the role she has been thrust into.

Y'shef visits periodically, delighted that his "sister" has found such a good home. Then, when the repairs are complete on his ship, he continues his journey north, promising to return each year.

Her "sisters" enjoy the quiet comfort of the temple life for some time, but after a few months they realize that the group will not be traveling on and they, too, must become teachers and healers in their own right. Martha, in particular, feels called to the wandering teaching life that they had known with Y'shuh. She arranges with one or two of the novices to let her travel with them to their homes, then returns to announce that she has found her calling in a town called Tarascon, several days' walk from here. There is a joyful, tearful parting, during which Sarah promises to come stay with her "aunt Martha" as soon as she has completed her language studies at the temple.

Soon after, Salome receives word from her mother that her step-father's villa is unoccupied and available for her. She puts off leaving for as long as possible, but, finally, the pain of staying is greater than the pain of departing, so she, too, moves on.

Mara and Sarah are left in the temple, learning the new language and new customs even as Mara is expected to preside over the seasonal rituals of the Goddess and provide healing and counseling for those whose complaints are beyond the skill of the other women. Word about her visit in the garden has traveled far and she is aware of a level of respect that she never felt in Jerusalem or Galilee. Men and women come to the temple to observe the rituals and, as she becomes more fluent, they invite her to come bless their homes and boats and tools, and to teach them.

Sarah grows up in the new surroundings, rapidly picking up the language and learning the lessons of the novices along with them. She still spends a lot of time outside in the Mediterranean sun, so remains darkly tanned. As Mara had anticipated, she begins her menses soon after the Daystar has completed its cycle and, with the other young novices, she is honored as the Goddess in her maiden form. Mara, seeing her daughter in the customary white gown, wonders if Y'shuh can see his beautiful daughter—and immediately, the spot on her forehead where he last touched her throbs, as if to say, "Of course! I am always with you."

Y'shef comes to visit soon after, with the news that the man once known as Saul of Tarsus now calls himself Paul and his Greek ideas are causing some friction with the more traditional messianic Jews of Jerusalem. He's telling people that they don't have to follow Mosaic law to follow Y'shuh and experience his Spirit. Y'shef also tells her that her mother-in-law is safely in Ephesus, working with the priestesses in the temple there—much as Mara is here.

The next months rapidly turn into years. Mara's power is now legendary across *Provincia* and into *Iberia* and the Frankish territories. Sarah, a priestess in her own right, is preparing for the *hieros gamos* with the son of the region's Prince and Princess—a man who is younger than her, having been born soon after they arrived, when Mara healed his parents of their barrenness. As the date approaches, Mara realizes that she is ready for this; it's time to retire from her public duties and focus on her own spiritual development—much as the elder Mara, her mentor and mother-in-law, had done before her.

After weeks of careful planning to ensure that all is in balance above, below, and within, the joining occurs. The feast goes on for days, as all the region rejoices in the renewal this union brings. Sarah is radiant as the bride, and speaks her part—the ancient lines spoken by all the Innanas and Ises before her and documented in the ancient "Song of Solomon."

Her handsome partner, her beloved Anointed One, is resplendent in his royal robes. They are perfectly matched and Mara is pleased. More, even as she watches, she feels a warmth on her forehead that tells her that her own beloved is pleased, as well. And of course, the Goddess smiles on the day with radiant sunshine and a light, cool breeze. The lunar eclipse that night is perfect and the Daystar the next morning shines in all his/her glory.

Now Mara needs to find the next step in her life. She arranges for Sarah and the other women of the temple to manage without her and embarks on the long-delayed journey with Y'shef northward into Brittany and Eire. There he settles her into his home at Avebury in Cornwall, while he tours his tin mines and arranges the trade of the goods he has brought for the metals needed by his Greek and Roman clients. Mara uses the time to meet with the local wisewomen and learn their ways. They show her their well, which sometimes runs red, recalling to her mind the pool of Shiloam at the Temple in Jerusalem. She shares some of her own understandings and introduces them to the Sabbath ceremony of wine and bread, explaining how her beloved Anointed One had transmuted water into wine and wine into the "blood of life," demonstrating the oneness of the Goddess' fruits, women's menstrual flow, and the blood of the sacrifice.

As the harvest time ends and the nights become long, Y'shef turns his loaded ships southward, and Mara joins him on the journey homeward. She spends most of the journey on the deck of the ship, watching the waves and dolphins during the day and the stars at night, feeling pulled to a new life, a new way of being.

The trip is uneventful and they arrive safely at the familiar harbor. Mara is pleased to see that Sarah is thriving and the temple is doing well. She rests a few days, advising and counseling as requested, then feels that call again.

In response to this deep restlessness, she packs up and begins to travel northward along the river, toward the town her "sister" Martha has called home these many years. Though they have corresponded, they haven't seen each other since those first weeks after their arrival in this new land.

On the way, she stops to visit her "brother" Lazarus, who came out with Y'shef on one of his annual trips in order to be with his "sisters" and is now teaching and healing in a little town not far up the river. It's been years since they spent any time together and Lazarus expresses some concern: Mara is aging and tired; her energy is disturbingly low; she needs to reconnect with her Source— not just in the feminine, as the Goddess, but with the masculine, as her beloved Y'shuh and the Father God.

So Mara makes a little side journey, up into the woods, where a sacred well and a cave have been dedicated to the Goddess since time immemorial and where, tradition has it, the sacred union takes place each high summer. Early the next morning, in the ancient woods, nestled against the base of the rock escarpment, she leaves her attendants behind. Walking up the trail, she feels that same sense of peace that she used to feel in the garden when Y'shuh would visit. She finds a log to rest on near the spring and looks down at the ground, feeling the spot on her forehead where he last touched her, simply appreciating the bond between them.

After a moment, she becomes aware of a shadow. She looks up and there, before her, is Y'shuh, beckoning to her to stand next to him. Without hesitation she leaps to his side. He takes her hand and, wonderfully, they begin to lift above the trees until they are looking into a large cave—the cave of the Goddess. Y'shuh points and says, "this will be your new school and I will once again be your teacher." He takes her into the shelter of the great cavern and shows her the public area, where she will be able to teach the many who come there each year, and a hidden area at the back, where she will be able to sleep and bathe. Mara, whose life is filled with miracles of healing and transformation, is nonetheless overwhelmed by the experience. She hardly sees anything but the eyes of her beloved and, again, must rely on the disciplined mind to track and recall what is being said, for she is not consciously aware of anything except his presence.

Finally, they descend again to the spring in the woods below the cave. As their feet touch the ground, Y'shuh says, "there's so much I want to share with you! You have done your work well, but now we can go even further! Together!"

As before, the light of the sun seems to light the air around her beloved and, as he steps away, she can barely see him for the glow. She watches as the glow fades away and then she rests there, in the silence, taking it all in.

After a while, Mara hears the voices of her attendants as they clamber up the trail, speaking excitedly, asking about the man she was with and inquiring as to her safety. But they stop as soon as they see her. It's clear from the expression on her face who was here, and with one voice they say, "The *Maximus!*" And she nods. Immediately, they go to their knees before her, aware that something truly wonderful has happened here, while Mara sits there with them in a deep prayer of thanksgiving.

The trip to see Martha is aborted and they return to Sarah at the temple to plan for Mara's retirement to the holy grotto. In a matter of days, all that she will need is packed and ready. The time has come and Mara feels as excited as if this were her own *hieros gamos* all over again—which, she realizes, it may well be. As the two of them embrace, Sarah promises to visit her at midwinter on the feast of the nativity and at high summer on the feast of the crowning—transferring these ancient temple rituals to the grotto so they can do them together in the place where they had been done in the misty past.

So Mara begins her last journey—up the river, then up into the deep mountain forest, and along the steep, winding, cliff-side trail to the grotto where she will once more be united with her lover. She realizes that much of what he is experiencing now is due to her teaching, that he now has much to teach her—and that, united, they have always accomplished far more than either could alone. Her attendants help her to set up the space that will be her new home, then retire to a small farm below, where they will grow the food to nourish themselves and her, along with any pilgrims coming through, and remain ready to assist at any time, but not in any way to intrude on her isolation.

The days of settling in pass quickly. Mara develops a comfortable routine of pre-dawn prayer, a light meal of dried fruits and water, more prayer, a few hours tending herbs she's planted around the grotto and working on the ancient scrolls she has been studying and translating, more prayer, a light mid-afternoon meal of cheese and herbs and water, a few more hours of study, more prayer, and then appreciating the sunset and stars until sleep. Some of her prayers are the ritual prayers she has used since childhood, spoken as a way to begin to feel that state of union with the divine that is so much a part of who she is. Some of her time in prayer is spent focusing on the people in her life who seem to be calling her attention; bringing them into that same state of union. After years of being surrounded by people, she finds the silence somehow comforting, and the small creatures of the air and soil quickly become her friends.

The days and nights become a blur, one running into another in this easy routine. Sunny days, stormy days, incredibly clear nights, gray and foggy nights—they all begin to feel the same, and life is good.

Toward the end of one such peaceful pre-dawn hour, Mara senses she is not alone. She opens her eyes and there, once again, is her beloved! "Welcome," he says, "to the kingdom of heaven." His warm, loving eyes fill her heart with both peace and longing; comfort and desire, but most of all, with a deep sense of love. This time they embrace, as they used to in her youth. "Come," he says, "I will show you the world as I see it."

Mara rises to her feet and almost at once realizes that her feet no longer touch the stone. They are flying out of the cave, above the still-dark valley floor below. Higher and higher they go, until she can see the curve of the horizon and the endless sea. Always at the edge of the dawn, they fly over forests and mountains, lakes and rivers, cities and deserts. She sees the Roman troops marching along, flocks of sheep on hillsides; cattle and horses at pasture; farmhouses and villages; bears and deer at the edges of forests, and whales rising from the sea. Holding the hand of her beloved, she is enraptured by the beauty and the scale. So much life! The Mother is truly great!

They return to the grotto as the sun begins to rise. In the shadow of the cave, she can still see him clearly as they talk of possibilities for the future. Then, as he rises to go, the sun's light reaches him and again, the air around him seems to glow as he fades from view.

The weather turns colder and Mara continues with the new practices and exercises Y'shuh has given her. More and more, she feels the power of the Spirit enlivening the cells of her body—and moving out beyond her body to touch the lives of those who enter into her awareness as she prays. She begins to feel her sense of Self moving with the power, until she can actually see and touch the people she is thinking about. They don't see her, but they seem to respond to her healing touch.

The days are much shorter now, and Mara realizes that the feast of the nativity is drawing near. She sets out the flag that is her signal to her attendants to come assist her in preparing the grotto for the annual event. Dozens, if not hundreds, of people will make the pilgrimage to this site, as they have for thousands of years, to honor the birth of the new Son of the Sun. All must be made ready for them.

The feast day arrives. The sun has "stood still," rising and setting in the same place, far to the south, for three days now: the night is very long and the day is gray. It's time to call forth the new sun. As promised, Sarah arrives with her beloved, and Mara is delighted to see that she will be bearing a child come spring. All of their attendants plus dozens of local farmers participate in the ritual with them. With fire and prayer and song they join their will and intention together—with all of humanity—to call the new sun into their lives. In the middle of this ritual, Mara becomes aware that Y'shuh is standing among them; unnoticed except by her, smiling and singing with the others. Then, just as the sun's first rays touch the sky, he signals to her that he will return and disappears out of the cave into the light.

Over the next weeks and months, Mara continues to grow in power and skill. She learns to visit each of the people she loves, projecting her awareness into the form of her body wherever she chooses to go, visiting the other Miriams she's known, including her mother-in-law, and even dropping in on Y'shef one evening, at his home in Arimathea. By spring she is able to monitor her daughter's pregnancy and to reassure her that all is well with the child. She is even able to attend the birth without leaving the grotto—and she's not at all surprised when she sees Y'shuh there, as well.

One day, Mara feels an urgent call from her mother-in-law—something important is happening at Ephesus! Almost without effort, she feels her Self standing in the presence of the elder Mara and her younger "brother" John. Roman soldiers are trying to get into the house where they have been living and teaching, to imprison them for not bowing before the emperor's statue. Mara sees it all and acts immediately, without thinking. She walks out the door of the house to the soldiers, telling them there is nothing they want here; she will go with them to show them what they seek.

At first, they seem confused; the voice seems much more powerful than the woman they see. Then, when she continues to walk toward them, they get angry, telling her to stop. She does so, but their fear and anger have begun to have an effect on her: the sense of being there, talking to them, wavers a little; she lacks full control of the projected image. One of the men shouts, "Where'd she go?" Another answers "over here!" and plunges his sword into her. Mara is so shocked by this that she faints—in both places. Her projected body in Ephesus collapses onto the ground, but begins to fade into the light. Her physical body in the grotto is collapsed in a heap on the chill stone floor.

Slowly, Mara comes into awareness; she's still in both places, but the Ephesus projection is very weak, she opens her eyes there and realizes that her projection is barely solid, almost transparent. She blesses all who are present—soldiers and bystanders, alike. Then she with-

> draws her awareness from that place and back into the cave, clutching the ache in her side where the Roman sword pierced her projected body. Slowly, painfully, she crawls toward her bed, knowing she must remain conscious long enough to heal this psychic wound, and warm enough to prevent physical damage to this body.
> She pulls blankets over her and leans back, feeling the Life that is the Goddess flow through her and into every muscle and bone and organ. As she has every day since she moved here, she visualizes a shower of light flowing over her and through her, touching and healing every part of her body. Then she extends the healing out beyond her body through the forest and across the valley, giving to the world that which she is ready to receive. Finally, feeling that deep peace that tells her the work is done, she curls up and sleeps.
> When she awakens, Y'shuh, now known by those around her as *Maximus*, "the Great One" is sitting by her bed, looking at her with pride and the deep love that they share. She realizes that he knows what she has done and is pleased. They smile at each other in wordless communion as he offers her a sip of wine from a crystal cup. All is well, and the best is yet to come.

Consider the possibility. "The Underground Church of Mary Magdalene" in the South of France is alive and well, and tied to the legends of her arrival there, her teaching at the Diana temple in Marseille and her long residence at *Ste. Baume*, on the escarpment above the town called St. Maximin. Hundreds make the pilgrimage up the cliff on *Lammas*, the 1st of August, the ancient day for crowning the king, as well as Christmas, the feast of the nativity, following the winter solstice.

Still, Picknett wonders,
> Which came first? Were the legends the product of the cult invented in order to establish a connection with the historical figure, or did the cult derive from a movement established by, or centered on, the real person?[65]

---

[65] Picknett, Lynn. *Mary Magdalene*. New York: Carroll & Graf, 2003, p. 97.

Or, perhaps, these images and stories of the Magdalene, like those of the Mother Mary, are not representations of a person, at all, but are depictions of the matriarchal form of the Goddess, the divine feminine, *Shekinah, Sophia,* the archetypal *anima* that resides within all and calls us to honor her. Perhaps all of the Christian stories are simply adaptations of pre-existing stories of the Goddess, as the Greek story of Demeter and Persephone was drawn from the ancient Sumerian story of the search of the God-Mother for her lover.

> Mary Magdalene is so much a part of the culture of Provence that thousands of shell-shaped cookies called "Madeleines" have been baked there on her feast day (and now all year!) since the Middle Ages.

Or maybe the stories we hear today are slightly distorted or misunderstood versions of events and people that actually existed. *La Madeleine* was clearly a major figure in Medieval France: a source of great power and authority. Perhaps the story of the Magdalene was adapted to make her fill the place of an actual "Queen Mother," which is what *La Mader Reine,* means. Or it may have been adapted so this Christian character would replace the ancient Mother who had nurtured the region's inhabitants for millennia. Consider the possibility.

We are one in the Spirit, we are one
... and they'll know we are Christians by our love.[66]

A HOLY COM-UNION

One of the more significant events in my life was when I sat at my (converted) Jewish aunt's Sabbath table on a Friday night and heard her and her husband repeat the words I had heard in a Catholic mass with my college roommate the previous Sunday.

> Blessed are you, Lord God of Creation, for through your goodness we have this bread to offer...
> Blessed are you, Lord God of Creation, for through your goodness we have this wine to offer...

As I accepted the bread that had been broken and shared, I was in a mild state of shock. Until that moment I hadn't really grasped that Jesus was, indeed, a practicing Jew, fulfilling the Law of Moses. Nor had I truly understood the extent to which Christianity was an extension of Judaism.

Under Paul's guidance, the people who called themselves Christians in the Greco-Roman cities were not Jews following Jewish law and tradition, so most of them didn't know that this simple ritual had been practiced for hundreds of years before the man they called *Iesu* performed it with his followers. They merely knew that it had power in it—the power to unite those who participated in it. This holy communion was celebrated almost daily by practicing Chris-

> Paul's insistence that it wasn't necessary to go to the temple, or even be circumcised, to be a Christian was in direct contradiction to the practices and teachings of the Apostolic leaders in Jerusalem—who kicked him out of their community as a result.

---

[66] "We Are One in the Spirit," American Catholic folk hymn.

tians, with the full expectation that in doing so, they too, would become part of the divine Union: One in Spirit with the Anointed One, blessed with the same gifts, experiencing the "kingdom of heaven" in his holy *shem*, or name.

Before Constantine adopted Christianity as the religion of the failing Roman empire, Christians met in each others' houses and reenacted the blessing and sharing of bread and wine "in remembrance of" the Anointed One who had fulfilled the Law of Moses and become one with the Deity. Through this process of communing together, they overcame their differences and formed one community.

The Bridegroom

One of the more disturbing questions that inquisitive students have asked their Sunday school teachers is: "If Jesus is the bridegroom, who is the bride?" Church doctrine states that Jesus is the bridegroom and the church as a whole—its congregants and its priesthood altogether—is the bride. Interpretations of the various biblical texts, especially John's *Revelation*, also called "The Apocalypse of John," nearly always emphasize this role for the church.

Yet, even within the Roman church, this interpretation gives way—in the practice of nuns "marrying" Jesus in their commitment ceremony. And if one looks at the biblical texts from the outside, it's hard to justify this interpretation. More, if one studies them in the context of the "rural conservative" culture in which Jesus lived, it's nigh on impossible.

The bridegroom in that time and place was not a metaphor. The "church" did not exist—not even as an idea. Jesus was a temple-going Jew. The Greeks were temple-going pantheists. Following Jesus' crucifixion the disciples formed a community of families and individuals under the leadership of the senior disciples but with an egalitarian approach to decision-making—and still went to the temple, in accordance with Moses' law. The concept of an institution or organization or community as a "bride" was only conceivable to the

Romans who thought of *Roma* as feminine, a mother, and fought and died for "her."

The bridegroom in that time in place was exactly that: a man who was in the process of being married to a woman. The "Bridegroom" with a capital "B" was the man who had been chosen to participate in the *heiros gamos* with the current representative of the Goddess. He was the "anointed one" who would be united with the Goddess and have "all power in heaven and in earth" until he became the "sacrificial lamb" whose blood must be sprinkled on the earth to restore life to it, and was entombed to become the "resurrected Son of God," one with his Father in all ways.

As described in earlier chapters, this was what those people in that place had practiced for thousands of years and, for these "rural conservatives," the coming and going of the Temple and the ark and the law and the prophets was just a backdrop for this, their "true" religion.

Sacred Marriage

The reenactment of the Sacred Marriage was, for virtually all rural populations across Asia and Europe, the focus of the annual cycle of renewal, and the means by which balance was maintained in the community. Extended family wedding feasts celebrated among the villagers today imitated the public wedding service. The wedding feast at Cana described in John's gospel had gone on for several days before they "ran out of wine" and the Queen Mother Mary worked with her Anointed Son to manifest the needed beverage.

We can see the pattern in private weddings still, across Asia. The elders decide who will be anointed as the bridegroom for a particular virgin. The virgin is dressed in the finest available clothes—usually red in color—and is decorated with gold and gems and painted almost beyond recognition. In the meantime, the bridegroom and his friends form a "raiding party." They are expected to "steal" the bride from her home and carry her off to the groom's family's home, where a great celebratory feast will be held, sometimes lasting for days, in which the bride and groom are honored as "king and queen" of the event. Typically, a priest is brought in to bless the event—and the lives of all present. Toward the end of the feast, the bride is taken to a room in the home and prepared for the consummation of the marriage. When all is prepared, the men, with much ado, escort the bridegroom to the bridal chamber and lock them in. The party continues as the two come to "know one another" and, the next morning, the bloodstained sheet is presented to all as proof that the bride was indeed a virgin and the groom did indeed fulfill his duty. Only then is the wedding feast complete and the groomsmen and families of the couple are free to return to their homes. They do so comforted in the knowledge that balance and harmony have been maintained through this truly sacred event.

So too, for the people attending the wedding at Cana. And so, too, for the people attending a certain feast described in the New Testament as occurring at the house of "Simon the leper" in Bethany. For there, if we are to fill in the missing pieces from the gospel stories, a scarlet-clad virgin anointed *Y'shuh ben Yusuf* as her Goddess' Son and Bridegroom, and with that action, fulfilled the requirements of her people for becoming a *Mrym*, a representative of the Goddess in her Matron (meaning "mother") phase. From that day forward, they traveled together, and he increased in power and authority.

The marriage of two people is the symbol for the union of heaven and earth, sea and sky, mountain and valley. It is the union of the active and receptive, light and dark, powerful and submissive. In Chinese culture, since about 600BCE, it is the Yin and Yang, the combination of which is the *Tao*, the Way:

A Holy Com-Union

The sacred union is internal and external at once: the man takes on the qualities of the woman and the woman takes in the qualities of the man; both must develop new understandings and skills in order to "become one." Both must develop the internal *animus*, or masculine nature, and *anima*, feminine nature. It's an alchemical process in which two elements, through a series of transformations, become a new, totally different element. Ultimately, it is the shift from the duality of earthly existence into the primordial ONE.

> The great surrealist painter, Salvador Dali, believed this so deeply that he used his wife's face as his model for Jesus.

The sacred union is, for a man, discovering the Goddess:
> The symbol of the Goddess allows men to experience and integrate the feminine side of their nature, which is often felt to be the deepest and most sensitive aspect of self. The Goddess does not exclude the male; She contains him, as a pregnant woman contains a male child. Her own male aspect embodies both the solar light of the intellect and wild, untamed animal energy...[67]

So the Mother, as well as the Father, is to be found within, by both men and women.
> The love of the Goddess is unconditional. She does not ask for sacrifice ... fulfillment becomes, not a matter of self-indulgence, but of self-*awareness*. ...
>
> For a man, the Goddess, as well as being the universal life force, is his own, hidden, female self. She embodies all the qualities society teaches him *not* to recognize in himself. His first experience of Her may therefore seem somewhat stereotyped; She will be the cosmic lover, the gentle nurturer, the eternally desired Other, the Muse, all that hi is not. As he becomes more whole and becomes aware of his own "female" qualities, She seems to change, to show him a new face, always holding up the mirror that shows what to him is still ungraspable. He may chase Her forever, and She will elude him, but

---

[67] Starhawk, (Miriam Simos), *The Spiral Dance*. Harper San Francisco, 1979. p.10

through the attempt he will grow, until he too learns to find Her within. [68]

And the result of the seeking, we learn in both the New Testament and in *Wicca*, is to embody the gifts of the integrated, formless Spirit: the power to

- heal the sick,
- preach the "good news" of freedom from wrongdoings through forgiveness,
- embody the eternal living Word of Wisdom, and
- raise those who have appeared to die into the life of the Spirit.

With the Passover Communion ritual, Jesus, as the Anointed One, the Son of God and Bridegroom of the Goddess, with "all power in heaven and in earth," was offering his followers the opportunity to experience the power of union without the *external* ceremony of *heiros gamos*. He was telling them that "the Way, the Truth and the Light" are *internal*, in the "I AM," just as he had often told them that "the kingdom of heaven" is "within" and "close at hand." He taught that we reach "the Father"—the nurturing, protective Presence, the transcendent Goddess' divine Consort and father to her Son—*through* the self, that which we call "me."

A New Covenant

At the Passover feast that is known as the "Last Supper," Jesus established a new covenant "for all humanity." This covenant included a mandate; "This do in remembrance of me." It also required the breaking of an old covenant in order to be established.

> It's from this mandate, in Latin *mandati*, that the name Maundy Thursday likely came.

---

[68] Flinders, Carol Lee, Rebalancing the World, why women belong and men compete and how to restore the ancient equilibrium. New York: HarperCollins, 2002. p. 84-85

A Holy Com-Union

By handling wine in public, Jesus was making it clear that his days as a Nazarite, dedicated to the God of the Temple, were over, and he did so while explaining that he, himself, was both the "perfect Lamb" being offered and the priest doing the offering to complete his vow of dedication. Now he was replacing his old covenant with a new one, which, as the Anointed One, meant that he was creating a new covenant for all of Israel. This was consistent with Hebrew tradition: the Anointed Noah received the rainbow as a sign of his covenant and whose first act after the flood was to plant grapes; the Anointed Abram, whose "children would number as the stars" and occupy the land "from the Jordan to Egypt;" and the Anointed Moses, whose tablets became the sign of the new covenant that brought his people back to the land "of milk and honey."

The sign of Jesus' new covenant was the visible presence of the Holy Spirit--in the wind and flames of Pentecost and in the "gifts of the Spirit" described by Paul:

- Healing
- Teaching
- Prophecy
- Capacity to perceive and minister to the needs of others

The fulfillment of the New Covenant would be in the heart and mind of "he who has ears to hear." Only those who could interpret Jesus' stories, who could see the meaning in his symbols, and let themselves actually experience the truth in his words, would be participants in this New Covenant. It would be available to all of the children of Israel—and to all others, such as the Roman centurion and the Samaritan woman, who recognized the work of the Spirit as it brought forth the kingdom of heaven—and accepted it.

Having declared this New Covenant, Jesus had completed his task as the Anointed One. Now he instructed his trusted first lieutenant to "do what you need to do quickly."

It's clear from his words and actions that Jesus believed that, if his offering was to be accepted, it must happen within a certain timeframe—in fulfillment of the prophetic scriptures. He must die as the "first born son" of God on the Passover—the day when all the "first-born" of Egypt died and the Israelites were sent out of that country. More, he must die before the solar eclipse, which, since all the *Magi* ("mages," Wise men") who had protected him in his early years were astrologers and astronomers, he knew would happen on this particular Passover. Finally, his death must be public, and in the accepted form: the ancient "hanging man on a tree," with the tree, or in this case Roman cross, penetrating the earth as a phallus penetrates the woman's body, as one more symbolic representation of the consummation of the Sacred Marriage.

He knew also that he must be resurrected from this death three days later, both to fulfill the ancient tradition of the consort of the Goddess, and to occur on the 17th of the month of *Nissan*, the anniversary date of all the major events in Hebrew history: the landing of Noah's ark, the crossing of the Sea of Reeds by Moses, and the crossing over the Jordan into the Promised Land by the first Joshua/*Y'shuh*. He prepared carefully for this, timing his challenges to temple authority and his ritual ride into town as "the Anointed One" to ensure that things would unfold appropriately. So it was, that as the phallic cross pierced the womb-soil of Golgotha, the divine marriage, the holy communion was consummated and all was fulfilled, in accordance with the scriptures. And he declared it so while hanging on the cross.

The fulfillment of the New Covenant is a recognition that "as above, so below," that all of the universe is one harmonic whole, in which events unfold in harmony with one another, so that what one person thinks and does is reflected in the earth and the stars. Only those who understood that they were part of this whole would be truly free—for they would, as he did, use thought and action to affect the world around them and then work with that shift to achieve their dreams for the good of all.

In today's world, this means that we need both "right brain" *and* "left brain" thinking—that is, both the intuitive, holistic, and relational mode *and* the linear, rational, analytic mode, if we are to be whole. It means that while we recognize that there are gender differences, no one need be limited by socially determined gender roles. It's an acceptance of the feminine, responsive, receptive, and nurturing qualities in everyone, as well as the powerful, active, creative masculine qualities. Most of all, it is the realization that "Mother-Father" God is all-inclusive, totally accepting of everyone, regardless of gender or social standing: the fulfillment of the Way.

Hail, holy queen enthroned above! Hail mother of mercy and of love!

...

Salve Regina![69]

OUR LADY ARISES ANEW

Although Jesus taught his disciples to ignore gender, we have seen that the men of the Roman church, as had their Greco-Roman forefathers, determined to wipe out any possibility of women as leaders, along with any trace of ways of thinking and believing that differed from theirs. From the early women bishops to the Cathars to the "witches," to the indigenous peoples of other continents, the Roman church sought to justify the Greco-Roman belief system on which it was built, using whatever means it could. Still, as St. Augustine pointed out around 350CE, one can't always force someone to change religions. Sometimes it's necessary to adopt and adapt what's already in place. Hence the church's conversion of local heroes, heroines, gods, and goddesses into Christian "saints," as well as the use of the Germanic Maiden-goddess name for Easter. Even its acceptance of the "gothic" cathedrals dedicated to *Notre Dame* "Our Lady" was part of this process: where She couldn't be destroyed, She was adopted and adapted.

A "New Style" Emerges in France

The first building traditionally said to be built in the "New Style" was the Chapel of St. Denis in Paris, part of the royal palace compound, the east side choir of which was built by Abbot Suger in 1144. Its soaring arches and tall win-

---

[69] "*Salve Regina*," ("Saving Queen") traditional Roman Catholic hymn—brought to modern audiences in *Sister Act*.

Finding a New Balance

dows were considered the wonder of their time. However, notes and drawings for Cistercian churches, and the somewhat older plan of construction of the cathedral at Sens, suggest that Bernard of Clairvaux was instrumental in developing the design we know today as "Gothic" well before his colleague Suger came along.

Bernard of Clairvaux, abbot of a major Cistercian monastery and designer of the Templar monastic Rule, was clearly on par with his predecessor, Fulbert of Chartres. He designed several abbey chapels, with the goal that musical and visual harmony be united in their architecture—demonstrating his mastery of the Liberal Arts by once defining God as "length, breadth, height, and depth."

So it's not too surprising to discover that the "new style" of architecture embodied in the final rebuilding of Chartres' cathedral largely followed his inspiration and leadership. In form, it was not so different from the ancient Roman basilica—a long nave supported by rows of pillars on each side with a series of chapels along the aisles and a rounded apse at the east end. The big difference was that every proportion followed precisely the ancient ideal, the "golden mean," so that the proportions of the body of the cathedral precisely match the proportions of the *mandorla*, or *vesica piscis*, and the human body—both horizontally and vertically. Also different was the tremendous height achieved, and the amazing amount—and quality—of light throughout, made possible by distributing the weight outside the building, through a system of columns and arches which we know today as "flying buttresses."

The soaring arched ceilings and tall windows made possible by these buttresses were a significant departure from the dark, cave-like Romanesque churches that had been built up till then. But perhaps the most obvious difference was that the many arches used in the construction were not round, as Roman arches had been, but pointed—as were the entrances to Arab mosques, particularly Al Aksa Mosque, which the Templars helped to build on the Temple Mount in Jerusalem.

"Gothic" Arches of Al Aksa mosque on the Temple Mount, Jerusalem

They are, today, considered the defining characteristic of this form of architecture.

Main entrances: Notre Dame de Chartres (top) and Notre Dame de Paris.

Finding a New Balance

These arches, and the "sacred geometry" by which they were formed, were taught to Templar builders by Sufis (members of the mystical orders of Islam) during the years they occupied the Temple Mount in Jerusalem. The harmonious form of these pointed arches fit well with Bernard's insistence that spaces be visually as well as musically harmonious. They also made it possible to build larger structures with fewer materials than the old Roman style. More importantly, however, they shifted the visitor's perspective. No longer would the Christians who entered these spaces be encouraged to focus on their lowly, sinful nature; now their gaze—and attention—would be drawn upward, to the new heights and possibilities of the divine.

Cathedrals, whose name comes from the Latin *cathedra* ("throne" or "seat"), are the "seats" of bishops. Medieval cities vied for them because of the number of people who would have to support the work of the bishop and who would come to visit the city because it was there. Once in place, cities were in some competition as to whose building was largest or which spire was tallest. The "New Style," able to support great heights with its massive "flying but-tresses," lent itself beautifully to this competition. Jean Gimpel, in his book *Medieval Machine*, describes some of the ingenuity involved in their construction:

> The medieval master builder was really a master of all phases of the work, familiar with each operation and constantly in immediate touch with it. They were as much engineers as architects ...
>
> These architect-engineers fulfilled one of the ambitions of the medieval citizen, which was to have a more outstanding building than any in the neighboring city, with a higher vault, a higher spire...
>
> Gothic churches were full of "inventions." ... At Chartres there were no less than nine staircases or vices. ... The vices, built inside the masonry and very economically made in that they were practically prefabricated, played a further role ... As the building went up, the vices followed, and therefore could be used to bring men and materials up the stairs to the level reached by the walls.

These vices allowed the builders the economy of not erecting extensive scaffolding inside and outside the building. ....[70]

The "New Style" was uplifting, harmonizing, and baffling, all at once. Observers loved it or hated it. The thousands of people who participated in the construction of these manmade mountains were appropriately proud of their achievements and celebrated them as the center of life in their cities. Bernard of Clairvaux, with his personal commitment to Notre-Dame in the form of a Black Madonna, had, with the aid of the Templars and their friends the Sufis, transformed the western concept of church from a dark "cave" to a soaring palace of the "new Jerusalem." Integrating architectural principles from Arabs, Greeks, Romans, and Druids, he shifted the locals' focus from the Mother Earth to the Queen of Heaven.

> The descriptor "Gothic" as applied to these amazing structures was a nineteenth-century pejorative, suggesting the barbarian backwardness of the ancient Visigoths who had once occupied France. For the same reason, the '80s fad of focusing on vampires and gargoyles was called "gothic."

The form was so effective and the combination of the Templars, Cistercians, and Sufis so powerful that the "New Style" rapidly became the norm. After Sens and Chartres came Reims, Amiens, Paris, and more. Each site was carefully chosen to meet ancient and modern building requirements. It had to be on or adjacent to a living *source* or spring. It had to be aligned so that its altar faced the proper direction. It had to have sufficient support for the weight of its massive structure. It had to be in the right place to ensure the Lady's blessing on what was then the kingdom of France.

---

[70] Gimpel, Jean. *Medieval Machine: The Industrial Revolution of the Middle Ages.* New York: Barnes & Noble, 2003.p. 114-116, 121.

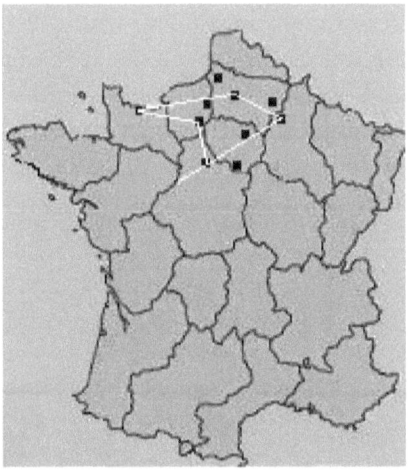

Locations of Notre Dame cathedrals in modern France forming the constellation of Virgo

Notre-Dame de Chartres is the first and, many say, the greatest of these buildings—with the richest symbolic meanings. At the level of the building-as-a-whole, we have, from a distance, a mighty ship sailing upon the plain, its towers great masts with furled sails.

Notre Dame de Chartres viewed from the train.

As we approach, we see a palace, an awesome structure to house and honor a glorious being who calls us to worship and praise. Then, up close, as we take in the number of life-sized people and scenes depicted here, and experience the light and the harmonious balance, we realize that we are entering the "New Jerusalem," a true place of peace (the meaning of the Hebrew word *Jerusalem*).

Approaching Notre Dame de Chartres from the *hotelerie*, a former convent and dormitory for students on the south east corner of the complex.

A Symbolic Journey

Each of these figures and setting has its own symbolic meaning, as well as its historical interpretation. The Mother and Son enthroned; the blessing Christ in the *Mandorla* (or *vesica piscis,* illustrated in Ch. 1 of this book), the figures of the apostles and prophets, and all the other figures that make up the pillars and archways around the entries have their own meaning, as well—in number, form, and substance.

For example, the three-fold archway of the entry speaks to the trinity in both the human (body, mind, spirit as well as head, heart, hand) and the divine. Then there are the 4 beasts

Finding a New Balance

representing the 4 gospel-writers, the 4 seasons in the zodiac, etc. The number 5 was equally sacred:
> The triad of the moon becomes the pentad, the fife-fold star of birth, initiation, love, repose, and death. ... The pentacle [5-pointed star], all five-lobed leaves, and five-petaled flowers are saved to the Goddess as pentad. The apple is especially her emblem because, when it is sliced crosswise, the embedded seeds form a pentacle. ... [71]

And so forth, all the way to the 12 apostles and signs of the zodiac. Each number itself has meaning—related from ancient Sumerian and Egyptian times, and continued into the Celtic traditions that were the foundation for the Chartres community.

All the new buildings were intricately constructed and filled with images in every possible space—images that evoked an emotional response because of their use of sacred geometry and their harmonious integration in a web of symbolic meaning. Among the important symbols woven into the "fabric" of these new buildings were three categories: form, number, and substance or story. They are interwoven in each image, each space—every aspect of the whole.

These symbols and the images in which they are presented give the experience of the cathedral multiple layers of meaning and depth. René Querido points out that the layers include:
> 1. The Story: Told through the pictorial representations of the statues and images of the windows...
> 2. The Beauty: Experienced in the details and the overall impression of the building...
> 3. The Symbolism: Seen...when one understands how, where, and why they are depicted, knows their traditional attributes, and recognizes their relation to one another,...

---

[71] Starhawk, (Miriam Simos), *The Spiral Dance*. Harper San Francisco, 1979 pp. 79-80.

4. The Meaning: Evoked through the iconography...about Christ, Mary, the spiritual world, the nature of man.
5. The Path of Initiation: ... to one who allows the cathedral to be a source and guide for inner development leading gradually to an *experience* of the divine...[72]

**(left) The north entrance to Notre Dame de Chartres.
(right) the Ste. Anne window (holding the infant Virgin Mary) above the north entrance.**

So what we call today a gothic cathedral is not merely a building. It's a library; a palace; a temple; a gateway to a new dimension. The zodiac signs with their depictions of appropriate tasks for the season on the main, West, or Royal Por-

---

[72] Querido, René, *The Golden Age of Chartres: the teachings of a mystery school and the eternal feminine.* Fair Oaks, CA: Rudolf Steiner Press, 1996. pp. 50-51.

tal act as a calendar. The clock tower nearby and bells above provide a public timepiece. The well that was built into the clock tower provides access to the divine *source*, which is the French word for "spring" or "well." But more, simply entering the space requires a shift in consciousness. As Jean Markale explains,

> During the Middle Ages, every visit to a sanctuary was a long initiatory journey. There was no expectation that it would be possible to abruptly enter a church, fall to one's knees, and start to pray. It was first necessary to *reach this stage*. ...a cathedral like Chartres does not allow itself to be entered so easily. It is necessary that we remain long on the outside to become imbued with the message left by its builders before we dare to bury ourselves in what could be called the "holy of holies"—the interior...[73]

Suddenly, for the first time since the Aryan invasions of Anatolia, the peaceful ways of the ancient Goddess were seen by the nobility as an ideal to follow. The mystical union of earth and sky, masculine and feminine, darkness and light were appreciated and honored in these noble edifices. Our Lady was honored again—within the framework of the male-dominated Christian church.

The Mother Mary's Role in Christian Life

Though God was defined in purely masculine terms and women were denied access to leadership roles, it's impossible to ignore the tremendous power and prestige granted to the image and ideal of the feminine embodied in Mary, the mother of Jesus, in the history of the Christian church. From Ephesus to Marseilles, Ireland to Istanbul, her influence cannot be ignored. Virtually every Catholic, Episcopalian/Anglican, and Orthodox church has a chapel dedicated to

---

[73] Markale, Jean, *Church of the Black Madonna*. Rochester Vermont: Inner Traditions, 2004. pp.46-47.

her. Millions of people pray the Rosary every day, and many more have altars and images of the Madonna in their homes. For these, she is the gentle supportive presence who can lift some of the suffering they've been experiencing or are afraid of; she is the understanding bridge, protecting their sinful hearts from the vengeful Father God.

> The Rosary is an ancient prayer device: a string of beads used in many cultures as a way to focus the attention and still the mind to take one into the deep state of communion that is true prayer.

Catholicism and Eastern Orthodoxy describe Mary, the mother of Jesus, as a living person who can intercede with her Son, Jesus, on behalf of humanity. Mary is also described by Ambrose as "the prototype of the Church." The traditional prayer is the *Ave Maria* ("Hail Mary"):

> Hail, Mary, full of grace! The Lord is with thee.
> Blessed art thou among women and blessed is the fruit of thy womb, Jesus.
> Holy, Mary, Mother of God, pray for us sinners now and at the hour of our death. Amen

These Marian devotions play a key part in the ritual and liturgy of both Western Catholicism and Eastern Orthodoxy. However, many of the traits attributed to her and devotions given her by Christians who adhere to Rome are not found among the Eastern Orthodox.

The earliest known Marian prayer is *Deipara, Dei Genetrix* ("God-birther, God-generator...") dating from late 2nd century Egypt, written in Coptic and Greek, and is a clear derivative of references to the ancient Mother who bore a Son who was God. The teaching that Mary was the *Theotokos*, which translates from the Greek as "God-bearer" or more commonly, "Mother of God," is evident from very early on in the Christian tradition. It's supported by the biblcal Elizabeth's inspired salutation to Mary in *Luke* 1:43: "And how [have I deserved that this honor should] be granted to me, that the mother of my Lord should come to me?"

Finding a New Balance

The Council of Ephesus met in 431 and, amid great encouragement by the locals, sanctioned the idea that Mary was predestined from all of time to be *Theotokos*, Mother of God, thus permitting the continued use of the local Temple of Diana (who had long born that title) and inaugurating the "Cult of the Virgin" and the creation of icons of the Virgin and Child.

Early representations show Mary as the "Throne of Heaven," with Mary and the Child Jesus both crowned as royalty, similar to Egyptian statues of Isis with the pharaoh on her lap. This image of Mary as Queen was softened somewhat by the image of Mary as the young mother of the infant Jesus. St. Francis of Assisi, in the 1200s, popularized the image of the Nativity scene using local people and live animals. His representation of the helpless infant Jesus being nursed by his mother brought Christmas into the hearts and homes of the people. Later, as journeys to the Holy Land became increasingly difficult, Mary's role in the Passion story as the Mother of the Suffering Jesus became one of the images in the popular Stations of the Cross.

As the foremost Christian saint and Mother of Jesus, Mary (like Bathsheba and other queen-mothers before her) was deemed to be a compassionate mediator between suffering mankind and her son, in his role as King and Judge. Biblical support for this position was found in the story of the Marriage at Cana where Mary asked Jesus to turn water into wine (*John*, 2). Although Jesus at first refused, his mother operated as if he would and the task was done. It was because of stories like this, that, during the great plagues of the Medieval period, Mary became greatly popular as intercessor and protector of mankind against the judgment of God.

As the goddess is at once maiden, mother, and crone, so Jesus' mother Mary is portrayed as all three:
1. the Virgin receiving the Holy Spirit;
2. the young, nurturing Mother, the advising Mother then the older, grieving Mother; and

3. the Elder teacher, supported by the youthful apostle, John.

It's a fundamental Catholic teaching that Mary remained a virgin her entire life. The perpetual virginity of Mary is linked to the belief in her sinlessness: her physical virginity is related to her spiritual virginity. The idea of Mary's perpetual virginity also stresses her exclusive love, devotion, and dedication to her offspring, Jesus. Several possible explanations may be offered to concerns raised by such verses such as Matthew 13:55 and Mark 6:3, both of which list *adelphoi* of Jesus. Jerome translated the ambiguous Greek term *adelphoi* that means certain types of close relatives as "cousins." Several early writers (e.g., Clement, Eusebius) suggest that they were stepbrothers of Jesus, sons of a previous wife of Joseph.

> For many people—Catholics and non-Catholics, alike—the idea of the Immaculate Conception is confusing. It's not that her parents conceived her without a sexual union, or that she conceived Jesus without sex.
>
> In the Roman church tradition, it's that she, by Grace, was conceived, born, and lived her life without the "stain" of the "Original Sin" of Eve and Adam that led to their expulsion from the Garden of Eden—and all human suffering. In other traditions, the idea is that the whole universe came forth out of one Creative Source, the divine feminine, without intercourse or intervention.

Catholic theologians have argued for years over the question of whether or not Mary had been subject to Original Sin along with other women. In 1854, Pope Pius IX effectively ended the debate for Catholics by stating that "the Blessed Virgin Mary in the first instant of her conception was preserved exempt from all stain of original sin by a singular privilege and grace granted by God, in view of the merits of Jesus Christ, the Saviour of the human race."

Finding a New Balance

Soon after, in 1858, a vision of "the beautiful lady" at Lourdes was said to announce, "I am the Immaculate Conception." Now the term is widely used to refer to the Mother Mary.

Pope Pius XII proclaimed the *Dogma of the Assumption*, in 1950, stating that "at the end of her earthly course, Mary was assumed into heavenly glory, body and soul." This was a belief held by Christians since the time of the early Church and is illustrated in several places in the cathedral at Chartres and others. In these images, a woman with all the iconic symbols that tell us she is Jesus' mother, lays dying, surrounded by as many of the apostles as are alive. Behind them stand the ones who have died and angels. Above all of them are flying angels, lifting the dying Mary upward, toward the Christ figure who is visible in the heavens. As an infallible pronouncement, the Assumption of Mary directly into Heaven is now a mandatory belief for Catholics.

Mary's name and role as Jesus' mother have not been sufficient to describe her influence on the Christian community. Her titles are many and all-encompassing. She is:

- The Queen of Heaven
- Queen of the Seas
- Mother of God
- Throne of Heaven
- Co-Redemptrix (with Jesus)
- New Eve
- Queen of the World
- Our Lady of Fatima (*Nossa Senhora de Fátima*)
- Our Lady of Guadalupe
- Our Lady of Doctrine (celebrated in Tarxien, Malta)
- Our Lady of Good Counsel
- Our Lady of Good Health
- Our Lady of Lourdes
- Our Lady of Loreto

- Our Lady of Sorrows
- Our Lady of Victories
- Our Lady of Mount Carmel (*Nuestra Señora del Carmen*)
- Our Lady of the Holy Rosary
- Our Lady of The Miraculous Medal
- Our Lady of Perpetual Help or Succour
- Our Lady of the Pillar (*Nuestra Señora Del Pilar*)
- Our Lady of Prompt Succor
- Our Lady, Queen of Ireland
- Our Lady of Solitude of Porta Vaga (*Nuestra Señora dela Soledad de Porta Vaga*, Patron of Cavite City)
- Our Lady of the Wayside (Patron Saint of California)
- Our Lady, Help of Christians
- Queen of the Angels
- Queen of Peace
- The Madonna of Consolation
- The Virgin of the Charity of Cobre (*Nuestra Señora de la Caridad del Cobre*)

These many names and titles (most of which have been the title of local goddesses, as well), along with the proclamations of her high status, have led to accusations of idolatry and "Marianism," the excessive veneration of Mary over Jesus. However, in Roman theology there is a clear distinction between the worship or adoration, called *latria,* which may be offered only to God, and veneration and praise, which is called *dulia*. Catholicism has traditionally accorded to the Virgin Mary the veneration of *hyperdulia,* which rests in part upon the angelic salutation, "Hail Mary, full of grace" (Lk 1:28), a phrase with momentous theological impact. The saints receive *dulia.*

Veneration and praise for Mary may take any of several forms. The Rosary of St. Dominic, which he declared was granted to him by Mary in a vision in the 12th century, is the most popular Marian devotional. In it, the "Our Father," ten

Finding a New Balance

"Hail Marys" and a "Glory Be to the Father" (together forming a "decade of the Rosary") are recited five times while meditating on the mysteries of the life of Jesus and his mother Mary (first the Joyful mysteries, then the Luminous, the Sorrowful, and finally, the Glorious). These are then followed by a prayer called the "Hail Holy Queen." *The Little Office of the Blessed Virgin Mary* is a weekly cycle of prayers said throughout the day, based on the Liturgy of the Hours. Other famous Marian prayers include the *Magnificat*, the *Angelus*, and the "Litany of the Blessed Virgin Mary." These are performed in monasteries and convents, and online and broadcast via radio and satellite tv, daily.

May and October are usually seen as Marian months. King Alfonso X of Castille, wrote in his "*Cantigas de Santa Maria*" ("Songs of Holy Mary") about the special honoring of Mary during specific dates in May. Eventually, the entire month was filled with special observances and devotions to Mary. This tradition of a month-long Marian devotion spread around the Roman Catholic world through the 19th century, together with a month-long devotion to Jesus in June and to the Rosary in October.

On May Day, images or likenesses of the Blessed Virgin Mary are ceremonially crowned as Queen of Heaven and the Mother of God. Young girls in white dresses carry flowers (traditionally Hawthorne) to adorn the statue. One of the girls (often the youngest) carries a crown on a cushion for placement by the May Queen (often the oldest girl) on the statue. The flowers are replaced throughout the month to keep them fresh. This is a direct descendent of the ancient honoring of the goddess as Mother: May Day is *Beltane* in the Celtic tradition, when the white-clad Maiden of early spring (February 1-2, *Imbolc*) gives way to one who is honored as the Mother, clad in green and crowned with blooming Hawthorne, blessing the fires that the herds pass through to be cleansed of insects and parasites as they depart for grazing lands in the cool hills.

One Marian website proudly declares that "every day, somewhere on this earth, is a celebration of the Blessed Mother," then lists the 365 feast days celebrated in different regions in honor of Mary. Among the Marian feast days in the standard Catholic Calendar are:

- January 1 Mary, Mother of God (Jesus' circumcision)
- January 8 Our Lady of Prompt Succor
- February 2 Purification of Mary in the Temple (also St. Bridgit's day & Candlemass)
- February 11 Our Lady of Lourdes
- March 25 Annunciation by Archangel Gabriel
- May 1 May crowning
- May 13 Our Lady of Fatima
- May 31 Mary, Mediatrix of all Graces
- June 27 Our Lady of Perpetual Help
- August 15 Assumption into Heaven
- August 21 Our Lady of Knock (*sic!* Knock is a town*)*
- September 8 Our Lady of Good Health, Our Lady of Charity
- September 15 Our Lady of Sorrows
- October 7 Feast of the Most Holy Rosary
- December 8 Feast of the Immaculate Conception
- December 12 Feast of Our Lady of Guadalupe

Not too surprisingly, these dates are very close to the traditional dates for honoring the Goddess in ancient Europe and the Middle East. Clearly, Mary has become the embodiment of the divine feminine in Roman Catholic culture. And, while Mary is not "worshipped" or "adored" but merely "venerated and praised," millions of men, women, and children pray daily to this gentle, loving Presence to relieve them and their loved ones of suffering and to help them achieve their desires, and, like every statue of Buddha in Tibet and every image of Kali or Krishna in India, virtually every image of Mary has flowers placed on it or in front of it as an act of appreciation and devotion.

Granted, this focus on Mary is not as intense in the Protestant denominations as it is in the Roman and Orthodox churches. Still, images of the Madonna and the Holy Family in the nativity scene are ubiquitous at Christmas, and few Christians of any variety do not feel a tender appreciation for the mother of their Lord, especially as represented in the *Pieta*, holding the body of her crucified Son.

Still, while the influence of Mary, the mother of Jesus, has long been profound in the Catholic tradition, modern observers are beginning to recognize that neither is she the only Mary that has been venerated, nor is the Lady being venerated always an image of a Christian saint named Mary.

The Dark/Black Madonna

Many people who have encountered a *Black Madonna* report a remarkably intense sense of connection. Some of them have returned again and again—may even have become "obsessed" with experiencing other, similar figures.

> The dark skin tone of these madonnas is in stark contrast to the images of the "white Virgin" that dominate so many churches, chapels, and altars—which, it seems, inspired the "Virgin Queen" Elizabeth I, to paint her face white for the majority of her reign.

My own experience with "Our Lady of the Pillar" in Chartres was almost overwhelming. As I settled into one of the kneelers in her chapel and simply opened myself to the experience of the moment, a bolt of "energy" "zapped" me, and suddenly there was no muscle tone in my body. I slumped there in the chapel for some time, aware that my companion was patiently waiting for me, but feeling totally unable to do anything about it. I was in a space of "empty-fullness," quite aware of my surroundings, but as if they were distant, not relevant. There was no voice, no vision, no sign of a particular being, just being-ness. After several minutes of this, I realized I had the power of volition and could choose to move my fingers and toes, then hands and feet, and so forth, until finally I could raise myself from that slumped-over position and let my companion know that all was well. Later visits to the same chapel were without incident, but I now understand the special devotion that the many people who visit "her" regularly feel for this figure.

Notre Dame de Pilar, Chartres, carved in dark wood c. 1600 and usually covered with fabric vestments.

Such images of a mother and child, or sometimes just a woman, painted with dark brown or black skin, or carved in a dark wood or stone, may be found all over Europe, from Poland to the UK. Over 60% of them are in France, mostly in the southern provinces. Most were made where they are located, and from the range of forms, they seem not to be copies. Locals dearly love them; Bernard of Clairvaux de-

Finding a New Balance

scribed his relation to one in the terms of a "spiritual marriage." The Roman church (except Pope John Paul II, who grew up loving one and visited several as cardinal and pope), however, does not approve—though they are typically located in churches and cathedrals. Church leaders offer no explanation for their color beyond the possibility that they were blackened by years of candle smoke—even for relatively new sculptures and paintings located away from candles, some of which are clearly painted.[74]

The church's silence on the subject is not too surprising, since history suggests that it's very likely that Black Madonnas were not originally created in homage to the Christian tradition at all. They're typically located on previously pagan sites—those honoring the Greek Artemis/Diana or the Roman Cybele or a Celtic tribal image of the Goddess, most of whom were "descendants" of Inanna/Ishtar and were often depicted as black long before Christianity moved into Europe.

Cybele was introduced into Rome in 205-4BCE. She was called *Magna Mater*, "Great Mother," by the Romans, and arrived by ship from Asia Minor in the form of a black meteorite. When it reached the shores of Italy, this beloved icon was passed hand-to-hand by Roman matrons to the emperor's throne.

The Egyptian Mother-Source, called *Isis*, is typically portrayed as black, also, and is the original "Madonna and child," holding Horus (or the current pharaoh, depicted as Horus)

> The Egyptian name *Eese*, translated by the Greeks as *Isis*, means "throne" in the feminine form. She held Horus, her divine son, on her lap and was often depicted holding an urn in funerary paintings. During Roman times her temples were built as far north as Hadrian's wall on the English-Scottish border.

---

[74] For a detailed exploration of Black Madonnas and their presence in the Christian churches of France, see Jean Markale, *Cathedral of the Black Madonna*, Rochester Vermont: Inner Traditions, 2004.

on her knee. Like Mary, Isis brought her son forth 'of herself' and her statues were found all over the Roman empire.

All of these icons were often referred to as "Holy Virgin," "Star of the Sea," and "Queen of Heaven," and in the latter form they were often shown standing on a crescent moon with a ring of 12 stars in their hair. These characteristics have led one French scholar to declare: "*The Black Virgin* is *Isis* and her name is *Notre Dame de Lumiere* ("Our Lady of the Light")."

In the *Song of Songs*, which is read on the Magdalene's feast day in the Roman church, the feminine character describes herself as seeking her love through the night and finding him in the garden; she is "dark and swarthy, but comely... Pay no attention to my black color, I have been burned by the sun." Usually described as Solomon's song of praise to the Queen of Sheba, these words are also part of the Egyptian sacred marriage rite of Isis and Osiris.

Given what we've seen so far of the imposition of the values and spiritual teachings of people who called themselves "Sons of the Light" on smaller, dark-skinned people who honored the ancient mother of all life, it's not too surprising that the deepest, most ancient veneration in many European communities is to a dark *Madonna* ("Great Mother") who evokes deep, almost genetic, memories of being held and comforted, when it was okay to be "dark and comely." In fact, French scholar Jean Markale suggests that these icons refer back to a time before memory, a mystical experience of the "creative darkness."

Markale also suggests that the black coloring is symbolic:
The shadow of the great Goddess of the Beginnings still lurks around the Virgin Mary. ... In all traditions, the color black is synonymous with night, darkness, death, chaos, or even, to use an Eastern term, nonexistence, which is not the same thing as death or chaos. ... The Virgin is potentiality, the *materia prima* that has not yet been organized but out of which everything may emerge. ...
In alchemical operations it was necessary to "cook" the primal matter under very special conditions that would

prompt the introduction of material heat as well as the flame of the spirit. The result of this "cooking" is ... the Black Stone... "burned by the sun."[75]

This interpretation helps to explain the importance of the study of alchemy at Fulbert's school at Chartres, which has two Black Madonnas: *Notre Dame de Sous-terre* ("Our Lady of Underground") is the focus of attention in "the crypt" that was Fulbert's church and is now below the cathedral (illustrated in ch. 1) and *Notre Dame de Pilar* ("Our Lady of the Pillar"), illustrated above.

It's also interesting to note that Black Madonnas are almost always located where Mary Magdalene is honored—at least fifty Magdalene shrines have them—in Provence, in the eastern Pyrenees, and mostly centered in the hills called *Monts de la Madeleine*, "the Mountains of the Magdalene." When we remember that in the ancient French, many words containing the letter "l" were written with an "r," and that therefore, *Madeleine* may well have been *Mater Reine*, or "Queen Mother," it all begins to make sense.

Visions & Apparitions

Since the 3rd day following Jesus' crucifixion, visions have played a tremendously important role in the Christian tradition. Visions of Jesus as the Christ and the Son of Man were, in the 1st century, a common theme of apocalyptic writings, such as John's *Revelation*, and, possibly, *The Gospel of Thomas* and *The Gospel of Philip*. The conversion of Saul of Tarsus into the Apostle Paul was, according to the New Testament, the result of such a vision.

Visions of Jesus' mother, however, were unmentioned in the New Testament and the other, lost gospels, and far less frequent in the life of the Roman church—at least until the "Cult of the Virgin" was launched at the time of the construction of the *Notre Dame* cathedrals. Suddenly, in journals

---

[75] Markale, Jean, *Cathedral of the Black Madonna*, p. 190-192.

and letters, and in trials of the Inquisition, thousands of people—popes, monks and nuns, kings and queens, priests and lay members of the church—all were describing visions in which they saw the Mother Mary appear to them. Many of these were unverifiable and were discarded by the church leaders as "the imagination of the devoted." A few, however, became the basis for yet another wave of construction: of shrines honoring sites of her visitation—one of the most recent of these being at Medjugorje in the former Yugoslavia.

Psychologically, this makes sense. Another phenomenon that began during the early 1300s was the appearance of *stigmata*: wounds on the body that replicate those described in the New Testament as having been inflicted on Jesus during the crucifixion. Historians have noted that such appearances began shortly after the Roman church began installing "crucifixes" in the churches, with their graphic depiction of the wounds, and before which the devout would kneel for hours each day and pray, longing to be "more like Christ." It's not too surprising, given the powerful effects of auto-suggestion and self-hypnosis, that some of the people who so intently focused on this idea actually began to experience the physical manifestation of their intention—St. Francis of Assisi being among the first to do so.

A similar explanation may be given for the sudden increase in "visitations" by Mary following the construction of shrines and cathedrals with dozens, and in some cases hundreds, of images of the Madonna. This is especially so when we consider that many of them were placed in chapels where people—especially pubescent girls—would kneel and spend hours praying.

Alternatively, it may be that people have always had visions of the Great Mother (the meaning of *Madonna*), but, in the world of the Roman church, didn't feel it was safe to talk about them until the Cult of the Virgin gave them a framework in which it would be acceptable.

In any case, there have been thousands of appearances, or visitations, of a "beautiful lady," the Virgin, or the Madonna, occurring on almost every continent—often during times of great tension in the world. Based on eye-witness accounts at Lourdes, Fatima, and Medjugorje, we can describe the experience:

> There is first a stillness in the area, as birds and insects become quiet, then the air feels charged with electricity, as if in a thunderstorm. Most people see nothing, but many feel a sense of peace, or relief from burdens. A few see whirling light around the sun. A very few, usually pubescent girls, clearly see and hear a "beautiful woman" radiating a light that feels wonderfully loving while telling them things they don't always understand, asking them to pray regularly for peace, and sometimes showing them images of possible events in the future—in a vision that seems remarkably similar to the vision described by John in *Revelation*. The "beautiful woman" is usually wearing blue and may have flowers or stars around her. She appears in the same spot for a few dozen occasions, appearing from nowhere and gradually fading from view at the end of the session.

In virtually every case, the children who have seen the vision have been quite ordinary—average or below-average at school, growing up in relatively poor, rural families. They have gone on to live quiet lives of love and service—usually including regular and frequent prayers in the Mary chapel at their local church. Several have become nuns or monks. Most have not lived into old age. In every case it's clear that their hearts and minds have been touched by something inexpressibly wonderful.

Neo-pagans: seeking to restore balance

Today, thousands of people have re-acquainted themselves with the ideas and traditions of the ancient Goddess cultures and are celebrating the ancient cyclical pattern of the sun and moon. Doing so, they seek to honor and restore the balance between masculine and feminine in their hearts, minds, and communities. These "neo-pagans" have given up on what they see as the religions of conquest and empire and seek a more harmonious path. For inspiration, they look primarily to the written and oral traditions of Brittany, Cornwall, and Ireland. Some also contemplate the spiritual literature of Sumer, Egypt, Babylon, and India. From these, they have put together a new, integrated mythos, using the names and qualities of the Goddess and her consort from these different cultural and language groups.

One of the most famous voices for this "neo-pagan" way of thinking is a woman from San Francisco known as Starhawk, who worked with (then Catholic priest) Matthew Fox at his Institute for Creation Spirituality (now Wisdom University). Starhawk has written a number of books on modern practice of the ancient traditions, using the controversial name, "witchcraft," or *Wicca* for the belief system she works with. Her conviction of the importance of reconnecting with the divine feminine comes from a deep concern about the imbalance in our culture, which has led to a sense of victimhood and powerlessness at every level. She says, "To invoke the Goddess is to awaken the Goddess within, to become, for a time, that aspect we invoke. An invocation channels power through a visualized image of Divinity."[76]

Starhawk describes the Goddess as:

... first of all earth, the dark nurturing mother who brings forth all life. She is the power of fertility and generation; the womb and also the receptive tomb ... The Earth Goddess is also air and sky, the celestial Queen of Heaven, the Star Goddess, ruler of things felt but not seen: of knowledge, mind, and intuition. ... Beautiful and glittering, She can never be grasped or penetrated; the mind is drawn ever further in the drive to know the unknowable, to speak the inexpressible. She is the inspiration that comes with an indrawn breath.

The celestial Goddess is seen as the moon, who is linked to women's monthly cycles of bleeding and fertility.

---

[76] Starhawk, (Miriam Simos), *The Spiral Dance.* Harper San Francisco, 1979 p. 85

> Woman is the earthly moon, the moon is the celestial egg, drifting in the sky womb, whose menstrual blood is the fertilizing rain and the cool dew; who rules the tides of the oceans... Mistress of Waters, ...the sea, streams, springs, the rivers that are the arteries of Mother Earth; of lakes, deep wells, and hidden pools, and of feelings and emotions, which wash over us like waves.
>
> The Moon-Goddess has three aspects: as She waxes She is the Maiden; full, She is the Mother; as She wanes, She is the Crone. ... [77]

This description is constant across all the spiritual traditions that have contributed to western culture, today—for both god and goddess, and the unnamable Essence that is the union of the two.

The people who are adopting these "neo-pagan" ideas and the rituals that go with them are, in their own way, seeking to restore the Anatolian-style community life that was all-but destroyed by the horseback-riding, sword-wielding Aryan herdsmen whose values formed the basis for western culture. By focusing on a nurturing, feminine Goddess who seeks fulfillment for her children rather than an angry, demanding God who requires sacrifice in atonement for an innately sinful nature, these people hope to re-establish a spiritual and material life that embodies Jesus' two-law: "love the Source/Power/Presence with all your heart, mind, and soul; love your neighbor as your self."

As Starhawk has put it:
> The myths, legends, and teachings are recognized as metaphors for "That-Which-Cannot-Be-Told," ... the inner knowledge literally *cannot* be expressed in words."
>
> The primary symbol for "That Which Cannot be Told" is the Goddess. The Goddess has infinite aspects and thousands of names—She is the reality behind many metaphors. She is reality, the manifest deity, omnipresent in all of life, in each of us. The Goddess is not separate from the world—She is the world, and all things in it: moon, sun, earth, star, stone, seed, flowing river, wind,

---

[77] Starhawk, (Miriam Simos), *The Spiral Dance*. Harper San Francisco, 1979. p.78.

wave, leaf and branch, bud and blossom, fang and claw, woman and man."

The symbol of the Goddess is not a parallel structure to the symbolism of God the Father. The Goddess does not rule the world. She *is* the world. Manifest in each of us, She can be known internally by every individual, in all her magnificent diversity. ... [78]

Among these people, in spite of all attempts to eliminate the divine feminine from, or minimize her role in our Aryan dominated, Greco-Roman western culture, she still appears. Through the ancient traditions maintained by rural conservatives, through the "new" discoveries made by modern, urbanized women and men, through the repressed but still present images and terms woven into our language and institutions, her power becomes known and her loving presence adored.

Women in Ministry — Embodying the Christ

Although, as described above, women played prominent roles in the first decades of Christianity, today's churches are at best split about the appropriate role for women in maintaining, nurturing, and expanding the faith. How can a woman stand in *loco Christi* (the "place of Christ") blessing the bread and wine? How can a woman—on whose shoulders the "original sin" of eating the wrong apple in the Garden of Eden has been placed for a thousand years, possibly not be a temptress? How can she, with all the distractions of motherhood, the need to be submissive to a husband (following Paul's injunction), and a mind that struggles with analysis, ever be an effective theologian or spiritual leader?

In the U.S. the shift in possibility appears to have begun with the Women's Conference of 1843 in Seneca Falls, New

---

[78] Starhawk, (Miriam Simos), *The Spiral Dance.* Harper San Francisco, 1979. p. 7-9.

Finding a New Balance

York. Though it was by no means focused on the issue, a number of secondary outcomes relevant to women and ministry resulted from this gathering. First, members of the group put together a "Women's Bible," which emphasized the role of women in biblical history. Second, the stated intention of finding more ways that women whose husbands were unable or unwilling to support the family might be able to led to an exponential increase of women in the professions—resulting in a larger percentage of women professionals in the 1870s than in the 1970s, the height of the next wave of "feminist" activity. It's difficult to believe a woman is incompetent when she's your surgeon.

One of those post-Seneca Falls professionals, Mary Baker Patterson, a divorced woman earning her living as a homeopathic physician, founded a school to teach women how to heal using the power of thought and prayer. In 1875 she wrote a book, then married her third husband, Asa Eddy, and moved to Boston, creating, with the help of "Mother-Father God," the Church of Christ, Scientist, and became its director and minister. She later determined that her teachings would remain purer if there were no ministers in Christian Science churches, so, at the dedication of the remarkable "Mother Church" building in 1903, she "ordained" her book and the Bible as its only ministers—as they still are today, around the world.

About the same time, a few hundred miles eastward, Ellen White began proclaiming her own brand of ministry—and drawing similarly large audiences into what became the 7th Day Adventist church. And a few thousand miles eastward, Madame Blavatsky, and later, Annie Besant, were opening minds and doors, as well, in the Theosophical movement.

These women were brilliant, charismatic, loving, absolutely devoted to their ministries, and trained many other women to be leaders in their churches. Many of their trainees then went on to form their own ministries—or to become active claimants for the role of women in the ministry of other churches. As a result, a fringe group of Protestant-based sects founded at the end of the 19th century became the basis, and proving ground, for a decidedly female orientation in the ministry. (And I, for one, am a beneficiary!)

All this was possible because of two characteristics of American political culture. First, the Constitutional requirement that Congress not establish a national religion—which has been interpreted and expanded to include the individual states. Second, the belief that no one person or organization has "a monopoly on the truth," making it reasonable and tolerable for individuals to break off from organizations in which they were trained and go on to create their own.

Today, women are among the top televangelists, women serve as bishops for the Episcopal and Methodist churches, many women work as rabbis, and over 70% of the several thousand New Thought churches (Centers for Spiritual Living, Unity, Divine Science, and Homes of Truth) are led by women or married couples. These women are spiritual leaders in the mainstream, restoring the qualities of the feminine in the "masculinized" Judeo-Christian tradition. They are embodying the balanced Christ, the genderless beingness that Jesus offered.

The Feminine Aspect of Modern Science

Even in the objectivist, male-dominated materialist "religion" of science, the feminine qualities of experience are becoming evident. The realizations that disciplines cannot be isolated, that relationships are as important as individual structures, and that change and flow, rather than stability, are the norm are rapidly transforming the scientific world. A few examples:

- Ecologists often refer to the totality of this planet's life and life-support systems as "Gaia," an early Greek name for the Mother-God that supports and sustains life as this world; while James

Lovelock, the chemist who wrote the book *Gaia Hypothesis* with microbiologist Lynn Margulis, has indicated he's not sure using the name was a wise decision, it was a turning point—with the name came a sense of connection that the term "biosphere" simply didn't provide, the potential for a new respect, and transformed behavior.

- The new emphasis in medicine on "holistic" health, with methods and ideas that complement the accepted medical model, honors the role of nurses in the healing process and focuses on the feminine quality of strengthening relationships within the body-mind system rather than on fixing individual parts, often using the ancient Goddess-related method of visualization.

- Embryologists and geneticists are realizing that the essential form of each being is female, modified by the introduction of "male" hormones as the DNA in the "Y" chromosome starts to function, several weeks into the development of the fetus.

- My own academic discipline, cybernetics, though usually applied in computers and control systems, has been called "the feminine science" because it emphasizes relationships and flows between matter, energy, and information within a system, rather than its form or structure.

- Even in physics, the most techno-rational of disciplines, the feminine is beginning to emerge: Dana Zohar, the physicist-philosopher who wrote *Quantum Self* and *Quantum Society*, suggests that subatomic physics would be more accurately defined as a science of overlapping relationships, rather than of colliding particles.

- Medical researcher Joan Borysenko's description of the difference between masculine and feminine spiritual paths, with which we started this book, came out of years of research on the use of meditation in addressing health challenges, and the shifts in consciousness, behavior, and wellbeing that result.

So, in the material sciences, as well as in art, psychology, and religion, western culture is slowly coming to the realization that human beings are not whole and complete without the feminine qualities of receptivity, nurturing, acceptance, intuitive-holistic thought, focus on relationships, and emotional expression. As 19th-century philosopher Wallace Waddles put it, "To live a full life means the complete expression of all three: intellect, body, and spirit." [79]

---

[79] W.D. Waddles, *The Science of Getting Rich*, 1910.

Let there be peace on earth and let it begin with me!
...we are one family. Let us walk with each other in perfect harmony![80]

FOR THE FUTURE: A NEW BALANCE

For thousands of years, we've been living a life out of balance. We've been told that the universe is a "man's world" in which feminine values and processes have no place. We've been taught not to trust our intuition and to treat the mythic as lies, rather than as another way of knowing. We've raised boys to be one-sided in their use of power, and raised girls to think that they are unworthy of power and incapable of wielding it.

To their credit, the Roman church has preached this doctrine while maintaining a vestige of balance in the form of veneration of Mary and the female saints. Protestants, scholars, and intellectuals, on the other hand, have attempted to completely turn their back on the "sinfulness of woman" and the "dark ages" of "mysticism," admitting only the "light" of "rational thought" to guide them.

Today these approaches have brought humanity to the brink of destruction, covering the planet with a culture that destroys and exploits, then asks "why me?" when the natural consequences unfold. Today, we see the extent of those consequences in the destruction of the planet's very infrastructure for life—which can only lead to the break-down of the global political and economic systems, as well.

Pagans around the world have gone to the other extreme, choosing to live by their own myth and metaphor.

---

[80] "Let There be Peace on Earth," traditional hymn used as the closing song in most New Thought churches.

Urban and suburban Neo-pagans focus almost solely on the Goddess and encourage mystical ecstasy and celebrating the creative darkness of the womb. The few remaining Earth-centered cultures have turned inward in their attempts to survive the constant onslaught from the increasingly dominant culture of Empire. Over the years, this approach has tended to lead them to withdraw from political and economic power. As a result, their wisdom practices have barely survived, offering minimal guidance to the rest of us, even as the now-global Empire culture destroys itself. Fortunately for all of us, the internet is making it possible for more of their teachings to reach the rest of the world, but theirs is still a tiny "voice in the wilderness"

Finding a New Synthesis

As the great German philosopher Hegel taught, the human mind always seeks balance. In our thoughts and in our development, we move from one extreme (what he called a "thesis") to another (his "anti-thesis") until we find, somewhere in the middle, a point that includes the best of both. Hegel called this a "synthesis."

If the thesis is the masculine-dominated view, and the antithesis is the feminine-centered view, what would a synthesis look like?

The men we call Buddha, Krishna, and Christ were undoubtedly models of a life of balanced thought and power. If we read their teachings from the perspective I've suggested here, we can see that their great strength was in their capacity to rise above the cultural norms and integrate feminine values and perspectives into their Aryan masculine histories and value systems.

Even in traditional understandings of the gospels, it's clear that Jesus the Nazarene hoped and believed that, through his teachings and resurrection, balance would be restored in the world. He expected that the masculine energy of the Romans and the appointed priesthood in the Temple

Finding a New Balance

would see that the power of the masculine must be balanced by that of the nurturing, healing feminine to achieve its full, seemingly miraculous capacity. And it's possible that he had some success in doing so. Rabbi Lynn Gottlieb says,

> *Shekinah*, the feminine Presence of God, is a central metaphor of divinity in Jewish mystical and *midrashic* texts from the first millennium CE onward. I was amazed to discover this focus on the feminine divine when I began to read the texts myself. I felt like an orphan who uncovered documents that proved her mother was not dead. [81]

A few sentences later, she goes on to say that "everything written about *Shekinah* appears to have been authored by men," pointing out that in the early texts, the word is used interchangeably with other names of God, referring to the "abiding Presence" (in Christian terms, the Holy Spirit, or Comforter). She goes on to say that early descriptions of *Shekinah* are overshadowed by the cultural antipathy toward the feminine, but that many later traditions recognize the power of the feminine and call for the unification of God (*JHWH*) as the active, creative force with the *Shekinah* receiving that energy and bringing it into form.

This is consistent with the pagan, or Goddess, traditions, as well. Starhawk's description, quoted above, makes it clear, and Carol Lee Flinders describes it further in her *Rebalancing the World,*

> The Goddess is the Encircler, the Ground of Being; the God is That-Which-Is-Brought-Forth, her mirror image, her other pole. She is the earth; He is the grain. She is the all-encompassing sky; He is the sun, her fireball. She is the Wheel; He is the traveler. His is the sacrifice of life to death that life may go on. She is Mother and Destroyer; He is all that is born and is destroyed. ... The God is Eros, but He is also Logos, the power of the mind ... The bodily desire for union and the emotional desire for connection are transmuted into the intellectual desire for knowledge, which is also a form of union. ...

---

[81] Gottlieb, Lynn, *She Who Dwells Within,* New York: HarperCollins, 1995; p. 20.

The God seeks for the Goddess, as King Arthur seeks for the Grail.[82]

Emma Curtis Hopkins, founding teacher of America's New Thought movement, was a product of the mid-nineteenth century, growing up at the same time as Louisa May Alcott in the early years of the Women's Suffrage movement. She understood the feminine aspect of the divine to be the working aspect, or Spirit:

> All the mysterious uplifting of men and the successes of nations are wrought by Spirit. Lay all your cause open before the Spirit. Tell Spirit that there is no failure for Her. Tell Spirit that it is in Her that you put your trust.
>
> Spirit is the Comforter. Spirit is the Holy Ghost. Spirit is the *Shekinah* of God. Spirit is the power of God, is the bounty of God. Spirit is the substance of God.[83]

In her many classes and publications, she taught thousands to listen to the voice of Spirit and find answers from within to any outward challenge, from healing to finances, then to act from a deep knowing that the power of the Spirit is doing the work.

From these and similar writings, it's clear that much of the language associated with the Divine Feminine is metaphoric and analogical. A familiar word or idea is used to describe or refer to something that is far too unfamiliar in nature, complex, or expansive to describe directly.

Such is also the essence of what is called "systems thinking," the field in which I earned my doctorate. Systems scientists seek to understand one situation or set of elements through its similarities to other, more familiar, sets. We use an analogy to analyze it,

> Margaret Wheatley's books on leadership and Peter Senge's studies are very effective introductions to systems thinking.

---

[82] Flinders, Carol Lee, *Rebalancing the World, why women belong and men compete and how to restore the ancient equilibrium.* New York: HarperCollins, 2002. pp. 95-99.

[83] Hopkins, Emma Curtis, *The Gospel Series.* Vancouver, WA: WiseWoman Press. 2006.

then apply the tools that work with one system to another, testing each step of the way to see how well the analog works. Using this method, models and simulations of very complex systems have been developed, such as an urban power grid or the world economy, providing very useful insights for future design and management. Using a new kind of logic and powerful computers these models encourage the integration of linear with relational thought.

Applying this mindset to the problem at hand helps to bridge the gap between "science" and "religion." The emerging science of Noetics, particularly as practiced at the Institute of Noetic Sciences, where they study how mind and matter interact, is another powerful approach.

What would happen if we, as a global culture, accepted *both* the metaphoric/mythic understanding *and* the rational, analytic understanding as valid? An analysis of historically sustainable cultures, combined with the discipline of systems thinking, suggest that such a synthesis is definitely possible.

Toward a Balanced, Sustainable Culture

A culture that is in balance accepts equally both material and spiritual aspects of being, active and receptive modes of being, and both orderly and chaotic processes of being. Such a culture has the potential for sustaining a healthy, comfortable, life for all its members over many generations.

In spite of what most of us have been taught, such cultures have existed on this planet, and life in them was good, with comfortable homes, beautiful clothing and art, healthy food, and powerful ceremonies. In fact, many of those cultures continue to thrive, but they are isolated and, as a result, limited in the ways we can learn from them. And, today, with corporate globalization and militarization, the few remnants that remain are rapidly disappearing.

Today, we have a unique opportunity: we can (and some say, must) transform our own culture. Using the lessons of the past and the tools of the present, we can create a sustainable, balanced global culture, rich in technology and in harmonious balance with the cycles of the earth and the amazing potential of the human spirit. [84]

As we unite our masculine and feminine natures, we can acknowledge that our inner power for healing and transformation is potentially as great as our capacity to manipulate outer forms, which may well be (and some indigenous prophecies say it must be) the defining discovery of this new millennium. Our power to heal, to perceive beyond the senses, and to unite with the soul of another being could, if combined with our capacity to create, to form, and to move matter, open an amazing new range of possibilities for all of us—individually and collectively.

Most of the "possible interpretations" and "explanatory stories" presented in this book have pointed in the direction of such a balanced, sustainable, integrated life. I believe that the man and woman we call Jesus Christ and Mary Magdalene—whether mythic or "real"—are models of living and teaching such a balance. It looks as if the Cistercians and Templars, the Gnostics, and the Cathars, all attempted to create such a culture. Then, more recently, the Shakers and Quakers, and today, the New Thought and some Neo-pagan traditions, have sought to move in the same direction. To a large extent, I think that the grand medieval gothic cathedrals are a testimonial and invitation to such a life.

Even today, many people are aiming in such a direction. Consider this possibility for the future:

> In this story ke and kem are offered as neutral pronouns in place of he & she, him & her,

> Tammy took a deep breath: ke was done with kem morning chores and was free to go! Wiping kem hands on kem playsuit, ke turned from the closet where ke'd

---

[84] My book *Home, Creating Humanity's Future* (Portal Center Press, 2018) offers a model of what such a culture might look like.

Finding a New Balance

just put the tools ke'd been using and skipped over to the garden-room where Mother was weaving to share kem plans and ask what to take for a midday meal. Mother had felt ke was coming and handed kem the desired packet of food, smiling her approval of kem plans. Just a few moments later, meal in hand, Tammy skipped out the door of the thick-walled cottage that had always been home, and on down the path toward the village center and the gathering-place beyond.

Today Tammy turned 7 years old. It was the day when all children began the process of discovering their inborn gifts, talents, and tendencies; a time of exploring possibilities prior to the trainings available during their adolescent years, preparing each child for the long life - maybe as long as 200 years, ahead.

And so, today, Tammy wanted to go look at the men's training grounds. Like all children, ke had been sheltered in the home by mother and grandmother since birth so ke understood the life of a woman in a home. Now ke wanted to see what kem father and brothers and uncles did when they went off to their work and play - as had every child in the village for generations.

On the way to the village center were all kinds of interesting things to explore: the pond with ducks and catfish, where all the run-off from nearby houses and barns was purified; the beautifully colorful wind-columns turning slowly in the light breeze of late morning to generate electricity for the water pumps and path-lights; the fruit and nut trees that lined the narrow road, offering shade and the joy of picking some ripe fruit in season to any who passed by, along with fun-filled harvesting of nuts in the fall. The old squirrel chittered as Tammy passed by and ke sent a silent greeting to calm its fears.

At the village center stood a lovely fountain, providing water for birds, bees, wandering pets, and passers-by as it aerated the water from the several ponds around the village before it was returned to the river. Around the fountain, paving stones with short, green grass and moss growing in the cracks between them formed a large square, on the edges of which were thick-walled homes and shops. Tammy had been in all of these over kem short life, with Mother, Grandmother, or Father as they traded for items to use in their garden and home. Normally, ke would be excited to see what was there, but today, the men's training ground was kem goal, so ke continued to skip down the road toward the other end of the village.

The late-morning light was just right - not too hot and not too bright. Tammy delighted in the feel of the air, the smell of the growing things, the patterns the shadows made on the road. The only sounds were the chattering of birds and squirrels against the faint hum of bees and other insects pollinating the flowers. Ke knew this was a special day, the beginning of something entirely new, and both curiosity and excitement grew as ke approached the open, stone-lined circle that was where the men were trained and the village adults gathered for sacred celebrations.

Now Tammy was in a totally unfamiliar part of the village. Ahead ke could see the trees along the road opening up. Soon ke could see where they joined together at the back of a large circle.

Tammy's skip slowed to a walk as ke began to feel the presence of other people and hear the men's voices ahead. Ke walked closer to the trees, not wanting to be seen while observing this other way of living. The voices grew louder and ke could hear kem father, and maybe an uncle, shouting instructions - as happened sometimes at home.

With that familiar sound, Tammy was less apprehensive. Feeling a little safer, ke continued toward the open area. Soon ke could see the rows of benches forming a large circle, some parts of it shaded with awnings suspended from the trunks of young trees planted between rows of benches. Then, as ke drew closer to the open area, ke began to see the men and boys, scattered around a large clover-covered area in front of a raised platform. They were all doing different things – all very strange. Some seemed to be dancing; some were lifting large objects; others were throwing things; a few were huddled together, talking. To the left, Tammy could see kem father sitting on one of the benches, with several others sitting in the short, green clover, listening intently to whatever Father was saying. To the right ke recognized one of kem brothers throwing things at a large straw bale.

Tammy was so intrigued with all these goings on that ke forgot to remain hidden. There was so much to see and try to make sense of!

Finding a New Balance

As the sun hit its zenith, the men and boys stopped what they were doing and climbed up the rows of benches to the trees around them, where each had set their belongings and a meal.

Tammy was startled to hear kem sibling's voice from a few feet away. Tod had felt Tammy's presence and climbed the benches to join kem in the trees. Ke congratulated Tammy on this important day and invited kem to share a meal – along with maybe some explanations of what was happening.

Tod was much older – had just turned 14 years of age - and was now completing the process that Tammy was beginning. Ke had explored many possible paths of work and study over those years, and when it was clear that kem gifts and tendencies made the path of healer the preferred direction for the next stage of life, ke was given kem adult name: no longer Toddy, but Tod. Soon ke would be leaving the village for an apprenticeship.

The two sat in the shade of a walnut tree where they could see the whole space. Eating their fruit and cheese, and drinking the clear, cool water from their *botas*,[85] they quietly reviewed what happened in this circle of stone and greenery, and why. Tammy was fascinated: a place where one could push one's body as hard as possible, learn from others how to hunt and fish and swim, and gain the skills to ward off predators without harming them! Amazing!

Tammy had heard some of the stories of elders' journeys, trials, and accomplishments, sitting around the fire on long nights. Now ke was seeing how they prepared for such experiences.

As they finished the meal, Tammy heard a bell ringing in the village and knew it was time for afternoon lessons. The two youngsters picked up their things, making sure no trace was left of their meal-break, and went back to the village center and the Hall where indoor gatherings and classes took place.

Usually, they went to separate areas for their lessons. Today, though, Tammy was seven, and that made kem

---

[85] A *bota* is water-bag or wineskin shaped so that the mouth piece is at the top of a narrow neck, above a rounded bottom, usually made of animal tissue and occasionally covered in fabric.

the youngest member of the life-prep classes instead of the oldest member of the basics class. So, Tammy went with Tod to a new part of the Hall, where one of the elders was waiting, congratulating kem as ke entered this new phase in life. From the next seven years Tammy would be encouraged to explore any aspect of life in the village, and soon would be visiting the market town, a few miles away, as kem world continued to expand.

That afternoon went quickly, with new possibilities opening up every few minutes. The elder and kem brother monitored Tammy's state closely, to minimize overwhelm in the face of change. Then, suddenly, lesson-time was over. Tammy and kem brother were leaving the building and their younger sibling Tilly was waiting for them outside. Together, the three made their way back to their safe and comfortable home. Along the way, noticing some ripe cherries fallen by the path, they stopped briefly to climb a tree and pick a few ripe ones, saving some to take to Mother and giving thanks to the tree for sharing, as they resumed their way.

At home, the three emptied their pockets of the delicious treats and shared with Mother and Grandmother some of the happenings of the day while helping to prepare the evening meal.

Later that evening, Father called Tammy into his workshop and asked about the day's experiences. Tammy loved being in Father's workshop, seeing the tools in their places on the walls was like seeing old friends. Ke shared some of the exciting things ke had experienced on this special day, then asked Father what ke was saying to the younger men in the arena. Father laughed, saying that such things would make no sense at all at this time, but maybe, someday, they could explore them together.

Tammy was intrigued but knew better than to push. Soon it was time for sleep; the great day was over and dreams were calling.

***

Years later, Tam would look back on that day and realize it was the turning point of a lifetime. While all children are considered neutral until their seventh birthdays, some will follow genetic norms and some won't as their life plays out. For Tam, that day of venturing into the men's world had made it clear: Tam was destined to live

> as a man. The homemaking skills learned in early childhood were essential for all human beings, but the quiet arts of a woman's life held no appeal, while the challenges of a man's life thrilled every fiber of Tam's being. Now, turning 21, Tam was an accomplished woodworker and forester whose work could be seen in the village shops, and even in the market town down the road. Father happily shared the tools in the workshop, and together they built a small cottage in the woods outside the village for Tam to call home. It was a good life, and Tam looked forward to seeing how the next couple centuries might unfold.

Consider the possibility…

Imagine a world in which all are encouraged to discover who we are on our own terms, where parents and teachers are trained to help us develop our innate capacity to know our own soul, to heal and be healed, to express our innate gifts and talents, to see beyond the range of eyesight, and to experience and express our fullest potential as human beings. Imagine the kinds of relationships we would have with each other and with the world around us if we *knew* that there is no separation, no difference, because, though we are each unique, we all emerge from the One and return to it, equally.

The stories of the ancient past have been preserved so we might have a light to show us the way. The question is: are we willing to go where they point? Are we willing to give up the belief that violence is inevitable, and the drive to "divide and conquer" the world around us as we've been taught for so many generations? Can we rediscover the nurturing source that is only found inside? Can we accept that the only true power is power with – not power over?

As I completed the final review of the first edition of this book, my phone rang. It was the dear friend with whom I had travelled to Chartres and Ste Baume, calling from several hundred miles away. The night before, she had hosted a full moon ceremony in which twenty women—professionals, mothers, grandmothers, healers—gathered at her home.

They walked the labyrinth my friend had built on her land; they shared a meal and their dreams and intentions. Then they stood in a circle in the light of the rising moon and felt the energy of the moonlight and the life of the plants and animals around them. They acknowledged the power of life within and around them, sang songs, declared intentions for the coming month and year, and told stories of other women in other places and times. My friend is pleased: some deeply moving experiences occurred in that circle and she knows that much good will come from this event.

Whatever we call the loving, Mother-presence—Holy Spirit, Oversoul, Comforter—however we relate to her; She is here, now, inside and around each and every one of us. To the extent that we allow, She works in union with the active, masculine Father-presence that also surrounds and enfolds us—so that we may become, finally, fully human, developing inborn gifts and potentials that are far beyond what our current culture is aware of.

This union is essential as we move through these years, this "end of ages," out of the past 6,000 years of the Age of Invasion & Empire, toward a new Age of Inclusion and Regeneration—a world of balance in which the divine Feminine, with all her gifts of birthing, knowing, and healing, is honored alongside the divinely Masculine drive to create, challenge, and explore—a world in which "in our image… male and female" is once more understood and lived by.

AFTERWORD

As I completed the final draft of the first edition of this book a much-promoted television show raised the possibility that a tomb found in the 1980s may be the tomb of the man we call Jesus Christ, along with two women called Mary and another person who could be their son. The producer of the show, James Cameron, took the idea and played it out to the fullest possible extent. What would Jesus' life have been like if he had married and had children and died a "normal" death?

The "tomb" is in fact an "ossuary," a box in which bones were stored after the flesh had decomposed in a tomb. It's actually a set of ossuaries, one of which says (in Hebrew/Aramaic) "Jesus son of Joseph," one of which says "Miriam," and another says "Mariamene," which is usually the Greek reference to Mary of Magdalene. Another appears to have held a boy. While historians say that the name "Jesus" was cited by the historian Josephus 21 times, and that many women were named "Miriam," Yacobivici, the researcher who partnered with Cameron, had a statistical study done and found that the odds were "800 to 1" that all of them would be in one place at one time. He also had DNA testing done on bone fragments in the "Jesus" box and the "Mariamene" box and found them to be unrelated, suggesting to him that they were probably married. (The ossuaries are empty because when they were discovered in 1980, Israeli authorities had the bones buried, as they do with all such finds.)

Among the many criticisms of the show's interpretation are that a Galilean family wouldn't have a tomb near Jerusalem. Yet, if there is any merit at all to the idea that Jesus son of Joseph and Mara/Mariamene founded a religious movement that was strong in Jerusalem, it makes sense that he and his family would have spent a good deal of time there and that his family might have been buried there.

Neither Cameron nor Yacobivici pretend that there is anything like definite proof, but they do request that the ossuaries not be dismissed out of hand and that appropriate studies be undertaken. To do so, however, flies in the face of 1700 years of Christian tradition that Jesus, as the Christ, "was resurrected and ascended into heaven" as described in the Nicene and Apostles' Creed. It also contradicts a tradition in Kashmir, India, that Jesus lived out his life there.

My own research suggests that neither of the people we call Jesus Christ and the Magdalene were anywhere near Jerusalem at the end of their days on this planet, and that, in the years immediately following the events described in the gospels, it's very likely that there were several more people with the titles of Mara/Mariamene and Joshua/Jesus in Palestine, as they took on the roles of leader in their communities and honored the ancient sacred cycle of sacrifice and resurrection for the sake of all the people.

That such practices were no longer necessary would have gone unnoticed by people steeped in a millennia-old tradition. Only a few in each generation hear the words of the great spiritual teachers – and only a few of them actually attempt to live by them.

Fortunately for our generation, we have easy access to all their teachings, and the leisure to seriously explore them. Hopefully, we will apply them effectively so that all humanity will benefit, soon.

APPENDIX A: THE HISTORICAL RECORD

During the period between 12000 and 8000BCE, when the ice sheets were melting and the climate was warming up, the vast herds of reindeer and horses retreated to the north and into the mountains, while the great Pleistocene mammals, including the saber-tooth tiger and woolly mammoth, disappeared. Across Europe and Asia, trees grew and forests spread, and the larger game animals were replaced by red deer, wild pigs, and cattle. Following the herds and hunting them for food, clothing, and shelter, was no longer a viable way of life outside of the Arctic Circle and largest mountain ranges, and so hunting tribes were gradually replaced by sedentary communities along fertile river valleys. Throughout southwest Asia and into Asia minor, for about a thousand years before wheat and barley were cultivated, isolated villages were supported by what could be gathered nearby, along with small herds of sheep, goats, cattle, and pigs.

From Paleolithic Hunters to Neolithic Villages

Scholars agree that women were probably responsible for figuring out how to cultivate plants, as they had long done most of the plant gathering and have been observed, in modern hunter-gatherer cultures, to encourage the growth of certain plants by leaving seeds and clearing space around seedlings. Over the next few hundred years these villagers were growing two-rowed barley and emmer wheat in small, well-irrigated plots. Cereals were being harvested with flint-bladed sickles and ground on limestone in the Nile valley more than 15,000 years ago. Plants and animals were not domesticated for food until about 7000BCE in the "fertile crescent" of southwestern Asia, and soon after that in what is now China.

Women also probably invented pottery, spinning, and weaving, as these are activities long associated with maintaining hearth and home. Pottery vessels, which have been found in Japan dating as early as 12000BCE, became widespread in the Near East by 6500BCE and in Europe by about 5000BCE. The use of fired pottery expanded and, by 3000BCE, fired bricks were used to build walls and fortifications across Asia.

As populations grew, more farmland was needed, and wood-handled stone axes were used to cut down trees and harvest wood for building houses. At first houses were round waddle-and-daub (also called cob) huts, but, with increased population, rectangular structures allowed more houses to fit in small areas, and permitted additional rooms to be added to individual homes.

The combination of systems for moving and storing water and compact architecture made village settlements possible. These, in turn, reduced even further the need for such manly skills as hunting, fishing, and herding, and encouraged the development of skilled artisans, each following their own specialty, very much as they had in the ancient hunting teams. In addition to pottery manufacturing, other specializations included stonecutters, bricklayers, metal-smiths, weavers, leather-workers, and sailors.

The oldest "city" discovered so far is Jericho, which had 2,000 people between 8350 and 7350BCE. A large stone wall and ditch surrounded the settlement and carved stone was used for containers and tools. There were a number of shrines with plaster statues and decorated skulls, and the presence of stones and shells from faraway places, indicating a wide range of trade connections.

Appendix A

Somewhat later, between 6800 and 5400BCE, the terraced apartments of Catal-Huyuk in the central plain of Anatolia (now Turkey) had a population of about 5,000. Here again, are many indicators of a broad trading range. Sophisticated pottery and woven textiles were in common use and all forms of plants and animals were cultivated, using rainfall and ground-water. Large frescoes decorate the walls, and one room is lined with plastered skulls of bulls, with their crescent-shaped horns intact (a shape that mimics a woman's uterus with fallopian tubes). There are no ditches or walls surrounding this community.

Large-scale irrigation began along the Euphrates River around 6000BCE, at a time when people living around the Nile and the Indus were using dikes and ditches to protect their homes and crops from floodwaters. Over the next two thousand years, these simple "back-up" procedures were expanded and systematized, making it possible for thousands of people to live where once the land had supported only a few dozen.

About 3200BCE, this proved a necessary capability, as a solar flare (or, some suggest, a meteor) changed the climate of North Africa and the Arabian Peninsula from lush prairie, dotted with lakes, to harsh desert, dotted instead with small oases. Soon, heavily populated agricultural settlements were appearing along all the major river plains across Asia and northern Africa.

Stone axes were replaced by copper-headed axes at about the same time, throughout Anatolia, across central Asia, and up into the Balkans. While shining bits of metal had long been used for jewelry and decoration, the capacity for generating the high temperatures necessary for melting ore and creating alloys was only developed as pottery-making advanced. High-fired pottery was common in Catal-Hayuk and across northern Anatolia and copper ore was located just northward, into the Caucasus mountains, opening the way for metal smelting. For the next two thousand years, while most of the metal work in settled areas across the region was focused on decorating religious objects, the more mobile hunters and herders focused on developing weapons, becoming warriors in the process.

Ironically, before women's pottery-making made it possible to use metal for tools rather than simply decorative purposes, there seems to have been equality between men and women and little warfare between communities. But with the development of metal tools and weapons, the age of patriarchy and empire began.

Harrapans of India

People have occupied the Indian sub-continent since the earliest humans walked the planet, at least as far back as 200,000 years ago. Several different racial groups have settled there, the first directly from Africa in the dawn of human pre-history. The first real cities developed around the Indus River, particularly at the sites now called Harappa and Mohenjo-daro. By about 3000BCE people were building mud-brick houses in the area, burials in the houses included funereal objects, and pottery had fine designs and potters' marks in a script unique to the Harappan culture. After 2500BCE, farmers moved onto the alluvial plain of the Indus River valley and built full-sized villages using fired bricks. Tools found in their homes include copper and bronze pins, knives, and axes; figurines of voluptuous women and cattle appear early on, as well.

The urban phase began about 2300BCE and lasted for about eight hundred years, during which about 500,000 square miles were dotted with elaborate cities built in uniform grids, with about 40,000 inhabitants congregated in well-built houses with private showers and toilets that drained into municipal sewer lines. Located on a flood plain, and suffering from occasional flooding by the Indus river, Mohenjo-daro was rebuilt seven times. High citadels marked each urban area, though the largest structures were the elevated granary for shared storage and the great bath (or swimming pool), which was 12 by 7 meters (about 40' x 24'). Around the pool were dressing rooms and private baths.

The people of the Harappan culture hunted wild game and domesticated cattle, sheep, and goats. Wheat and barley were the main foods grown, supplemented by peas, sesame, and other vegetables and fruits, beef, mutton, pork, eggs, fish, and milk. They traded widely, particularly with Oman ("the land of Magan") and references to them are found in early Mesopotamian texts. The houses were of nearly equal size, indicating an egalitarian social structure made up of merchants, farmers, and priests. Toward the end, carts were used and children played with miniature toy carts.

Cotton and wool were grown there and made into clothing. Metal was used primarily for decoration. A bronze figurine was found of an expressive dancing girl with her hand on her hip, naked except for jewelry. As in most such communities around the world, there are numerous figurines of the Mother Goddess.

Harappan culture had greatly declined by 1500BCE. With no written histories, the decline of this civilization is subject to much speculation. One theory focuses on deforestation, because of all the wood needed for the kilns to make the bricks used to build and rebuild the city, as well as to keep out the floodwaters. Another explanation depends on overgrazing by extensive herds of cattle and the resulting degradation of the ecosystem, including pollution of water supplies. This practice would lead farmers to move on to greener pastures, leaving behind abandoned villages and depopulated cities.

The traditional theory, well documented by the ancient hymns of the *Vedas*, is that a people calling themselves *Aryans*, or "noble ones," moved into the area with their herds of horses and cattle, conquered the native peoples of India, and destroyed their fields and structures to make more grazing land, which was then overgrazed, completing the destruction.

The hymns of the *Rig Veda* (See Appendix C) are considered the oldest and most important of the *Vedas*, having been composed between 1500BCE and the time of the great *Bharata* war about 900BCE. Essentially, the *Rig Veda* is a set of hymns praising the Aryan gods for giving them victories and wealth plundered from the local people, the *Dasas*, through warfare. The Aryans apparently used their advances in weaponry and skill in fighting to conquer the agricultural and tribal peoples of the fading Harappan culture. Numerous hymns refer to the use of horses and chariots with spokes, which must have given their warriors a tremendous advantage, even over a well-trained infantry. Spears, bows, arrows, and iron weapons are also mentioned.

As a nomadic and pastoral culture glorifying war, they established a new social structure of patriarchal families dominated by warriors and, eventually, with the knowledge woven into the *Vedas*, by priests. This social stratification was maintained well into modern times, throughout India, as the caste system, in which priests and warriors dominate, merchants and farmers follow, the lighter-skinned the better, and the dark-skinned people who originally occupied the region became "Untouchables."

The Mysterious Phoenicians

The *Rig Veda* also tells us that the civilization emerging as Assyria, Babylonia, Egypt, Greece and other ancient countries owed its origin to the union of Aryans with the seafaring traders of the Harappans into what became the Phoenicians. Upon being driven out of the Indus Valley, these highly civilized urbanites migrated westward. They had long traded with and colonized the coastal communities of the Red Sea and the Mediterranean, which, up until about 2500BCE, appear to have been connected by a strait through which Indian goods were taken to Europe. In later centuries, that passage gradually silted up and the connection between

Appendix A 313

India and Europe broke off, leaving the seafaring Phoenicians stranded, away from their homeland.

Many of their colonies were either expelled or were simply absorbed by successive waves of Aryans. Finally, they took hold of the coastal plain of what is now Syria and Palestine and developed the highly advanced civilization that gave us, among other things, the alphabet. Carthage, the magnificent seaport in North Africa, was founded about 900BCE as a Phoenician colony and became the dominant presence in the Mediterranean until the Roman Empire finally duplicated their vessels, destroyed the city, and salted its surrounding agricultural plain.

Urban Empires

Like all other river basins, the valley of the Euphrates attracted farming people who sought rich soil and reliable sources of water, and for several thousand years, scattered mud-brick villages, pastures, and gardens were the only sign of human habitation in the area. Then the invading settlers came.

Wave ONE

What is called the Ubaid culture, referring to the tribal peoples who moved into the area from the northwest, Aryan territories, developed along the lower Euphrates starting about 5800BCE. The resulting culture had the potter's wheel, high levels of metalworking, and refined irrigation methods, along with a rudimentary set of pictograph characters used in religious centers and to mark the work of specific artisans. The first city established was Eridu, about 5400BCE, which a Sumerian creation story, similar to those in the early *Vedas,* calls the first city to "emerge from the primeval sea." The oldest known temple was constructed there.

Most settlements by this time were fortified, with ongoing conflicts between the city-states of Uruk, Ur, Umma, and others along the river and its tributaries. They were united as Sumer about 4500BCE. The city of Uruk, begun about 5000BCE, had about 10,000 people in 3800BCE, and eight hundred years later 50,000 people were protected by its defensive walls and worshipped at its towering temple ziggurat.

Archeological evidence shows that Ur, which had become the capital city of Sumer, was completely inundated by a calamitous flood about 4000BCE. A thick layer of sandy mud and clay separates the remains of the more recent buildings from those of the earliest settlements all along the Euphrates river, which some believe lends credence to the story of Noah in the Bible and to some parts of the earliest known written epic story: "The Epic of Gilgamesh."

The first written records, appearing about 3,300BCE, were in the uniquely Sumerian cuneiform script, in which wedge-shaped letters were incised in damp clay and then dried as permanent records. According to the thousands of surviving tablets from the Sumerian culture, a ruler was called a lord (*en*) and was often deified. Each city had a governor (*ensi*) or a king (*lugal*, meaning "great man") who lived in a great house (*egal*), and their religious duties included building and maintaining temples. The wife of the king was called Lady or queen (*nin* or *nan*), and she managed the affairs of the temple, dedicated to the service of Inanna, the Goddess equated with the Moon. Some young women were "married" to the god in the temple; some were acolytes or priestesses who offered initiations through sexual union with the Goddess, and any children they bore through this service were often legally adopted by the men who fathered them. The tablets included poems, epic tales, and lists of all the kings who ruled along the Euphrates river, which, when compared with the records of other cultures, provide a remarkably coherent overview of Sumerian politics.

Appendix A

From the tablets and the many tools, decorations, and servants buried in the "royal tombs," it's clear that the Sumerians believed in an after-life for the spirits of the dead. It's also clear that people believed that each god or goddess lived in the temple built to them.

Wave TWO

The dynasty to take over the region after the deluge was from the Akkadian region northwest of Sumer in the city of Kish, ten miles east of what became Babylon. By about 3000BCE, a group of Semitic-speaking tribes had taken over the northern plains of the "fertile crescent," occupying Shinar and Akkad. And, over the next several centuries, they moved, individually and collectively, southward along the Mediterranean coast and along the river valleys of the Tigris and Euphrates. By 2400BCE, their tribes and herds were interspersed with most of the river communities. Except for language, they were virtually indistinguishable from the Sumerians. So it's not too surprising that twelve of the kings' names in this dynasty were Semitic rather than Sumerian.

The first legendary ruler during this period, Etana, was seen as a savior, and is said to have ascended to heaven on the back of an eagle. The earliest historical king, Mebaragesi, ruled Kish about 2700BCE and was described as having carried away the weapons of the neighboring community of Elam as spoil. The second dynasty, at Uruk, the original capital of Sumer itself, must have overlapped with the first, because it was the legendary fifth king of that dynasty, known as Gilgamesh, whose unbridled sexual adventuring and boisterousness was said to have so offended the values and norms of his people that they sent him off on a quest, described in the famous "Epic of Gilgamesh," during which he met the then-immortal sole survivor of the famous flood and managed to incur the wrath of Inanna by refusing to marry her because she "killed off her lovers."

Several generations later, in 2414BCE, Lugalzagesi became king of Uruk and greatly expanded Sumer's boundaries—from the Persian Gulf, including the Tigris and Euphrates, all the way to the Mediterranean—under the god Enlil. However, to do this he had to ally himself with the cup-bearer to the king of Kish. As a result, his reign of 24 years was to mark the end of that Sumerian empire in about 2390BCE, for the name of that Akkadian cup-bearer was Sargon.

Wave THREE: Sargon, the First Semitic Emperor

Sargon's story is classic myth: he "did not know his father and claimed his mother was a changeling." A Neo-Assyrian (7th century BCE) text recounted how his mother, vowed to the temple, bore him in secret, put her baby in a basket of rushes sealed with bitumen, and cast it upon the Euphrates River. The river carried him to Akki, a drawer of water, who reared Sargon as a son and appointed him as his gardener. As a gardener Sargon had an experience that he described as "receiving the love of the goddess Ishtar." This then gave him the power and authority to become a military and religious leader. Older inscriptions describe him as cup-bearer to the king of Kish whom either he or Lugalzagesi overthrew.

In 2350BCE, Sargon built a new capital that he called Agade on the Euphrates, with temples dedicated to Ishtar (the Akkadian name for Inanna) and to the warrior god Zababa of the Kish. He began to introduce centralization, appointing Akkadian governors in all the city-states, placing Semites in authority over the Sumerians and setting the Semitic Akkadian language as equal to the ancient Sumerian—in both written and spoken forms. Then, following Sumerian religious traditions, he appointed his daughter to the position of high priestess and was himself anointed as priest of the gods Anu and Enlil.

Appendix A

In ancient Sumerian tradition, the queen of heaven, Inanna, was not only the goddess of love but of battle as well. Sargon's daughter, as high-priestess of Inanna, wrote a poem in which she called her deity, "radiant light" and "queen of all the divine decrees of civilization." She described her as a goddess who could be terrible by destroying vegetation, bringing floods from the mountain, fire over the land, destroying foreign lands, attacking like a storm, burning down gates, causing rivers to run with blood so that people had nothing to drink, driving off adult males as captives, and in cities which were not hers keeping her distance so that its women did not speak of love with their husbands nor whisper to them nor reveal the holiness of their hearts to them.

At the same time, in an Akkadian text, we can see elements of the Aryan *vedas* and kernels of modern Semitic rules of character:

> Let your mouth be restrained and your speech guarded;
> That is a man's pride - let what you say be very precious.
> Let insolence and blasphemy be an abomination for you;
> a talebearer is looked down upon....
> Do not return evil to your adversary;
> requite with kindness the one who does evil to you;
> maintain justice for your enemy;
> be friendly to your enemy....
> Give food to eat, beer to drink;
> grant what is requested; provide for and treat with honor.
> At this one's god takes pleasure.

Ambitious to expand his new empire and gain material resources, Sargon crossed the Tigris River to make the kings of Elam, Barshashe, and other neighbors his vassals. He then went northwest, where he prostrated himself before the grain-god Dagan, who "gave" him the region of Mari, Iarmuti, and Ebla, all the way to the cedar forests of Lebanon and the Taurus mountains, giving him access to ample timber and precious metals. Some even suggest that Sargon crossed the western sea and landed on Cyprus and Crete—giving rise to the Greek legends of the golden age of "Arcadia." The Akkadians valued independence of households and building of wealth as private property. Sargon's military officers and bureaucrats controlled their own lands and served their emperor only as it suited them. Still, Sargon ruled over this vast empire until his death, still fighting battles, and destroying a vast army in revolt.

He was succeeded by his son, Rimush, who put down the revolts in Sumer, Iran, and Elam. He, however, became victim to the ancient ritual sacrifice, for after only nine years, they "killed him with their tablets." His brother Manishtusu, was next in line. He continued these wars and boasted how he had secured silver mines and diorite for many statues from southern Elam.

A palace revolution ended the next man's reign in 2249BCE, and over the next three years the classic list of Sumerian kings includes four names. Eventually the Guti, another Aryan tribe, invaded from the north, destroyed the city of Agade and put an end to the Akkadian empire.

Wave FOUR: The Rise of Ur

In the confusion of city-states that followed the crumbling of the empire, Gudea, governor of Lagash from 2197 to 2178BCE, rebuilt the Sumerian city of Girsu, which had been burnt to the ground prior to Sargon's rule, adding fifteen or more temples. He was inspired by a dream he had:

> ...a man as tall as the sky and as heavy as the earth told him to build a temple. A woman also appeared holding a stylus of flaming metal and a tablet with the good writing of heaven. To understand this dream, Gudea consulted his "mother," the goddess Gatumdug, and he went by boat to the temple of the goddess Nanshe, who interpreted dreams. Nanshe explained that the man was the god Ningirsu and the woman the goddess of science, Nisaba. The wisdom of Ningirsu, the son of Enlil, would

reveal to him the plan of his temple. Gudea obeyed and tried to unite the people of Girsu "as sons of the same mother" by purifying the city with encircling fires, putting clay in a pure place; making bricks, he purified the foundations of the temple and anointed the platform with perfume.

About 2176BCE the governor of Uruk, Utu-hegal, revolted against this Guti "serpent of the hills" and, in time, with the help of other cities, defeated the foreigners. However, Uruk was not able to hold the power, so seven years later, in the ancient pattern, Ur-Nammu, the governor of Ur, was proclaimed king of Ur, Sumer, and Akkad.

Ur-Nammu, ruling from 2112-2095BCE, is credited with building the great ziggurat at Ur, freeing the land of thieves, robbers, and rebels, and, using "principles of equity and truth," promulgating the oldest known code of laws. According to the ancient texts Ur-Nammu established "equity in the land and banished malediction, violence, and strife." Not as harsh as the later laws of Hammurabi and Moses, crimes involving physical injuries were not always punished by death or mutilation but often by paying compensation in silver instead.

His son, Shulgi, ruled for 47 years. Calling himself "King of the Four Quarters," following tradition, he was worshipped as a god. The first half of Shulgi's reign was spent completing the temples and ziggurats, reinstating the gods in their shrines with newly appointed high priests, supporting the schools, and reforming the calendar and the standards for measuring grain. Then Shulgi

> Interestingly, this title reappeared among the Etruscans in Italy, over 1000 years later, suggesting that it was always in use in the "underground" or pagan culture.

began a series of military campaigns in the plains and mountains north of Diyala. He pacified other regions by marrying his daughters to governors in Barshashe, Anshan, and Susa.

Shulgi described himself as the trustworthy god of all the lands; he claimed to be endowed with wisdom by Enki, loving justice and hating evil words. He boasted of straightening the highways, planting gardens along them, making travel safe, and establishing resting places. He took charge of the music in the temple and brought bread-offerings, claiming as his spouse the maid Inanna, queen and vulva of heaven and earth. From 2150 to 2094BCE Shulgi and his son, Amar-Sin, ruled over an empire even more unified than the Akkadian empire of Sargon. The state had now merged with and overwhelmed the importance of both temple and private property. The government owned and operated large factories, workshops, and trading posts, and oversaw thousands of laborers in agriculture, industry, public works, civil service, and police. Workers were freemen who paid taxes in both coin and military service.

Amar-Sin was succeeded by his brother, Shu-Sin, who ruled for eight years, coming into conflict with an "uncivilized" people coming in from the northwest called the Martu or Amorites, who were contemptuously described as not knowing about grain or agriculture or houses or burials but were mountain boors eating raw meat.

Shu-Sin was succeeded by his son, Ibbi-Sin, and the empire soon disintegrated. Esh-nunna and Susa in the southeast broke away, and then the Amorites attacked from the north. An Amorite had already been crowned in Larsa near Ur. Then the Elamites invaded Sumer. Ibbi-Sin, facing a famine and enemies on two fronts, tried to ally himself with the Amorites against Ibbi-Irra and the Elamites. However, this too failed, and in 2060BCE the glorious city of Ur, starving under siege, was attacked and burned down, a catastrophe that scribes attributed to the wrath of their god, Enli. This Third Dynasty of Ur lasted just

> Today, the use of "Sin" in the name suggests a connection with China, which, in the Indo-European languages, is "Sin-, Sino-, or Sing."

Appendix A

over a century, until 2060BCE and is considered the final glory of Sumerian civilization. It's also the period during which the biblical patriarch Abram grew up and left Ur for Canaan.

Ibbi-Sin was depressed by the bad omens and believed that the god Enlil hated him. Then his general, Ishbi-Irra, asked his sovereign for permission to defend the two cities, and defeated the Amorites. Believing he was favored by Enlil, Ishbi-Irra proclaimed himself king in 2073BCE, and, in spite of a number of significant invasions—including one in 1925, when the Hittites plundered Babylon—his dynasty lasted until 1850BCE. In large part, it is due to the effort of his grandson, Iddin-Dagan, named after the wheat-god Dagan of Mari before whom Sargon had prostrated himself and where his grandfather Ishbi-Irra had begun his conquests, that we have this detailed a record of the history of the Sumerian culture. While he occupied Sippar and ruled over the entire southern Euphrates region, this Semite ruler used the Sumerian language in official inscriptions and gathered a huge collection of Sumerian literature into a library at Nippur.

During his reign, the city-state of Assur joined with Nineveh to form an Assyrian kingdom, which along with the kingdoms of Mari, Babylon, and Larsa, surrounded Eshnunna. Under the Amorites, the kingdom of Mari extended as far west as the Mediterranean Sea. The son of a ruler near Mari named Shamsi-Adad became an outlaw and was exiled to Babylon; but when his brother succeeded to the throne, he gathered a force to take and attacked Assur, replacing his brother, and led his army to the west as far as Lebanon. Then, with his sons' help Shamsi-Adad ruled the first Assyrian empire from 1869 to 1837BCE, overlapping with the reign of Hammurabi in Babylon. Someone warned him about Hammurabi, but another advised him not to, and so he ignored the threat.

Wave FIVE: The Amorite Hammurabi's Babylon

The Babylon (the word derives from the Semitic *babi-lu*, "gate of the gods") that Hammurabi inherited from his Amorite father in 1848BCE was a relatively new city-state, quite limited in size and power. Then, after being king for five years Hammurabi began to attack his neighbors, capturing Isin, moving down the Euphrates to Uruk, and expanding in other directions. In 1820BCE Babylon was attacked by Elamites, Guti, Assyrians, and Eshnunna, but Hammurabi was victorious "through the great power of the gods," and "encouraged by an oracle" the next year, he invaded and defeated Larsa. The year after that a new coalition of the same old enemies formed and was again defeated by Hammurabi's forces. Apparently caught up in a warlike mode, the very next year Hammurabi attacked his ally and took control of Mari and parts of Assyria, making them his vassals. Two years later, Hammurabi returned and destroyed the city of Mari and, over the next few years, defeated all his enemies in that country. In less than ten years Babylon had conquered almost all of Mesopotamia.

Hammurabi ruled through provincial governors but also allowed cities to make local decisions and collect taxes by councils of elders. Diverse religious traditions were tolerated, and many temples were rebuilt, even at Nippur, although Marduk was made the chief god. This was a significant shift in attitude, for Marduk, unlike other gods, was not a loving son of the Goddess, but her destroyer:

> Marduk harnessed his terrible storm chariot and went to challenge Tiamat to single combat. He enmeshed her in his net; when she opened her mouth, he drove in the evil wind, which distended her belly. Then he shot an arrow, which split her heart. When her life was destroyed, he stood on her carcass. Marduk imprisoned her followers and broke their weapons. Then binding Kingu and taking from him the tablet of destinies, Marduk put his seal on it and fastened it on his breast. He split Tiamat into two parts, half in place as the earth and half for a roof as the sky.

Appendix A

This violent poem was clearly a means to foster Babylonian patriotism and the patriarchy through the worship of the ultimate masculine god.

On the surface, though, things were not much different. With the exception of this version of Marduk the Babylonians continued to worship the Sumerian gods, with Semitic names. Temples were still important and contained the usual lodgings, libraries, schools, offices, workshops, stores, cellars, and stables. Religious ceremonies were performed every day with music, prayers, and sacrifices. Priests had sons who were taught in the schools. Clergy included chanters, exorcists, and dream interpreters. Priestesses could marry but were not allowed to bear children in the temple, where sacred sexual initiation continued. Houses were still built in the Sumerian manner with enclosed courtyards and a family chapel for the household gods and a place for burials.

Hammurabi is best known for the code of laws he promulgated near the beginning of his reign and had carved in stone in temples shortly before he died. The stated purposes of these laws were noble:

to cause justice to prevail in the country,
to destroy the wicked and the evil,
that the strong may not oppress the weak.

However, Hammurabi's code is far more severe than previous Sumerian laws. What had been created to settle quarrels and private conflicts by means of arbitration had become law for everyone, instituting a system to resolve private conflicts by public standards that included various forms of capital punishment, where once fines were considered sufficient; they reflected the new culture's penchant for using retaliatory violence as a reaction to problems. Moreover, the laws supported social and economic inequalities: classes and castes, not to mention genders, were treated differently, with higher penalties often imposed on lower classes and women.

Hammurabi's Babylon dominated the Mesopotamian region. He died about 1806BCE and was succeeded by his son,

Samsuiluna, who ruled until about 1768, but had to handle numerous revolts. In the south, Larsa rebelled for two years and then Iluma-ilu claimed independence for Sumer south of Nippur, fighting a bloody war against Babylon in which several cities, including Ur, were burned down. This was about the time that the Hittites, called Hyksos by the Egyptians, were using their chariots and compound bows to take over the Nile delta.

Waves SIX – TEN: Kassites, Hittites, Mitanni, Assyrians, Hurrians

Babylon was invaded again by the Hittites and captured by king Mursilis in about 1650BCE, but he soon left Babylon and returned to Hattusas in Asia Minor. The Kassite ruler, Agum II, filled this power void, establishing the Kassite dynasty in Mesopotamia that was to last until about 1157BCE. The Kassites had been moving into the Babylonian area from the time of Hammurabi and had adopted many Babylonian traditions, while maintaining their earlier Aryan influence, as evidenced by their Vedic deities, among them Surya and Marut. Among other things, 24 years after the Hittites had carried it off, Agum II brought back and restored the statue of Marduk to its temple. They restored the ancient temples of Nippur, Larsa, Ur, and Uruk and their scholars wrote in Akkadian, establishing it as the standard language of the region for a millennium.

About 1370BCE, the Hittite king Suppiluliumas plundered the Mitanni capital of Wassukkanni and conquered the western region of Aleppo and Kadesh, which had been at the northern edge of the Egyptian empire. This was when Egyptian influence in the area was in decline, while Akhenaten, the monotheist, was pharaoh.

About 1360BCE, Ashur-uballit I was declared Great King of Assyria. He called Akhenaten his brother and gave his daughter to king Burnaburiash in Babylon; but the grandson

Appendix A

of this match was murdered, causing a civil war and, with Ashur-uballit's intervention, resulting in Kurigalzu II becoming king of Babylon.

The followers of Ashur, or Assyrians, turned against the Hurrians, advanced to the Euphrates, and eventually wiped out the Mitannian kingdom that had built up around the Sumerian region. The greatest defeat was administered by the Assyrian Shalmaneser I about 1265BCE, who claimed to have destroyed 180 of their cities and blinded 14,400 captives. The Kassites tried to make new boundary agreements with the encroaching Assyrians, but the Assyrian Tukulti-Ninurta I, about 1220BCE, conquered Babylon, declaring frankly, "I forced Kashtiliash, King of Kar-Duniash, to give battle." (Kar-Duniash being the Kassite word for Babylon.) After seven years of Assyrian domination, the nobles of Akkad and Kar-Duniash revolted and put the Kassite heir on the throne. Ramses II was pharaoh in Egypt at this time and maintained a strong military presence on the borders.

In 1146BCE Nebuchadnezzer I (*Nabu-kudurri-usur*)took the throne and led Babylon, once again, to a position of power and respect in the region. The Assyrians took it back about 200 years later.

Nebuchadnezzer II defeated the Assyrians just over 200 years after that and it was under his reign that Jerusalem and Zion were captured and Solomon's temple was destroyed, in 596BCE.

Waves ELEVEN -FIFTEEN: Persians, Greeks, Romans, Turks, and Mongols

The Persians, under Cyrus the Great, conquered the region about 70 years later, and established their religion, Zoroastrianism, and their language, now known as Aramaic, as the primary language and religion in the region. Even when Alexander, the Aryan king of Macedon came along, conquering the region in the name of the Greeks in 350BCE, these traditions did not change among the rural population—many of whom still speak and write Aramaic and still practice the ancient rituals of that period.

The Romans conquered the Greek empire over an extended period that ended about 50BCE, and controlled the region until about 300CE. Then Constantine became emperor and moved his capital from a badly deteriorating Rome to Byzantium in Asia Minor; a new, Christian, Byzantine Empire controlled the region, and, following the ancient tradition of spiritual leadership, Constantine's mother, Helena, went to Jerusalem and surrounding areas to identify and establish the new sacred sites for the newly established religion.

The Byzantines lost control of the region to the Muslim Arabs who established their Caliphate about 700CE and remained in control of the region until Genghis Khan came sweeping through from Mongolia, in the early 1200s.

Wave SIXTEEN: Ottomans, Iranians, Spanish adventurers, Bonaparte & Englishmen

The Ottoman Empire grew out of a synthesis of the Muslim and Mongolian cultural traditions in the late 1300s. What started as a pesky state on the edge of the Mongol-Muslim region very quickly took over the Byzantine empire and grew into a major world power that remained in place until World War I, when the British, seeking petroleum reserves, took over the region.

Wave SEVENTEEN: Iranians, Spanish adventurers

Meanwhile, in the years that Columbus discovered the New World and Gutenberg built a printing press, a whole new empire was formed in Iran, the Safavids, and the kings of England Spain began to dream of Empire—sending armies out to conquer the Americas. This wave lasted until the 1700s.

Appendix A

Wave EIGHTEEN: Bonaparte & Englishmen

Bonaparte of France emerged as the next major empire-builder, extending his reach all the way into Egypt and parts of Russia and upsetting the Ottomans in the process. Then England defeated Bonaparte and used trade as the primary vehicle for maintaining control well into the 1900s, when it all dissolved.

Wave NINETEEN: American Hegemony

Today, the United States of America has taken on the mantle of world-domination, in the name of "bringing democracy" to other peoples. The price? Constant presence of U.S. troops, preferential pricing for exports, acceptance of U.S. technology and infrastructure for the local economy. Over 40 countries in the world today are part of this "globalization" process with the expectation that, by the end of the 21st century, American-owned corporations will control the economies of over 2/3 of the world.

Anatolia/Asia Minor, Base of Operations for the Hittites

Though people had been living in Anatolia for several millennia, little is known of its history until Assyrians settled on the central plateau about 1900BCE. Their Aryan heritage can be seen in the name of their ruling city, Purushhattum, which is very close to the Sanskrit word meaning "highest person."

The Hittites accepted the deities of all the cultures they conquered, which they added to their own Goddess Arinna, who was also sometimes seen as a supreme God. Mursilis II thanked the goddess for helping him to destroy his enemies, and Hattusilis III justified his taking of the throne from Urhi-Teshub to the omniscient Ishtar, explaining that Ishtar had told his wife in a dream that he would be king. As throughout the Middle East, great festivals were celebrated every spring and autumn, and it was essential that the king be present.

Hittite custom said that the queen retained her position after her husband's death while her son usually became king, and in some diplomatic letters she is addressed independently of the king, as Queen Mother. Laws were strict against incest with a mother or daughter and even among in-laws except after a death, but, as in Egypt, a brother could marry a sister.

An ancient document attributed to Anittas described how a king of Kussara took the city of Nesa at night by force but did not harm anyone. Anittas took Hattusas by force, fortified Nesa, and campaigned against Salatiwara. The city of Purushanda sent him gifts, and he made one of their leaders his advisor.

About 1700BCE King Hattusilis I moved the Hittite capital from Kussara to Hattusas and fought several wars to expand his kingdom and acquire silver. He first took control of the north to the Black Sea and then raided Alalakh in north Syria and Arzawa in the west; but then Hurrians attacked from the east, and only his capital at Hattusas remained loyal.

Praying to the goddess, Hattusilis went southward to battle again in north Syria, destroying Ulma, Zaruna, and Hassuwa. After three battles he took Hahhum and claimed that he freed their slaves and gave them to his goddess, Arinna, along with silver, in carts pulled back to Hattusas by the captured kings of Hassuwa and Hahhum. Discovering a plot to replace him by the heir apparent, his nephew, and his nephew's mother (his sister), whom he called a snake, Hattusilis did not kill them but designated his grandson Mursilis as successor, counseling him to consult the assembly (*panku*).

The Hittites then proceeded southward into Egypt, where they were known as Hyksos, or "shepherd kings." Riding their chariots and wielding iron swords, they easily overtook the Egyptian foot-soldiers and drove the Egyptian king, or pharaoh, south into Thebes. For nearly two centuries, from 1720 to 1552, Hittite/Hyksos rulers controlled the northern Nile, occupying pharaoh's palace and taking on the role of the god-king there.

Finally, in 1552, Kamoses, rightful heir to the Egyptian double-crown and throne, amassed enough power to throw out the impostors and he and his successors, Amosis I, Thutmose II and III, chased them back to Asia Minor and to the Euphrates.

During the 1400sBCE, the Hittite code of law was developed while the Mitannian kingdom spread into north Syria. About the time Egypt's Thutmose III invaded Mitanni, the Hittites regained control of Kizzuwadna and began sending tribute to Egypt, including people from Kurushtama. When Mitanni and Egypt became allied by the marriage of a Mitannian princess to Thutmose IV, the Hittites were attacked from Gaska in the northeast and Arzawa in the west, and they lost control of Kizzuwadna in the south. While his father Tudhaliya III was still king, Suppiluliumas regained some of the eastern lands but lost the capital at Hattusas, which he recaptured and fortified about the time he became king in 1380BCE.

Using diplomacy to regain control, Suppiluliumas brought the king of Kizzuwadna back under Hittite influence, made an agreement with Tushratta's Hurrian rival Artatama, and congratulated Amenhotep IV (Akhenaten) on his accession to the throne of Egypt. Then Suppiluliumas invaded the Mitannian areas of north Syria, establishing his son in Kumanni and making Aleppo a vassal. This stimulated Amorite revolts against Egyptian hegemony by Abdi-ashirta and after his death, by his son Aziru, who was called to Egypt by Akhenaten and, having seen there the strange pharaoh's weakness, made a treaty with Ugarit upon returning and joined the Hittite camp.

Provoked by Mitannian attacks, Suppiluliumas also made a treaty with Ugarit and invaded the Mitannian capital at Wassukkanni; Tushratta fled and, as a losing king was killed in a coup involving his son Kurtiwaza. Suppiluliumas then ravaged north Syria as far as Apina (Damascus), which, at that time, was under Egyptian influence. Suppiluliumas established feudal states, taking some reigning families to his Hittite land, returning them to Syria later. After a siege, the city of Carchemish was taken, and he installed his son there as king Shar-Kushuk and made Telepinus, another son, king of Aleppo. When Tutankhamen died in Egypt, his widow wrote to Suppiluliumas asking to marry one of his sons; but after some questioning and delay, the son that was sent was killed.

Hittite soldiers returning from a vengeance attack on Egypt brought a plague, which killed Suppiluliumas and probably his son Arnuwandas II, who ruled for only one year. Mursilis II became king but was occupied with responding to revolts in Arzawa for ten of his 26 years as king, and the capital was moved south to Tarhuntassa.

Muwatallis became king of the Hittites about 1320BCE. Then, about 1300BCE a major military confrontation occurred at Kadesh between the empire of Egypt led by Ramses II and the Hittites. Both sides claimed victory, but the result was a stand-off, which was ratified in a treaty sixteen years later between Ramses II and Hattusilis III, who had supplanted Urhi-Teshub in the traditional fashion, after seven years of internal strife.

Over the next century Hittite power declined, and about 1200BCE the Sea People invaded and destroyed the remains of the Hittite empire.

> Many people believe the "Sea People" documented by Hittites, Egyptians, and others, to be the Phoenicians or even Etruscans.

Appendix A **331**

The Etruscans, Founders of Italy

Somewhere between 900 and 800BCE, the Italian peninsula was settled by a mysterious people called the Etruscans. They founded their civilization in northeastern Italy between the Appenine mountain range and the Tyrrhenian (which is the Greek name for the Etruscan people) Sea, in the area now known as Tuscany, also the "birthplace of the Renaissance."

We don't know where the Etruscans came from, but archaeologists suspect that they came from Asia Minor. Excavations on Lemnos turned up a community there dating around 600BCE with a *stele*, or marking-pole, inscribed in a language similar to Etruscan. It was found in a warrior's tomb with weapons and pottery that are very similar to early Etruscan ware. The necropolis, or cemetery, of the city contained 130 cremated burials. In the women's burials an early form of Etruscan *Bucchero* pottery was found (*Bucchero* clay was used both by the people of Asia Minor and by the Etruscans). In the men's sites were found daggers and axes of Cretan and Etruscan model. This, then, is a small community with strong cultural ties with the Etruscans. The date, however, is an issue: the Lemnos *stele* could represent an isolated colony of Etruscan sailors or even pirates.

The theory of Northern origination, which bases its evidence on the similarities of Raetian and Etruscan languages, has one major flaw: Raetian Alpine inscriptions are much later, and are more consistent with later Etruscan influences, suggesting that they're associated with the scattering of the Northern Etruscans following invasions.

Although the Etruscan language is by no means totally decoded, we now know enough to see that the language is not of Indo-European base. Still, many words of Etruscan origin found themselves into Latin and from there into English. So quite a few Etruscan words look very familiar.

In the Proto-Villanovan period (Bronze Age) and the following early Villanovan (Iron Age), no signs of distinction of classes have been noted. Then, after about 750BCE, archeologists notice a marked differentiation among individuals, evidenced by increased numbers of items in burial outfits and by the presence of status symbols, besides imported ornaments and jewels (vitrified gypsum scarabs from Egypt and golden Punic pendants) and ceramics (such as painted jars from Greece). About this time we find bits for horses, associated with warriors and kings—the first sign of Aryan influence.

Etruscans were largely an agrarian people, but when they built a strong military, they used that military to dominate all the surrounding peoples. These dominated populations did the agricultural labor on Etruscan-held farms, so the Etruscans had time to devote to commerce and industry. In the 600sBCE, the Etruscan military had subjugated much of Italy, including Rome, and some regions outside of Italy, including the island of Corsica.

The birth of a "middle" class took place in the Archaic Age, in the 500sBCE, when craftsmen and merchants began to work for themselves instead of for rich princes. There were also the slaves imported from far-off countries or captured during the numerous battles for the domination on the Tyrrhenian trade

Etruscan women enjoyed greater respect and freedom than in the Latin and Greek world. For the Latins the woman had to be *lanifica et domiseda*, sitting and spinning the wool in her home, and, in more ancient times, the *paterfamilias* (head of the family) had the right to decide her death if she was found drinking wine. In contrast, among the Etruscans, a woman could take part in banquets, lying down on the same *kline* (couch, or *chaise longe*) with her companion, or be present at sport-games and spectacles. This was scandalous for the Romans who branded, without hesitation, this equality as a sign of licentiousness and poor morality, so the adjec-

Appendix A **333**

tive "Etruscan" became a synonym of "prostitute." Clearly, the social condition of women in the Etruscan civilization was really unique in the Aryan-dominated world, and maybe that was due to the different descent of the peoples: Etruscans appear to have emerged from pre-Indo-European cultures while Latins and Greeks were definitely Indo-European, or Aryan, in origin.

Etruscan women could transmit their family name to their children, especially in the highest social classes. Sometimes in the epigraphs the woman's name (we would say the family name today) is preceded by a first name (the personal name); this distinguished her individually within the family group, unlike the Romans who commemorated only the name of her *gens*, the line of descent.

Etruscan religion was, like Christianity and Judaism, a revealed religion. An account of the revelation is given by Cicero (*On Divination* 2.50).

> One day, says the legend, in a field near the river Marta in Teruria, a strange event occurred. A divine being rose up from the newly ploughed furrow, a being with the appearance of a child, but with the wisdom of an old man. The startled cry of the ploughman brought *lucomones*, the priest kings of Etruria hurrying up to the spot. To them, the wise child chanted the sacred doctrine, which they reverently listened to and wrote down, so that this most precious possession could be passed on to their successors. Immediately after the revelation, the miraculous being fell dead and disappeared into the ploughed field. His name was Tages, and he was believed to be the son of Genius and grandson of the highest God, Tinia (or Jupiter as he became known to the Romans).

This doctrine, known to the Romans as the *disciplina etrusca*, seems to have comprised three categories or books (*libri*). The first was the *libri haruspicini*, which dealt with divination from the livers of sacrificed animals; the second, the *libri fulgurates*, the interpretation of thunder and lightning; the third, the *libri rituales*, which covered a variety of matters. They contained, as the Roman historian Festus said,

...prescriptions concerning the founding of cities, the consecration of altars and temples, the inviolability of ramparts, the laws relating to city gates, the division into tribes, curiae and centuriae, the constitution and organization of armies, and all other things of this nature concerning war and peace.

Among the *libri rituales* were also three further categories: the *libri fatales*, on the division of time and the life-span of individuals and peoples; the *libri Acherontici*, on the world beyond the grave and the rituals for salvation; and finally, the *ostentaria*, which gave rules for interpreting signs and portents and laid down the propitiatory and expiatory acts needed to obviate disaster and to placate the gods.

Such a broad doctrine naturally required long study. For this, the Etruscans had special training institutes, among which the school at Tarquinii had the highest reputation. These institutes were much more than seminaries in the modern sense. They were a kind of university with several faculties. Their curricula included not only religious laws and theology, but also the encyclopedic knowledge required of the priests, which ranged from astronomy and meteorology through zoology, ornithology, and botany to geology and hydraulics. This last subject was the specialty of the *aquivices*, members of the priesthood who advised the city-states on all their hydraulic engineering projects. They were expert diviners who knew how to find subterranean water and how to bore wells, how to dig water channels, supply drinking water to the towns, and install irrigation and drainage systems in the fields. In addition they created artificial reservoirs and collaborated with other priests who specialized in constructing subterranean corridors and tunneling through mountains. In Etruria, as in the ancient Middle East, theological and secular knowledge were not separated. Whatever humanity set out to do on earth must align with the patterns of the cosmos.

The Etruscans even evolved a system of town planning based on these religious concepts, which were likewise re-

Appendix A

flected in the elaborate ritual prescribed for the foundation of a new city. In Etruria the town laid out in accordance with the sacred rules was considered a minute portion of the cosmos, harmoniously integrated with an all-embracing order governed by the gods.

In all community ritual, the priesthood played an important role, ensuring that only good powers were present and all others were removed. The priest, after fixing the north-south and east-west lines by the sky, turned to the south and pronounced the words: "This is my front, and this my back, this my left and this my right." Then wearing his conical hat (which survives today in the form of the Bishop's mitre) and holding his *lituus* (today's Bishop's crook), he solemnly used his right hand to mark out the cross of the *cardo* and the *decumanus*, top to bottom and left to right.

A number of symbols often ascribed to Rome, including the *Lictor* and *Fasces* as symbols of rule, were of Etruscan origin, as were the purple robes worn by the emperors and the white robes of the high priest.

Each of the cities in the Etruscan league of twelve, together with the Po Valley cities to the North of Italy, was an independent state. Houses were laid out in streets with sewage lines located under the roads. Early Rome, founded by the Etruscans, was laid out in a similar fashion. The Etruscans reticulated water by means of underground water pipes and pressure boxes—a technology not passed on to the Romans. Under-floor heating was used in homes and bathhouses, which the Romans continued in later years.

The pillars used by the Etruscans to support temples and other public works were built according to long pre-defined ratios, and modern computer models show that they were a significant improvement on the Greek Corinthian, Doric and Ionian models. At the same time, arches, unknown in Classical Greece, were originally used in Mesopotamia, and were introduced to Italy by the Etruscans.

As a result, homes of the Etruscan ruling classes were typically characterized by a wide central courtyard, entered from what the Romans called an *Atrium Tuscanicum*. The word *atrium* comes from the Etruscan word for entrance or harbor, as in the Etruscan port of Atrii, which gave its name to the Adriatic Sea. Several other rooms led off from this central courtyard. These Etruscan *villas* were the precursor to the later Roman *villa* (a group of which came to be called a "village").

The buildings were single story and were built with blocks of stone as a foundation. The walls were constructed with frames of wood and clay plastering. The typical roof had eaves, but terraced roofs were also built. The exterior and interior walls of the houses were frescoed with geometric patterns or with molded terracotta. Painted scenes adorned the interiors. It was common to have murals painted in frame-like sections, giving an overall effect of pictures hanging on a wall.

The Etruscans, like the Basques, the Irish, and a few other isolated groups, have significantly contributed to Western culture simply by maintaining their Anatolian roots and language in the presence of Aryan culture. Much of what made Rome unique derived from Etruscan influence and remains alive in our culture today.

Appendix B: Church Commentaries on Mary Magdalene

In the 200s, an early church leader and interpreter of scripture, Origen, associated Mary Magdalene with Luke's sinful woman, and she became a symbol for the contemplative life *(La Vie Contemplative)*.

Augustine, c.410, suggested that the Wedding at Cana was in fact, the disciple John's wedding—only he was so impressed by the wine miracle that he gave up marriage and went to follow Jesus. Several later sources, including St. Anselm, suggested that Mary Magdalene was the abandoned bride and that she either fled into Jerusalem and became a prostitute, or stayed with Jesus' mother.

In 441, Cyril of Alexandria, of the Eastern Church, proposed that Mary Magdalene's penance freed all women of Eve's transgression, and all women were honored through her witness of the resurrection.

Pope Gregory I, the Great (author of Gregorian chants), in a sermon on 9/14/591, united the penitent sinner and Mary of Magdalene with the woman who washes Jesus' feet with her tears and dries them with her hair; he later uses her as a model of repentant conversion. His sermons are common in sermon-collections so many other priests told their congregations the same story, making it the Official Story of the Roman church. Shortly after, related art appeared.

Around 650, a Byzantine calendar listed Mary Magdalene's feast day as July 22 and her sepulcher was honored at

Ephesus, where she's said to have journeyed with the Virgin and the young disciple, John.

Around 750, British historian Bede listed her in his book of martyrs and includes her in his commentary on Luke's gospel, entitling the section: "The most blessed Mary; the story of her repentance" He unites her with Mary of Bethany and the sinful woman who washed Jesus' feet with her hair, and describes in great detail the source of the alabaster jar containing the spikenard used in anointing Jesus.

c. 970, a book of martyrs described Mary Magdalene retreating to the desert for thirty years, fasting and praying and being lifted by angels into heaven for spiritual sustenance several times a day.

About the same time, prayers to be used on her feast day were printed and distributed to the abbeys and churches, and altars were built to her and to Martha as her sister-saint.

In 1050 Pope Leo IX declared her remains to be at the monastery at Vezelay, in Burgundy.

In 1058 Pope Stephen IX named her as the Vezelay Abbey's sole patron, supplanting the Virgin Mary. Pilgrims came from far and wide to touch her tomb and experienced miracles. Kings were crowned there. Crusades are launched from the cathedral's steps.

In the years 1060-1250 churches and abbeys across Europe were built and dedicated to Mary Magdalene.

In 1215, the Fourth Lateran Council decreed that every individual must make annual confession to a priest. Mary Magdalene was portrayed as the model of "holy sinner," "beloved penitent," and her Saint Day, July 22, became an opportunity for people to free themselves of past sins and reunite with Christ through penitence and devotion.

The Bishop of Genoa in 1250, Jacobus de Voragine, a Dominican, published *The Golden Legend,* a book of the saints that detailed Mary Magdalene's arrival in Provence, along with her retreat to the cave.

In 1267 Louis IX, "St. Louis," declared the long-revered relics at Vezelay to be truly the remains of Mary Magdalene's body and took some home to add to his collection of sacred relics. His nephew was not convinced and continues to search for them.

In 1279 the monks at St. Maximin, a monastery and basilica in Provence, near the Holy Grotto (Ste Baume) where she is said to have spent her last years, unearthed a sarcophagus that they declare contains the true remains of the Magdalene's body, which had been hidden to protect it from the Saracen invasion of 710. Louis' nephew Charles concurred. An annual festival carrying the skull through the town on her Feast Day was inaugurated. The monastery and chapel were turned over to the Dominicans.

In 1297 the Dominican order adopted Mary Magdalene as their patron saint.

Der Saelden Hort, a German poem written in 1298, stateed clearly that John and Mary Magdalene were bride and groom and that their descendants are among the European royalty.

Around 1500, with the printing of the Bible in local languages and the Protestant Reformation, all ideas of sainthood were called into question, and particularly hers. Calvin uses Biblical passages to criticize the tradition of uniting Magdalene, Bethany, and the sinner, and scorned the claim of her body being in three places. French humanist Lefevre distinguished the 3 women, based on study of the original sources—and was lambasted by the orthodoxy.

After the Councils of Trent, 1545-61, Mary Magdalene remained "a symbol of penitence, salvation, and mystical love" within the Roman Church, and religious art being understood as the "bible of the illiterate," greater realism and theological accuracy was encouraged in her depictions.

19th century Evangelicals stressed Mary Magdalene's presence at the foot of the cross and her announcement of the resurrection, separating her from the "sinner." At the same time, "Magdalene houses" were built and supported all over Europe as places to send girls who were pregnant out of wedlock, women who were arrested as prostitutes or adulteresses, and other women considered "undesirable." Residents of these homes did the laundry and sewing for the churches in their area—often under slave-like conditions.

Ernest Renan, a rationalist and skeptic at the College de France in 1870, denounced Jesus' miracles, called Mary Magdalene Jesus' "most faithful friend," though "very excitable," and declared, "the glory of the resurrection belongs, then, to Mary Magdalene."

Luis Duchesne, in the 1880s, publishes a skeptical study of the Magdalene's legends in Provence.

During the 1890s-1930s plays, paintings and poetry begin to depict Mary Magdalene and Jesus as lovers: D. H. Lawrence writes *The Man Who Died* and Kazantzakis, *The Last Temptation*. Martin Scorsese produces a film based on Kazantzakis' work in 1988—using the old figure of the Magdalene as repentant sinner; the Church deplored it and the faithful march against it.

In 1969, the Roman church officially relieved Mary Magdalene of the connection with Luke's sinner and Mary of Bethany.

In 1978, "Maria poenitans" and "magna peccatrix" were deleted from her description in the breviary.

From the 1970s Jungians suggest that the women around him, and Mary Magdalene in particular, helped develop Jesus' feminine side. Feminists began to suggest that there's more to the Magdalene's story than has met the eye in traditional literature.

Through the 1980s several books, fiction and nonfiction, offered alternative perspectives on her character and life. *Holy Blood, Holy Grail* (Baigent, Leigh, and Lincoln, 1983) suggested a staged crucifixion, with an impregnated Mary escaping to Egypt and later arriving in the south of France with an entourage who establish themselves in the Jewish community there. The authors share the Provencal belief

Appendix B

that her descendants intermarried with the family that became the Merovingian kings, a bloodline carried down through Godfroi di Bouillon (the founder of the Templars), as well as the European king of Jerusalem during the Crusades, the houses of Lorraine and Hapsburg, and the families known as St. Claire and Sinclair, who trace their lineage through the royal family of Assisi.

In 1988 Pope John Paul II's encyclical, *Mulieris Dignitatem* ("Woman's Dignity"), said of the Magdalene that: "she is the first to meet the risen Christ ... She came to be called the apostle to the apostles ... Christ entrusting truths to women as well as men." Nonetheless, he still maintained that the primary role of women is as mothers and that Jesus spoke only to "the twelve," thus telling only men to "do this [bless the bread and wine] in remembrance of me."

APPENDIX C: THE *VEDAS* - EARLIEST HISTORY OF THE ARYANS

The written scriptures of the Persian Zoroastrians and the Hindus date from sometime prior to 2000BCE and tell us much about the Aryan people who wrote them. The ancient Persian *Zend-Avesta* and the Hindu *Vedas* describe many of the same deities and beliefs (for example, both refer to the thirty-three gods), indicating that they come from the same root source. When the two groups split apart, later writers demonized the divinities of their adversaries. For example, in early verses of the *Vedas,* the *asuras* were revered as gods, but later were called demons, while *Ahura Mazda* became the primary deity of the Persian Zoroastrians. (Persian often uses an h where Sanskrit uses an s, as in *haoma* for *soma.*) The Hindu term for angels, fairies, and other spirits, is *devas*, used by Zoroastrians to describe the demons from which our English word "devil" is derived.

The word *Veda* means knowledge or wisdom, and the *Vedas* are considered the most sacred scriptures of Hinduism. They are grouped into four sections: *Rig, Sama, Yajur, and Atharva.* The Hindu tradition is that even these *Vedas* were gradually reduced from much more extensive and ancient divine revelations in the early years of the now-ending dark age, which is called the *Kali Yuga.* More recent *Vedas* include the *Brahmanas* or manuals to be used by members of the Brahmin caste for ritual and prayer, the *Aranyakas* for religious hermits, and the *Upanishads,* or mystical discourses.

The hymns of the *Rig Veda* are considered the oldest and most important of the *Vedas*, having been written between

Appendix C

1500 BC and the time of the *Maha-Bharata* war of about 900 BC. More than a thousand hymns are organized into ten mandalas or cycles, of which the second through the seventh are the oldest and the tenth is the most recent. They were probably passed on orally for at least a thousand years before they were written down.

Throughout these texts, the Aryans frankly boast of their conquest over the indigenous *Dasas* or *Dasyus* in northern India. The *Rig Veda* is dominated by hymns praising the Aryan gods for giving them victories and wealth plundered from the *Dasas* people of the fading Harappan culture in the Indus valley. Numerous hymns refer to the use of horses and chariots with spokes that gave their warriors a tremendous advantage. Spears, bows, arrows, and iron weapons are also mentioned. As the verses unfold, they describe how a nomadic and pastoral culture glorifying war established a new social structure of patriarchal families dominated by warriors, and eventually, through the power of the *Vedas* themselves, by priests.

In *Rig Veda* III:34:9 The great warrior god *Indra* killed the *Dasyus* and "gave protection to the Aryan color." The Aryans based their militarily won supremacy on the lightness of their skin color compared to the dark colors of the native *Dasyus*. *Indra* is praised for killing thousands of the abject tribes of *Dasas* with his arrow and taking great vengeance with "murdering weapons." (*Rig Veda* IV:28:3-4) One hymn mentions sending 30,000 *Dasas* "to slumber" and another hymn 60,000.

The basic belief is that prayers and sacrifices will help them to gain their desires and overcome their enemies, as in *Rig Veda* VIII:31:15: "The man who, sacrificing, strives to win the heart of deities will conquer those who worship not."

The first hymn in this book refers to the "iron-fashioned home" of the Aryans.

In the first book of the *Rig Veda* the hymns recognize *Agni* as the guard of eternal law (I:1:8) and *Mitra* and *Varuna* as lovers and cherishers of law who gained their mighty power through law (I:2:8). In the 24th hymn they pray to *Varuna*, the wise *Asura*, to loosen the bonds of their sins. *Indra* is thanked for winning wealth in horses, cattle, and gold by his chariot. *Agni* helps to slay the many in war by the hands of the few, "preserving our wealthy patrons with thy succors, and ourselves." (I:31:6, 42) *Indra* helped win the Aryan victory:

He, much invoked, hath slain *Dasyus* and *Simyus*,
after his wont, and laid them low with arrows.
The mighty thunderer with his fair-complexioned friends
won the land, the sunlight, and the waters.

(Control of the water was essential for agricultural wealth.) *Indra* is also praised for crushing the godless races and breaking down their forts. (*Rig Veda* I:174)

In the tenth and last book of the *Rig Veda* the *Dasyus* are still condemned for being "riteless, void of sense, inhuman, keeping alien laws," and *Indra* still urges the heroes to slay the enemies; his "hand is prompt to rend and burn, O hero thunder-armed." (X:22)

The first indication of the caste system is outlined in the hymn to *Purusha*, the embodied human spirit, who is one-fourth creature and three-fourths eternal life in heaven.

The *Brahmin* was his mouth,
of both his arms was the *Rajanya* made.
His thighs became the *Vaisya*,
from his feet the *Sudra* was produced.

The *Brahmin* caste is the priests and teachers; the *Rajanya* are the kings, heads of the warrior or *Kshatriya* caste; *Vaisyas* are the merchants, craftsmen, and farmers; and the *Sudras* are the workers. In hymn 109 the *brahmachari,* or student, is mentioned as also engaged in duty as a member of God's own body.

Appendix C

Finally, a hymn of creation is found in *Rig Veda* X:129: Beginning from non-being when nothing existed, not even water or death, the One breathless breathed by itself. At first this All was concealed by darkness and formless chaos, but through the energy of heat (*tapas*) that One came into existence. Thus arose desire, the primal seed and germ of Spirit, out of which all of creation was formed. And so the ancient question of how a male could produce offspring is addressed.

The *Vedas* are justly recognized today as including some of the most remarkably accurate descriptions of the nature of physical reality—based solely on observation, contemplation, and intuition. At the same time, sadly, they set a model for wanton disrespect for the lives of any but the light-skinned followers of Indra, Krishna, and their fellow-gods that has caused unbelievable distress for thousands.

REFERENCES AND RESOURCES

About Mary Magdalene and Related Stories

Ashcroft, Mary Ellen, *The Magdalene Gospel: Meeting the Women Who Followed Jesus*

Begg, Ean, *The Cult of the Black Virgin*. New York: Penguin, 1995.

Burstein, Dan & Arne J. de Keijzer, *Secrets of Mary Magdalene*, New York: CDS Books, 2006.

Harris, Anthony. *The Sacred Virgin and the Holy Whore*.

Haskins, Susan. *Mary Magdalen: Myth and Metaphor*. Orlando, FL: Harcourt Brace, 1993

Houston, Siobhan, *Invoking Mary Magdalene, Accessing the Wisdom of the Divine Feminine*, Boulder, CO: Sounds True, 2006.

King, Karen L. *The Gospel of Mary of Magdala: Jesus and the First Woman Apostle*, 2001

Picknett, Lynn. *Mary Magdalene*. New York: Carroll & Graf, 2003

Redgrove, Peter. *The Black Goddess and the Sixth Sense*.

Starbird, Margaret, *The Woman With the Alabaster Jar*. Rochester, VT: Bear & Co., 1996.

_____, *The Goddess in the Gospel*., Rochester, VT: Bear & Co., 1998.

_____. *Bride in Exile*, Rochester, VT: Bear & Co., 2005.

"Mary Magdalene: The Hidden Apostle" produced by Biography (DVD - Aug 10, 2004)

About Medieval Culture, Templars, Cathedrals

Beresniak, Daniel. *Symbols of Freemasonry*. New York, Barnes & Noble, 2000.

Butler, Alan. *The Goddess, The Grail and the Lodge*. New York: Barnes & Noble, 2004.

References

Gimpel, Jean. *Medieval Machine: The Industrial Revolution of the Middle Ages.* New York: Barnes & Noble, 2003.

Haagensen, Erling & Lincoln, Henry. *The Templars' Secret Island: The Knights, The Priest, and The Treasure.* New York: Barnes & Noble, 2002.

Holmes, George (ed.). *The Oxford Illustrated History of Medieval Europe.* London: Oxford University Press, 1988.

Holmyard, E. J. *Alchemy.* Middlesex England: Penguin, 1927.

Phillips, Graham. *The Templars and the Ark of the Covenant; The Discovery of the Treasure of Solomon.* Rochester, VT: Bear & Co., 2004.

Picknett, Lynn & Prince, Clive. *The Templar Revelation: Secret Guardians of the True Identity of Christ.* New York: Touchstone, 1998.

About Ancient Cultures & the Divine Feminine

Budge, E.A.Wallis, *Egyptian Religion: Egyptian Ideas of the Future Life.* London: Arkana/Penguin, 1987.

Clagett, Marshall, *Greek Science in Antiquity.* New York: Collier, 1959.

Contenau, Georges. *Everyday Life in Babylon and Assyria.* New York: Norton, 1966.

De Lubicz, Isha Schwaller, *Her-Bak: The Living Face of Ancient Egypt.* New York: Inner Traditions, 1955.

_____, *The Opening of the Way: A Practical Guide to the Wisdom of Ancient Egypt.* New York: Inner Traditions, 1979.

Diamant, Anita. *The Red Tent, A Novel.* New York: Picador, 1997.

Duby, George, Perrot, Michelle and Pantell, Pauline S. *A History of Women; from Ancient Goddesses to Christian Saints.* Cambridge: Harvard Press, 1992.

Eisler, Rianne. *The Chalice and the Blade: Our History, Our Future.* Harper San Francisco, 1988.

Ferguson, John. *The Religions of the Roman Empire.* New York: Cornell University Press, 1980.

Fletcher, Joann. *Chronicle of a Pharaoh: The Intimate Life of Amenhotep III,* London: Oxford University Press, 2000.

Forte, Maurizio and Siliotti, Alberto. *Virtual Archaeology: Re-creating Ancient Worlds.* London: Thames & Hudson, 1998.

Gimbutas, Marija. *The Civilization of the Goddess: The World of Old Europe.* Harper San Francisco, 1991.

_____. *The Living Goddesses.* Berkeley, CA: University of California Press, 2001.

Goodrich, Norma L. *Heroines: Demigoddess, Prima Dona, Movie Star.* New York: HarperCollins, 1993.

Johnson, Elizabeth A., *She Who Is: The Mystery Of God In Feminist Theological Discourse*, New York: Crossroad, 1999.

King, John. *The Celtic Druids' Year: Seasonal Cycles of the Ancient Celts.* London: Branford, 1995.

Knight, Christopher & Lomas, Robert. *The Hiram Key: Pharoahs, Freemasons and the Discovery of the Secret Scrolls of Jesus.* New York: Barnes & Noble, 1998.

Kramer, Samuel N. *Sumerian Mythology: A Study of Spiritual and Literary Achievement in the Third Millennium B.C.* New York: Harper, 1961.

Markale, Jean, *Sites & Sanctuaires des Celts.* Paris, Tredaniel, 1999.

_____, *Church of the Black Madonna.* Rochester, VT: Inner Traditions, 1988.

McEvedy, Colin. *The Penguin Atlas of Ancient History.* Middlesex, England: Penguin, 1967.

Meyer, Marvin W. *The Ancient Mysteries: A Sourcebook.* New York: Harper & Row, 1987.

Mireaux, *Daily Life in the Time of Homer.* New York, Macmillan, 1989.

Ogilvie, R.M. *Roman Literature and Society.* New York: Penguin, 1980.

Pearson, Carol Lynn. *Mother Wove the Morning, A One-Woman Play.* Walnut Creek, CA: Pearson Printing, 1992.

Sjoo, Monica and Mor, Barbara. *The Great Cosmic Mother: Rediscovering the Religion of the Earth.* Harper San Francisco, 1987.

Stone, Merlin. *When God Was A Woman.* New York: Barnes & Noble, 1976.

_____, *Ancient Mirrors of Womanhood: A Treasury of Goddess and Heroine Lore from Around the World.* Boston: Beacon Press, 1979.

Torjesen, Karen Jo. *When Women Were Priests.* Harper San Francisco, 1995.

Walker, Barbara G. *The Woman's Encyclopedia of Myths and Secrets.* Harper San Francisco, 1983.

About Christ & the Divine Feminine

Butler, Willis. *The Other Bible; Ancient Alternative Scriptures.* Harper San Francisco, 1984.

Freke, Timothy & Gandy, Peter. *Jesus & the Lost Goddess: The Secret Teachings of the Original Christians.* New York: Three Rivers, 2001.

Knight, Christopher & Lomas, Robert. *The Book of Hiram: Freemasonry, Venus, and the Secret Key to the Life of Jesus.* London: Harper Collins, 2003

Picknett, Lynn & Prince, Clive. *The Templar Revelation: Secret Guardians of the True Identity of Christ.* New York: Touchstone, 1998.

Starbird, Margaret. *The Woman With the Alabaster Jar.* Rochester, VT: Bear & Co., 1996.

_____. *The Goddess in the Gospel,* Rochester, VT: Bear & Co., 1998.

Fiction:

Brown, Dan. *The DaVinci Code,* New York: Doubleday, 2003.

Cunningham, Elizabeth, *The Passion of Mary Magdalene*

De Lubicz, Isha Schwaller, *Her-Bak: The Living Face of Ancient Egypt.* New York: Inner Traditions, 1955.

Diamant, Anita. *The Red Tent, A Novel.* New York: Picador, 1997.

Kinstler, Clysta, *The Moon Beneath Her Feet,* HarperSan Francisco, 1991.

McGowan, Kathleen *The Expected One: A Novel* (Magdalene Line), 2006.

Index

Abraham 4, 20, 91-95, 97, 109, 188, 227
Abram 34, 92, 93, 94, 259, 323
Age of Invasion and Empire .... viii, 35, 64
alchemy 20, 207, 210, 283
Alexander the Great ... 80, 113
Anatolia ... 35, 40, 41, 48, 53, 59, 64, 154, 271, 311, 329
Anatolian . 36, 37, 54, 56, 62, 66, 72, 76, 85, 110, 117, 134, 196, 287, 338
anima ... vii, 11, 181, 189, 252, 257
animus .. vii, 11, 181, 189, 257
Anna 30, 56, 119, 126
anointing .. 124, 127, 128, 143, 195, 196, 226, 229, 340
Apostle to the Apostles 134, 222
Aryans 63, 65, 72, 82, 85, 88, 228, 313-315, 344, 345
Asia Minor 35, 64, 85, 91, 98, 152, 153, 199, 281, 326, 328, 329, 331, 333
astrology 20, 22
Augustine 24, 79, 90, 154, 155, 262, 339
balance 11, 14, 34, 41, 52, 54, 57, 66, 71-75, 82, 84, 95, 109, 111, 112, 117, 134, 138, 139, 147, 233, 245, 255, 256, 268, 285
Bernard of Clairvaux 160, 198, 204, 263, 266, 280
Bible ... 13, 14, 16, 58, 89, 124, 126, 148, 149, 151, 153, 154, 167, 177, 188, 193, 289, 316, 341, 351
Bride 4, 128, 206, 224, 226, 348
bridegroom . 72, 138, 143, 195, 254, 255
Buddhist 148, 225
Caesar 73, 75, 86, 87
Catal-Huyuk .. 35, 36, 311
Cathars 159, 160-162, 174, 200, 201, 262
cathedral .... 2, vi, 14, 15, 19, 21, 23, 26- 29, 32, 33, 188, 192, 207, 214, 227, 263, 269-271, 275, 283, 340

Catholic vi, 3, 8, 11, 127, 153, 253, 262, 271, 274, 277-279
Caucasus...63, 65, 67, 69, 79, 85, 91, 224, 311
Celtic ..17, 28, 29, 50, 72, 86, 87, 154, 167, 203, 208, 210, 212, 228, 231, 269, 277, 281, 350
Celts ...41, 50, 85, 86, 87, 88, 192, 350
Chartres....2, i, vi, 14-18, 21, 22, 24-30, 32, 33, 80, 87, 129, 161, 188, 189, 192, 210, 214, 215, 219, 263- 271, 275, 279, 280, 283
Christian.....2, 3, 7, 9, 10, 13, 17, 21, 29-32, 50, 79-81, 84, 115, 127, 151-154, 158, 159, 162, 166-169, 173, 175, 177, 181, 182, 186-188, 193, 208, 210-213, 216, 252, 262, 271-273, 275, 279, 281, 283, 289, 290, 308, 328, 349
Cistercian..161, 198, 204, 205, 208, 210, 263
Consort..................56, 58
Coptic Christians......179, 180
Crete ..36, 37, 40, 62, 320

Crone.....39, 47, 226, 287
Crusades...156, 158, 174, 223, 340, 343
David......34, 76, 90, 108, 109, 110, 125, 126, 138, 142, 157, 203
Dead Sea scrolls..90, 178
Diana......52, 56, 80, 213, 218, 251, 272, 281
Dominican 161, 174, 216, 220, 223, 340, 341
Druids ..28, 87, 147, 266, 350
Egypt..20, 38, 53, 56, 59, 64, 72, 73, 90-92, 96-101, 102, 105, 107, 128, 134, 137, 147, 154, 179-181, 186, 188, 193-196, 213, 216, 222, 229, 235, 236, 238, 259, 260, 272, 286, 314, 327, 329-332, 334, 342, 349, 351
equinox 3, 41, 43- 46, 56, 75, 193, 238
Essenes.....116, 120, 121, 159, 191, 201
Etruscan 154, 333-338
Exodus 76, 78, 90, 98-105
farmer.... 70, 71, 148, 163
Father God ... 5, 246, 272, 289
Fatima ... 3, 275, 278, 285

Fulbert....... 15-18, 21, 25, 210, 263, 283
Gaia........................... 290
Genesis 25, 76, 91-95
Gilgamesh... 66, 316, 317
Gnostics ... 116, 159, 181, 182, 222
gospels 23, 119, 122-124, 128, 132, 134, 136, 139, 151, 153, 172, 190, 193, 196, 213, 220, 227, 283, 308
Grail .. 202, 204, 208-212, 225, 226, 230, 342, 348
grandmother......... 6, 9, 14
Greek vii, 2, 4, 16, 18-22, 51, 55, 77, 80, 84, 113-116, 119, 123, 138, 149, 153, 164, 173, 177, 179-184, 187-200, 224, 238, 244, 245, 252, 272, 274, 281, 290, 307, 320, 328, 333, 334, 337, 349
harlots 126
heiros gamos ...... 71, 138-140, 185, 190, 195, 238, 255, 258, *See* holy marriage; Sacred Marriage
herders ... 67, 72, 91, 204, 312

hierarchy.37, 55, 82, 101, 115, 134, 159, 161, 182, 186
High Priest.100, 118, 121
Hittites 65, 91, 97, 106, 323, 326, 329-332
holy marriage .55, 71, 73, 78
Holy Spirit...... 3, 11, 152, 180, 193, 259, 273
Hyksos.... 91, 93, 97-102, 106, 326, 330
Inanna..... 56, 70-74, 190, 281, 316-319, 322
Indo-European...... 65, 82, 333, 334
Inquisition 162, 166, 173, 201, 224, 226, 283
Isaac Newton.20, 26, 210
Isis 72, 111, 128, 207, 273, 281, 282
Israel. 90, 91, 95-97, 109, 112, 115, 117, 120, 125, 127, 143, 259
Jericho 36, 76, 90, 108, 125, 134, 310
Johannon 138
Joseph.4, 91, 96, 97, 122, 137, 141, 212, 216, 230, 274, 307
Kaaba 81
Koran 3, 14, 198
La Madeleine 210, 214, 215, 219, 226, 252
lamb........... 130, 131, 255

Liberal Arts....18, 19, 22, 207, 263
Maiden......39, 43, 47, 88, 262, 277, 287
Mara. 123-126, 128, 135, 139, 140-147, 196, 233-250, 307, 308
Marduk.56, 72, 324, 325, 326
Marija Gumbutas.........12
Messiah....120, 122, 127, 139, 141, 143, 178, 187, 193
Miriam.. 14, 88, 104-108, 123-126, 135, 257, 269, 286-288, 307
Monastery................204
moon 3, 4, 10, 19, 34, 38-40, 46-52, 57, 59, 61, 88, 107, 145, 195, 235, 268, 282, 285-287
Moses..... 5, 90, 100-107, 110-112, 116-118, 123, 126, 128, 129, 134, 227, 235, 242, 253, 254, 259, 260, 321
Mother of God..3, 29, 81, 173, 174, 192, 207, 272, 275, 277, 278
Muslim .79, 94, 156, 177, 328
myrrh..89, 106, 107, 124, 126, 128, 141, 211, 212

mystery school....16, 270
Nag Hammadi....90, 134, 149, 172, 178, 180, 189, 211, 222
Nazarenei, 115, 129, 130, 135, 139, 140, 144, 145, 194, 235, 243
Nazirite..................... 130
Neolithic..29, 34, 35, 36, 40, 57, 72, 224, 309
Neo-pagans...............285
New Testament.. 89, 108, 115, 120, 122, 123, 131, 136, 148, 151, 153, 178, 186, 189, 191, 222, 227, 229, 258, 283, 284
New Thought vi, 10, 175, 290, 361, 363
Nicea. 151, 153, 172, 186
Notre Dame...... 2, vii, 14, 22, 23, 24, 29-31, 188, 210, 215, 262, 264, 267-270, 280, 282, 283
Osiris............56, 72, 282
Our Lady vii, 29, 30, 173, 198, 227, 262, 271, 275, 276-279, 282, 283
pagan....3, 21, 72, 82, 83, 125, 128, 154, 155, 218, 223, 224, 227, 281, 286, 287
Paleolithic............35, 309
Paul....... 6, 119, 121, 136, 137, 151, 153, 167,

170, 172, 174, 178, 179, 186, 193, 211, 222, 244, 253, 259, 280, 283, 288, 343
Plato. vii, 17, 19, 25, 116, 161, 164, 222
priestess ... 61, 72, 73, 78, 93, 107, 190, 195, 233, 243, 245, 318, 319
prophetess. 106, 119, 126
Protestant vi, 3, 5, 7, 153, 167, 174- 177, 186, 222, 278, 289, 341
Pythagoras 19, 116
Qumran.... 120, 121, 189, 191
Red Tent 48, 107, 108, 349, 351
Resurrection............... 133
Royal Portal ... 21, 24, 26, 270
Sacred Marriage. 55, 128, 190, 255, 260
sacred site 28, 30, 110, 157
saints 5, 79, 166, 192, 218, 223, 262, 276, 340
Sarah 92, 94, 95, 210, 213, 216, 238-240, 244-249
Sarai 92, 93
Sargon. 77, 318-320, 322, 323

Shekinah ...4, 11, 81, 185, 252
shepherd 70, 71, 154, 330
Solomon ...30, 72, 76, 78, 89, 108-112, 117, 125-128, 138, 141, 197, 200, 245, 282, 327, 349
solstice 41-46, 50, 51, 88, 238
Son ...3, 4, 11, 30, 39, 42, 55, 56, 75, 81, 84, 138-140, 145, 152, 183, 227, 249, 255-258, 268, 272, 279, 283
Sophia.4, 5, 22, 149, 172, 183, 184, 185, 200, 218, 222, 226, 252
Ste Baume .... i, 214, 218, 219, 341
stone circle 38, 41-46, 50, 51, 58, 61, 62, 79, 85
Sumeria ..56, 64, 97, 185, 286
Tammuz....56, 72, 73, 74, 75, 84, 128, 140, 142, 238
Templars.. 162, 163, 197-201, 203, 207, 210, 264, 266, 343, 348, 349
temple-mound .38, 42, 45
The DaVinci Code . ii, 72, 187, 208, 351

Thomas Aquinas 90, 161, 173, 220, 230
Torah ...14, 102, 117, 136
Troyes 198, 203, 208
unbound hair 128, 228, 229, 231, 232
Vezelay..... 157, 213-215, 220, 223, 227, 340, 341
Virgin-Mother............. 30
Western Culture 77
women's court 120
Women's House... 47, 48, 235
women's hut................ 48
zodiac ... 22, 23, 268, 269, 270

About the Author

Ruth L. Miller, PhD, integrates scientific, spiritual, and cultural understanding to clarify metaphysical principles and practices for the modern audience.

With degrees in anthropology, cybernetics, environmental studies, and the systems sciences, she was a futurist and college professor before being trained and ordained as a minister. She now teaches in Unity, Science of Mind, and Unitarian churches and is Director of Gaia Living Systems Institute in Oregon.

Miller is the author of numerous books and reports. She is the editor of the Library of Hidden Knowledge series published by Beyond Words (Simon & Schuster/Atria), which "translates" the work of 19th century New Thought teachers into modern language and format and includes *The New Science of Getting Rich* and *Natural Abundance: Ralph Waldo Emerson's Guide to Prosperity*, among others. She is also the author of *Unveiling Your Hidden Power*, *Coming into Freedom*, and the Paths of Power series of biographies of New Thought teacher/healers published by WiseWoman Press. Her history and explanation of the New Thought movement – *The Science of Mental Healing;* her approach to dealing with stressful environments – *Making the World Go Away;* and her guides to spiritual practice – *Spiritual Success*, *Uncommon Prayer*, and *Unlocking the Power of the Secret*, are published by Portal Center Press.

Dr. Miller works with individuals and organizations who are ready to explore new possibilities in their life and work, applying the principles described in her books.
For more information about Dr. Miller, her work, and her schedule, see www.ruthlmillerphd.com.

Other books by Ruth L. Miller
- ✓ The Creative Power of Thought: Thomas Troward's Metaphysics Explained
- ✓ Discovering A New Way: finding a path to peace in patterns of the past
- ✓ HOME: Creating Humanity's Future
- ✓ Making the World Go Away
- ✓ The Science of Mental Healing: lives & teachings of America's New Thought healers
- ✓ Spiritual Success: a guide for daily practice
- ✓ Uncommon Prayer: connecting with the One Power
- ✓ Unlocking the Power of *The Secret*

Related books by other authors

Wake UP! our old beliefs don't work anymore,
by Andree Cuenod

Butterfly Soup: transformation from the inside out
by Aurora J. Miller

Miracles through Music: a harpist's odyssey
by Joel Andrews

To Rebalance Earth: Awakening an Inner Knowing
by Milt Markewitz (and Ruth L. Miller)

www.portalcenterpress.com

www.ingramcontent.com/pod-product-compliance
Lightning Source LLC
Chambersburg PA
CBHW030145100526
44592CB00009B/129